WALKING TO HOLLYWOOD

**WILL SELF** is the author of many novels and books of non-fiction, including *How the Dead Live*, which was shortlisted for the Whitbread Novel of the Year 2002, *The Butt*, winner of the Bollinger Everyman Wodehouse Prize for Comic Fiction 2008, and, with Ralph Steadman, *Psychogeography* and *Psycho Too*. He lives in South London.

# WALKING TO HOLLYWOOD

*Memories of Before the Fall*

## WILL SELF

BLOOMSBURY

LONDON • NEW DELHI • NEW YORK • SYDNEY

First published in Great Britain 2010

This paperback edition published 2011

Copyright © 2010 by Will Self

Illustrations copyright © 2010 by Will Self

The moral right of the author has been asserted

Bloomsbury Publishing Plc
50 Bedford Square
London WICB 3DP

www.bloomsbury.com

Bloomsbury Publishing, London, New York, New Delhi and Sydney

A CIP catalogue record for this book is available from the British Library

ISBN 978 1 4088 0994 5

10 9 8 7 6 5 4 3 2

Typeset by Hewer Text UK Ltd, Edinburgh
Printed and bound in Great Britain by CPI Group (UK) Ltd, Croydon CR0 4YY

*For Marti*

# Contents

# Very Little

'Miniature is one of the refuges of greatness'

– Gaston Bachelard, *The Poetics of Space*

# I
# Sherman Oaks

At three minutes past noon on 8 October 2007, I found myself standing listening to Sherman Oaks beside a dew pond on the crest of the South Downs in Sussex. A single cramped ash was reflected in the gunmetal disc of water, a disc that was ringed with pocked earth and cupped in a fold of cropped turf. Had an eavesdropper crept up on the pair of us, they might have thought Sherman's magniloquence prompted by the very finitude of this watering hole, that the way he lectured not only me but the thrushes flitting overhead was an attempt to break free of this claustrophobic scene: the sky closely sealed by a lid of cloud, cut-outs of hedge and woodland stuck on the receding crests of the downs.

I knew this not to be the case.

Sherman had always been a big talker. I remember him aged seven or eight, rolling around in the boot of my mother's car when it was her turn to do the school run, spouting a stream of wisecracks and making razor-sharp observations on the foibles of the world. A precocious anarchist, at thirteen Sherman told me he was going to strip naked, except for a skullcap and an attaché case, then stump into Grodzinski's, the Jewish bakery in Golders Green. When challenged he would say only this – in a thick, *mittel*-European accent: 'Can you tell me the way to Grods?'

It's barely worth remarking that the impact of this stunt would be hugely enhanced by the perpetrator's stature: at eight Sherman had been less than three feet tall, at thirteen he was perhaps three-foot-two, thirty-five years later he had gained, at most, an inch.

Assuming Sherman did do it – and I have no reason to doubt him – his dwarfism was the reason he got away with it, for in the North London of the 1970s the uneasy ridicule that disability once provoked had mutated into a tolerance that already verged on de facto acceptance of collective responsibility: we were all to blame for Sherman Oaks's restricted height. Not that our peers felt exclusively this way; after all, children are always in a state of nature – always nasty, brutish . . . and short. Sherman may not have been overtly persecuted, but he undoubtedly felt excluded – forever eddying while the life stream flowed forward all around him.

In my early teens I felt that way too. It wasn't commonplace spottiness – my face was mailed in acne. Then there was Dick Holmes, who could've used a D-cup bra. Together we formed a mismatched trio: the Small, the Fat and the Spotty lanky one. I daresay there are plenty of outcasts who sink into introspective angst, but with Sherman to goad us on there was no chance of that: he made me march into the chemist's, where I bought the useless salves for my hurting face and confronted the pharmacist, claiming that it was the product that had done it to me. He got Dick Holmes to dress up in his mother's frock and buy us booze, and he himself led us into the reference section of High Hill Bookshop, where he sat insouciantly on a table reading the *Britannica* aloud. When confronted, he said he was a five-year-old genius.

Still, as the lugubrious narrator of *La Jetée* would have it: 'Nothing tells such memories from ordinary memories; only afterwards do they claim remembrance on account of their scars.' Sherman, having none to spare, never gave an inch. I was in awe of his chutzpah – he was our own home-grown Vamana: Vishnu incarnated as a dwarfish trickster. As for me,

I had already imperfectly grasped an awareness that would harden within me even as my acne scabbed then flaked away: whatever the emotional scars I might bear my life would remain coddled and my instincts conformist – only a striving such as Sherman's against his crushing disability could be accounted an exercise of will at all.

On his sixteenth birthday Sherman threw a party at his parents' house on Norrice Lea. The studious entrepreneurialism of Mr Oaks – he manufactured cash registers in a 1950s block near Hangar Lane that looked like a cash register – had kerchinged the family this Lutyens villa, complete with redbrick loggias and a sunken garden. Twice-my-height privet hedges hid the mullioned windows, behind which lay an enormous open-plan kitchen – the first I had ever seen. Beneath track lighting (again, the first I had ever seen) gleamed two of every white good, for although Sherman bought ham at the deli then wolfed it straight from the wrapper, Mrs Oaks kept strict kosher.

The child of a ruptured family from the wrong side of the North Circular, I was awed by the opulence of the Oakses' home. Our kitchen window still had several broken panes patched with cardboard and Sellotape – the result of my parents' penultimate row. Our goods weren't white at all, but yellowed with sadness and neglect. There was less than one of everything and the family dog had had a nervous breakdown, while my older brother – having absorbed the force of Christopher Logue's clerihew 'When all else fails, try Wales' – had decamped. To Swansea.

I was awed by the Oakses' home – and captivated by the Oaks sisters. There were three of them, ranged around Sherman in age and each seemingly more lovely and gracile than the preceding one. The youngest, Tertia, was an outright stunner. My mother, whose own neuroses and phobias made her a lightning conductor for any distress sparking across the suburb, speculated on what quirk of heredity had produced Sherman. But, while it was tempting to think in terms of throwback, or kick sideways, or even adoption, he shared with his sisters the same white-blond hair, fierce blue eyes and highly wrought features; it was the parents who failed to jibe – their doughy pans were both dashed with liverish freckles, and their bottoms were as broad as the seats of the Mercedes in which they purred the 500 yards to Greenspan's in the Market Place, where they bought schmaltz herring and smoked salmon. While not discounting Mr Oaks's ability to drive a hard bargain, the notion that they had got the kids in a job-lot was preposterous.

Anyway, on this summer evening the old Oaks had been got rid of so that the teens could get drunk, dance and feel each other up shamelessly – either on the G-plan leather sofas in the living room, or at the top of the house, in a rumpus conversion fully equipped with snooker table, one-armed bandits and a 1950s jukebox loaded with 1970s rock 'n' roll revival singles. Showaddywaddy anyone? Unlike my own house, where cobwebs smeared the ceilings, here the only spiders were from Mars and locked up in the polished beech cabinets of a Bang & Olufsen stereo system, from where they screamed to us of slinking through the city, smarming in and out of sexes, before bawling teen abandonment to the rooftops.'

In the previous year the religious anointment of hydrogen peroxide had sloughed off my beastly mask. It had hurt, and no one – least of all me – believed that any great beauty lay beneath, so how to explain Tertia, who after two hours and twice that many Bacardi-laced Cokes, waltzed me backwards across the hall and into the oddly antiseptic gloom of her father's study, where, her neat denim behind aligned on the desk blotter, she grabbed hold of my crotch while exhorting me to 'Do it!'

The alcohol certainly helped, but, with hindsight and the benefit of career résumés – gobbets of gossip sucked up gummily in dentists' waiting rooms – I can only conclude that Tertia was practising on me. Of course, unlike her many subsequent conquests, I had no reputation to sully, family to alienate or assets to strip. Nor could she have wanted to humiliate me sexually – after all, she was only fifteen. Still, humiliated I was: it was all over in hundredths of a second, with four layers of clothing for prophylaxis.

I say I had no assets – but there was one: Sherman. I understood enough of the family dynamic to realize that he, by reason of his charm quite as much as his disability, was doted on by both his parents. He was also their only son, and moreover, although we may balk at such dispositional crudity, their daughters were already outsoaring them, while Sherman would always remain their little boychick.

My rapidly cooling semen pooling in my underpants, I recoiled from Tertia, who gave a precociously vicious laugh. There she sprawled, the diamonds of evening sunshine scattered across her bare belly, her father's obsessively aligned pen stand, his Dictaphone, and paperclip holder, etc. Is it only a currently felt scar, rather than the memory, that makes it seem now as if there was more pathos and eroticism on that desktop than I would ever fully grasp – let alone experience?

Then there was Sherman. So much was unsaid between us – could not even be framed, still. I knew these teen soirées were a nightmare for him; that as our hormones spurred us on, he felt he lagged further and further behind. Earlier that day, on the phone, he had said heavily: 'Stick by me this evening, will you?' Now I'd not only abandoned him but been seduced by his little sister.

I yanked my way out of the study, madly scanned the kids in the kitchen, the living room, pelted to the top of the house and checked there, then tumbled down a storey to Sherman's bedroom, where the sensitively truncated furniture and juvenile decoration belied the .22 air pistol and cubic inch of Pakki Black I knew he had hidden under the floorboards. He was nowhere to be seen – but had he seen us?

I eventually located him in the most sunken part of the garden, standing by the perfectly round pond fringed with marigolds and primulas. He had his back to the house, and before I heard the words of his bitter rant, I saw all the tension in his blocky shoulders; crammed into them were all conceivable miseries – for now, forever. Over and over he incanted, 'Fucking cunts, fucking cunts, fucking fucking fucking cunts . . .' – a bizarre accompaniment to Bryan Ferry's complacent yelp of 'What's her name, Virginia Plain', which was belting from the open french windows.

Worse was to emerge: first Sherman's handsome face uglified by tears, then Sherman's square fist raised like a pestle before being ground down hard into the mortar of his palm, again and again – 'Fucking cunts, fucking cunts, fucking fucking fucking cunts . . .' – while in that hand, already mashed, glistened the innards, the greyish braided and bloodied fur, of Max Headroom, Tertia's beloved mouse.

I let him wind himself down. I let him punch me in the stomach with his gory knuckles. I took the mouse's corpse and lost it in the compost heap. I took Sherman in through the side door and washed his Othello hands in the little sink in the little bathroom beside the great big kitchen. Then I got the hash. We sat back down by the pond and I stuck three Rizla papers together, split a Benson & Hedges and built a joint. We passed it between us, sucking up the smoke, acrid as Accra. Then Sherman said a lot of the unsayable things – about how it was for him, and how he feared it would be.

Inevitably, after that night we didn't so much drift as scamper apart. I never grew any more, only became annealed by a life that seemed at the time to have had plenty of significant events – addictions, affairs, marriages, children, the micro-mosaics of literary composition – yet which, when I came to in the dusty stalls of middle age, I realized had been altogether lacking in high drama: no blitz or pogrom had been visited on me; the angel of death awaited me in Edgware or Bushey, at a care home, in a cardigan.

Of Sherman I had picked up bits and pieces over the years – he had done a foundation art course somewhere in the north, then dropped out. Next I heard it said he was in Berlin, squatting in the Kreuzberg – and incidentally driving his parents to despair. Then he was back in England and at Goldsmiths completing his studies. All this seemed apt: he was merely another contemporary I had lost touch with, his life to be expressed through the bare bones of his curriculum vitae, rather than felt for, or loved.

Then, in the late 1980s, there began the inexorable rise of Sherman Oaks, the artist.

From the very beginning the Oaks phenomenon caught the public's imagination. His contemporaries may have been flashier and more pretentious – but, while they were conceptualists, at a remove from the fabrication of their works, he was an unashamedly personal actualizer, a *macher*, who hewed stone and wood; shaped, pummelled and spun clay; smelted and cast iron, bronze and steel. He created enduring facts on the ground – not airy abstractions of blood, meat and crumpled paper that had life only in temperature-controlled galleries. That he, a middle-class Jewish boy, should be working on such pieces alongside tough Northumbrian welders and phlegmatic West Country stonemasons made the enterprise seem that much more authentic. That Sherman was also a person of restricted height lent a greater poignancy to his monumental works, which, twice and three times life size from the outset, grew still larger as soon as he got the funding. And of course, every single piece derived from his own body.

For the masses, with their fractals of I-know-what-I-like ceaselessly yet variably replicated throughout the nineties then the noughties, this was narrative enough – but Sherman evinced a modesty that, if not exactly false, certainly didn't ring true to me. Not for him the dialectical twaddle of theorizers, or the *de haut en bas* of the new *Kulturkampf*. Instead, when interviewed he'd cackle disarmingly, 'I'm a very small man making very big things.' Then, if pressed, he'd add, 'Believe me, mine is an utterly content-free art: what you see is what you get.'

I tracked his progress, first through newspaper and magazine items, then larger features, then radio and television segments. Invitations to private views arrived concurrently – at first to group exhibitions, then solo ones and eventually retrospectives. The evolution of his 'content-free art' had almost amused me. More remarkable was his ability, unerringly, to produce a likeness of himself – even when it was a 64-foot-high basketry woven from steel struts. Nevertheless, I would scrutinize the pasteboards for a while, tracing the fine lettering with my own gross digit, then whirl the duff Frisbee away into the pile of waste paper in the corner of my writing room; a pile that I bagged up weekly, then deposited outside the house, so it could be carted away, pulped and turned into more invitations to private views.

I supposed we must meet again eventually – we revolved in interlinked circles of the social Olympiad – but I was in no hurry. I suspected that after the enormous success of Sherman's *Behemoth*, a 128-foot-high body form set astride the Manchester Ship Canal near Runcorn, he would – no matter how small – have become too big for his boots. 'Behold,' read the inscription on the plinth, 'he plunders the river and does not harden.' The sculpture had at first been the occasion for local scorn, then regional and eventually metropolitan. But inevitably, when it became internationally regarded as an icon of the new and prosperous Britannia, it was appropriated as a symbol of national pride. Sherman had accepted a gong from the government.

Really, it wasn't the outer man I feared but the inner. Whatever may be said about the indelible marks of childhood memories, mine, for the most part, were vague and unthreatening. I could recall sitting in an antique Silver Cross pram with a pillowcase full of dirty laundry as my mother pushed it up Deansway to the laundrette in East Finchley. Sometimes I thought of a promotional Esso T-shirt I had loved fiercely – its bold blue roundel the target all futurity should aim at – that I had worn until it disintegrated. And then there was my third birthday.

That morning, after breakfast, my jealous brother told me he was going to run away from home. I said I would come as well and carefully packed one of my mother's old handbags with toy cars, but when the time came to leave he said he wasn't interested any more, so I set off alone. I can see now the terror-annihilated face of the lorry driver as I dashed across the North Circular in front of his wheels, and also the police car pulling up at the bus stop where I was waiting with what I imagined was mature casualness. And lunging up from that car, her face mottled and cracked like a saltpan, my mother – she was only forty-four when I ran away, but I fancy the taint was already on her: green grave weeds, rotting at the edges.

The bus stop was right beside the synagogue, at the end of Norrice Lea.

*     *     *

About three or four years after *Behemoth* was installed, my brother – who knew my love for all things out of scale – gave me a 1:200 scale model of Sherman's sculpture. The metal figurine was dubbed a 'minumental' and had been made by Paul St George, an artist my brother knew. I've no idea whether St George is successful or not, but I thought it likely that it was his own massive sense of failure and envy that had been compressed into this, and the other teensy travesties he had made of his contemporaries' works.

I placed the minumental *Behemoth* in among the little wooden blocks and cylinders modelled on London landmarks – Big Ben, the Millennium Wheel, Telecom Tower – that my daughter had bought for me at Muji, and that I had ranged about the base of the anglepoise in the middle of my desk. Attached to the lamp was a tuft of wool I had picked up from a hillside on the Shetland island of Foula – this was the off-white cloud on the horizon of the diminished capital.

The memory that preyed on me was both definite and embodied; it visited me on waking, dissolving only imperfectly to reveal the expected things – penis sputtering, kettle whistling – then reforming into Sherman's rock-hard shoulders, the leaden disc of the garden pond, his pile-driving fist and the mouse mush.

I avoided Sherman because of my shame – and so Vamana played tricks on me. Over the years I betrayed an increasing preoccupation in my work with littleness, hugeness and all distortions of scale. Nobody gave a damn about the big stuff, but the wilful insertion of dwarfish characters into my stories was . . . insensitive. Worse still were the riffs on smallness I retailed to my cronies, and the paltry anecdotes they reciprocated with. How this one had attended the Little

People of America convention, where he had seen a primordial dwarf* brother and sister treated like film stars. While that one had written a play about the actors who played the Munchkins in *The Wizard of Oz*; they had stayed at the Culver City Hotel in Los Angeles during the shooting, and it was said they slept four to a bed, with predictably 'comic' antics.

Most shaming of all was the 'game' I devised for my children's amusement when they were small, 'Child or Dwarf'. Driving in the car, if one of us saw an ambiguous figure walking along the pavement we would cry out 'Child or dwarf?' and the others would make their guesses until we pulled past and turned to observe his or her face. What could possibly have been my motivation for this sick and derogatory form of 'entertainment', which was nothing less than laughing at someone's misfortune? What was the difference between my behaviour and that of the Victorian showmen who had exhibited Charles Byrne, the Irish Giant, or Caroline Crachami, the Sicilian Dwarf? Even those who had taken these poor folk's bodies when they died, dissected them, rearticulated their bones, then put their skeletons on show in the Hunterian Museum had science – or at least pseudo-science – on their side, but I had nothing but the sham jocundity of those who, having much to hide, expose themselves over and over again.

What did I expect to see when the car drew level with, then passed, the small and heroic figure that stumped between the elongated legs of the shoppers who *font du lèche-vitrines* along the King's Road? Had that jacket been purchased in the boys' outfitting department of Peter Jones by a parent or the person

---

* Of all the 200 syndromes associated with restricted height, primordial dwarfism results in smallest and most fairylike individuals.

who wore it? Was this a child, a dwarf – or Sherman, who, until I had the courage to confront him, would remain both for me?

When I eventually met up with Sherman Oaks again he was nothing but charm itself. His eldest sister, Prima, had a share in a Bond Street gallery. I'd seen her about town – she was in her fifties now, but not showing it. She'd been sending me her pasteboards for a while before she began personalizing them. Then one day she sent an invitation to an opening that was emphatic: 'Please come. Sherman will definitely be there, he so wants to see you again. Please.'

I went, and stood on the fringes of the openeers, a representative sample from the Venn intersection of Taste and Money that exhibited not much of either. The works themselves weren't too bad: they looked like enormous drinks coasters attached to the hessian walls, and bore the curved stains that had, presumably, been left there by enormous glasses. I couldn't identify the artist, but assumed he must be at the epicentre of a particularly dense thicket of tastefulness – assumed, until trunks parted and I spied Sherman holding forth.

I had seen photographs and television pictures of the great man; still, I was shocked. Sherman had always had the large head and short limbs associated with achondroplastic dwarfism. (I defer from using the term 'disproportionate'; after all, who is to say which body form represents the human mean?) As a child, on his broad face the precise nose, etched cheekbones and petaline lips he shared with his sisters had seemed a little lost – morsels on a fleshy plate. Now the blue eyes weren't just fierce but commanding, while the cultivation of neat moustachios and a stroke of beard accented his stronger features. He had, I realized, based his look on the Velázquez portrait of a court dwarf, Don Sebastián de Morro. This was typically Shermanesque chutzpah, then, as he came towards me, round-housing one leg then the other, I took in the well-cut dark clothes that allowed his face to float, as if disembodied, within its aureole of white-blond hair.

He came right up to me before saying hello. Sherman had always done this: tucked his short body inside the personal space of others, so challenging us to refute the idea that it was he who was the measure of all things. We talked easily and unaffectedly, although of what exactly I have no recall. Probably there was a deal of cynicism about the drinks coasters; I do remember laughing in a full-bellied way that I hadn't since I'd last heard his devastating wit. He drew you in, Sherman, and so drew you down. You began by bending your neck, but, as he continued rubbishing reputations and lisping shibboleths, you'd find yourself bending over, then hunching, then hunkering down, until finally you were squatting or even kneeling in front of him, mesmerized both by what he said and by his unusual intonation – a trifle old-fashioned – as he barked, 'Jolly good!' or affirmed 'Quite right!' about something he himself had just said.

After that initial meeting we fell readily enough into a pattern of regular contact, meeting up at a Chinese restaurant in Baker Street near his flat for long – and, on his part, bibulous – suppers. We reassumed the easy commerce of our teenage friendship, and it made me wonder if this was true for all men: that it was impossible to attain such proximity to another man, unless you had known him before the hardening of that deceptively transparent carapace: the ego.

There was more. At an experimental play we attended in a warehouse theatre – Sherman was friends with the stratospherically famous actress who was slumming in the lead – our seats were on a two-foot-high dais. When we arrived Sherman hoiked himself up on to this with no prevarication, then, when the lights came up at the end of the single act, he stood, turned to me and raised his arms. Responding involuntarily I lifted him down.

When Sherman visited our home for the first time, he descended the steep steps to the basement kitchen quite unafraid, despite our yapping snapping Jack Russell. I yanked the dog away and slapped it, but Sherman only remarked, 'I'm not too fond of dogs for obvious reasons.' He charmed my wife and saw fit to ignore our youngest son – then aged six – who, having been cowering upstairs prior to Sherman's arrival, saying he was scared of 'the elf', now tiptoed up behind him so he could compare their heights.

Grace is what my wife said Sherman possessed, and, although this was a quality I had never associated with him when we were young, I could concede it to him now. My own behaviour had by contrast been utterly graceless – was it any surprise that my children had been corrupted by my facetiousness? As I grew closer to Sherman once more, I tried to squeeze this bladder, inflated with mockery, into the smallest cavity inside of myself. The disappearing trick didn't work.

Dreams began to plague me. In them, trampolining children shot inexorably skywards from the back gardens of suburbia. In my reverie I saw first one, then two or four, their trainers skimming past the cherry blossom. Then my perspective changed: I was out on the marshes to the east of the city, and looking back could see a purple-grey cyclone hunched over the endless rooftops, rising up into the firmament, into which were being sucked a myriad vortices, each one comprised of a myriad children.

The children of London – they were being taken up. Yet this was no Rapture, for I knew there was nothing above them but the vacuum. I had to warn someone, but I'd lost my shoe and slashed my cheese-white foot on some razor wire. Up in the heavens the haemorrhaging had begun, tens of thousands of little lungs filling up with blood.

## 2

# Round the Horn

Sherman Oaks stood stabbing the end of his unlit cigar at the South Downs and described his latest project to me: a 30-metre-high iron statue that he wished plunked in the River Seine: 'It'll be ten times life size, knee-deep in those *bière*-coloured waters and slap-bang opposite the Bibliothèque Nationale. Unlike *Behemoth* this one'll be a hollow figure, the outer layer of which will be cut away in transverse sections – like an anatomical model – to reveal its interior.'

'And what will be inside?' I felt obliged to ask.

'Aha!' He sucked on the damp butt. 'Inside it will be hundreds – thousands probably – of smaller solid figures, varying in size from the very little to the twice life size.'

'So, the big figure is Pantagruel the giant, while the small figures it contains—'

'Are representative of all the odd distortions of his size in the novels – yes, yes, of course. You would've thought that in the city where Rabelais died there'd be enormous enthusiasm for such an exciting piece, but the planning committee are proving almost wilfully obstructive – banging on about the preservation of the skyline!'

I tried to be tactful. 'You have to concede, Sherman, that this would be a very, um, radical, addition, to a traditionally, er, traditional city. But, tell me, is there a Rabelaisian anniversary of some kind – I mean, what's the pretext?'

Sherman put his sculptural head to one side of his plinth of a body and scrutinized me. He seemed on the verge of a crushing put-down, but was interrupted by the cheap-bleep of his mobile phone, which he fetched up from one of the pockets of his self-designed silk waistcoat. He turned away and began barking into it:

'No, no, call Klaus in Stuttgart, he has the plans, he'll be able to email them to the Kapellmeister in Berne . . . What's that? No, I'm in Sussex . . . Suss-ex, not *having* sex – but I'll be flying to Bremen late this evening so have Heidi send copies to the hotel there for me, and make sure the tent's there too . . . Yes, and the crampons . . . Cramp. Ons, yes, quite right, jolly good!'

I wasn't certain whether I found Sherman's habit of punctuating our times together with these noisy one-sided conversations infuriating or endearing. Invariably it was me who proposed the excursions, then made the arrangements, and, while I was flattered that the Great Man dealt with me directly, unobstructed by the small tribe of factotums that staffed his growing atelier, I couldn't help but feel that his inability to cease from his Herculean labours was a message barked at me: See how busy I am! How sought after! How creatively fired up!

It was true that Sherman's career trajectory had become near-vertical in the fifteen years since *Behemoth* bestrode the Manchester Ship Canal. Now, not a week went by without an invitation arriving at my house to an Oaks opening in Seoul or Soweto, Kiev or Cancun. Along with executing smaller works for private galleries and public collections, Sherman politicked remorselessly: trying to arrange funding and permissions so that he could have body forms poised on Alpine mountaintops, or sunk in Norwegian fjords, or submerged where the Kattegat met the Skagerrak.

Taken in sum, Sherman's works were acquiring a peculiar sort of public reverence – as if they were secular votive objects.

Their very simplicity, combined with their creator's refusal to spout the usual arty-gnomic guff, seemed to inspire people's devotion. You might've imagined that the critics would have accused Sherman's big things of exhibiting the usual fanfaronade of the monumental, which, historically, has been a totalitarian mode, yet they said nothing of the sort; instead the notion took root that this was an individualistic, Neoliberal giganticism – besides, in a globalized world of ever taller buildings, longer bridges and thicker dams, Sherman's statues were, comparatively speaking . . . dinky.

That no one saw fit to remark on the way Sherman was populating the world with big Shermans I found inexplicable. Moreover, while it was well known that all the body forms were derived from casts of Sherman's own body that were then enlarged, what everyone seemed oblivious to was that the basic unit of Shermanness – one Sherman, if you will – was not his actual height, 3'3", but 6'4". That this was my own height may have been a coincidence – if an odd one.

On the first point, as a friend of sufficient long-standing to have seen him playing with clackers, I felt able to tackle the Maître: 'Isn't it a little egotistical,' I ventured across the table in the Heavenly Kingdom, 'the way that all your works are, um, you?' I was almost blown away by the vehemence of his rebuttal:

'For fuck's sake! Don't be so dumbly, simplistically, bruisingly, prosaically predictable, *mate.*' He speared a prawn ball with a chopstick. 'The works aren't *me*. It doesn't matter that they're based on my own body any more than it matters that pharaonic statues were all made using a single set of standardized measurements and dimensions of someone who wasn't even a fucking pharaoh! The point is that the body forms are archetypes – they are *every*man.'

The obvious rejoinder – as a person of restricted height Sherman was not *that* archetypal – died in my mouth. Had I uttered it when riled, I may have been unable to prevent myself asking him not only why he scaled up his own height to mine, but also why he thought no one else had done the calculation. This seemed especially bizarre, given a recent public exhibition had involved one hundred 'life-sized' Shermans being ranged right along Hadrian's Wall – yet nobody pointed out that all of them were six-footers.

It made me ponder whether my own guilt was only a subsection of a more widespread shame. Perhaps the unacknowledged six-foot dwarfs were evidence of a collective uneasiness about the sizeism that dare not speak its name? Or maybe – in Britain and, increasingly, the States as well – the scaling up of the small was registered, albeit unconsciously, as a just commentary on the misadventures of post-imperial nations that were in stature denial, and went on punching above their weight in the world arena, KOing hundreds of thousands of blameless everymanikins?

So, I said nothing in the Heavenly Empire, and I said still less up on the Downs; where we walked on, with Sherman fleshing out the impression of his next week's itinerary that I had been given by the phone call. The tent and crampons were needed for a trip up on to the Grosser Aletsch glacier, where the installation of an heroic group of Shermans – the central one standing 37 metres, and surrounded by five more half that size – was being strenuously fought by what the artist termed 'a bathetic coalition of tree-huggers and chalet maids', with whose positions, nonetheless, he sympathized.

It was at the core of Sherman's steely grace that he refused his disability the right to dictate his physical limitations. When he was young this had seemed feisty; now he was middle aged it had taken on an almost mystical character. Sherman Oaks couldn't gaze upon lake, river or sea without stripping off and diving into it. Confronted by a rocky wall or an icy defile, he would insist on scrambling up it. If on our rambles we came across signs prohibiting access or fences barring it, Sherman was duty bound to trespass.

Thus he kicked against the pricks – but they remained big ones. He had great energy but it was wearisome for him to walk more than a mile or two. So he was almost always attended by his driver, Baltie (short for Balthazar), a dim old Etonian, who, as Sherman put it – out of his earshot – 'Rather than being equipped with an elaborate and expensive education should've aged fourteen been packed off to deliver groceries!'

On this particular day Baltie had picked us up in the Range Rover where the train halted at Plumpton Racecourse. Then he drove us up a track on to the Downs, and Sherman walked with me to Ditchling Beacon; then, in his own coinage, he 'called in a Baltie-strike'. I next saw him at Saddlescombe, where he clambered down from the car and accompanied me to the Devil's Dyke.

Such a punctuated companionship did have its advantages: being with Sherman for more than an hour or two at a time was *de trop*. The constant phone calls, the bluster, the charging into fields with bulls in them – it all grew wearing; besides, I also needed time alone to process (the therapese is warranted here) certain psychological symptoms that had been latent in me for many years, and were now coming disturbingly to the fore.

Were those the shreds of black plastic bags caught on the legs of the pylons that strode over the hills? Or were they the clothes of plane-crash victims who in death had transgressed the first commandment of globalism: keep your belongings with you at all times? Was there any more distressing sight to behold than television news images of rayon blouses, frumpy brown skirts and smalls unlaundered for the entire fortnight, now caught in the bushes at the airport's perimeter? To say nothing of the holdalls and suitcases that lay ruptured like sickeningly burst boils. *Enfin*, the corpses, neatly packed away in body bags, all they once possessed having already been decanted.

In eleven days' time I was due to leave for a fortnight's book tour, heading first to Toronto and then on to several cities in the USA. Due to, but I was questioning whether I could go at all, since my as yet unpacked bag dragged on me like an anchor. Of course, I had long since dispensed with anything but carry-on and was taking only a small rucksack – and not one of those pantechnicons you see being hauled up the aisle, a shotgun marriage between human and trunk. The lapwing pee-witting up above me, the ladybird millimetring along the buttercup at my feet, the red kite swooping between me and Fulking, or the rabbit hopping across the chalky path – were they so encumbered? I yearned in my own life to re-create Duchamp's *Boîte-en-valise* by stylizing my impedimenta over and over again, each time reducing the scale of books, clothing and toiletries, until all I took with me was a sheaf of sketches slipped inside my wallet. Nowadays, the thought of carrying anything more seemed grotesque, making of my world an *n*th-class cabin into which – my greasepaint moustache shining – I manoeuvred the steamer trunk packed with the other Capitalist Brothers.

\*    \*    \*

At the Devil's Dyke, Sherman and I sat on a bench. I wanted to tell him the folk tale associated with this great V-shape gouged out of the chalk escarpment. How the Devil, bent on flooding the Sussex Weald so as to drown all its sleeping cotters, one night set to with his mighty spade, aiming to dig a ditch through the Downs. But an old woman living alone in a farmhouse awoke in the small hours and lit her lamp. Satan, fearing the dawn, cast his tool aside and with a howl leapt all the way across the Weald to the North Downs, where he landed, thus creating the enormous depression now known as the Devil's Punchbowl.

Wanted to – but couldn't, because Sherman, while chewing a pizzle of biltong I'd handed him, was on the phone to a powerful arts *Gauleiter* half a world away, etching with incisive verbalizations his plan to implant the crater of Rano Kau, the volcano at the south-west corner of Easter Island, with scores – if not hundreds – of carved basalt Shermans, latter-day moai that, like those celebrated statues, would awe visitors by the sheer implausibility of their being in that place at all.

'Make it happen!' Sherman cried, then turning to me said, 'So, what were you saying?' But then he was interrupted once more by the fo-fiddle-i-o of contemporaneity, so that while he exchanged yelps with some willowy curator in a Berlin bunker I was left to tell myself that the destination for this trip was Lancing College, which stood on its knoll on the far side of the River Adur. My father and uncle had been educated there, and the neo-Gothic pile loomed large in the family mythology, having been founded by my great-great-grandfather, Nathaniel Woodard.

His photograph – an original daguerreotype – had hung in the gloomy stairwell between the second and third storeys of my grandparents' house on Vernon Terrace in Brighton, throughout the interminable Sunday afternoons of my childhood. It now hung in exactly the same position in my own terraced house in South London. The High Anglican churchman, and apostle of public school education to the rising middle classes, sat, life sized, behind thick glass, edged in gilt and framed with black mahogany, his expression at once stern and soppy, his cheeks furry.

At Lancing we would find something pleasingly out of joint – another oddity to add to our collection. Together, Sherman and I had visited the Tradescants' monument at St Mary at Lambeth, and, rubbing away the lichen from the tomb, read the inscription: 'Whilst they (as Homer's *Iliad* in a nut) / A world of wonders in one closet shut' – a reference to the gardening family's celebrated 'cabinet of curiosities', the Ark, which in the seventeenth century occupied a site close to my house. In place of the long-departed Ark there was now a takeaway called Chicken World, which seemed painfully apt: a world of chickens in one box shut . . .

Another time Baltie had driven Sherman and me down the M3 to Painshill. Here we had wandered Charles Hamilton's landscaped park, surveying its grottoes, its ruined abbey, cascade and temple. Standing by the lake while Sherman bellowed at a banker in Shanghai, I was entranced as a flotilla of model dreadnoughts came cruising by, line abreast; then appalled, when one of these six-foot Edwardian warships was opened from within, the entire deck and superstructure flipping up to reveal the pasty face of the middle-aged boy who was lying inside.

I thought often of Claude Lévi-Strauss, still alive and buzzing at a hundred, an anthropological bee deep in the honeyed hive of the Sorbonne. It was his contention – made with reference to Clouet's portrait of Elizabeth of Austria – that all miniatures have an intrinsic aesthetic quality derivable from their very dimensions. So it was that Sherman and I set out for Godshill, a model village on the Isle of Wight, where we discovered a model of the model village inside of it, and inside this model, model village a third.

Not that we neglected the sublime; after all, Sherman's own works were themselves Burke's 'great objects and terrible', willed concretizations that forced us into submission – albeit democratically. So we visited Northern Ireland for the weekend, and Baltie drove us in a rental Range Rover back and forth along the lanes to the south-west of Belfast, until we were able to establish the exact location from which Swift had seen the Divis and the Black Mountain massif as a recumbent giant, the easternmost tumulus of Cave Hill being its nose.

I had also proposed a longer trip to the remote Shetland island of Foula, although, given the lack of network coverage, I very much doubted Sherman would agree to go. On Foula we could see thousand-foot sea cliffs, vaulting stone arches, plunging rocky gullies – and all of this natural giganticism crammed into nine square miles. It was the ultimate fantasia on the sublime themes of the very big and the very little.

Not that either of us mentioned the B or the L word. It may have been all right for Sherman to say in public that he was a very small man who made very big things, but that was a deflection that effectively stymied any more penetrating questioning. I didn't want to talk about it either – I enjoyed Sherman's company, his curious grace, his hunger for life, his all-devouring eye, but I knew that sooner or later we would have to confront what was going on, then there it would be, winched upright like one of his own body forms, my vast and artfully oxidized shame.

Sherman finished his call and after we'd settled on our next rendezvous he joined Baltie in the Range Rover and they bumped away. I went on alone along the ridge, past fields where cattle lay as brown and glossy as the pools of their own shit. Six hundred feet below lay the amiable farmland of the Weald, while up here I simply revolved in my cloudy ball. But between Perching and Edburton hills my moodiness fused into a certainty: I could no longer cope at all with the infantilizing demanded by intercontinental air travel. It was over: no more would I dutifully respond to those parental injunctions go here, go there, empty my pockets and take off my shoes. Never again would I take my underpants to see the world, which meant in turn that never would the world witness them espaliered on a hedge.

I say fused, but disintegrated would be closer to the truth. Of course, I had always performed certain . . . rituals, but doesn't everyone? Doesn't everyone count the cracks and divide them by the number of paving stones? Doesn't everyone ascribe numerical values to each action and every thing, then compute their way through the day? Doesn't everyone listen to the fridge intently so as to be certain that its vibration calibrates with their pulse and heartbeat? Doesn't everyone wash their hands because they touched the soap? Doesn't everyone *know* that each digit has its own personality – feckless 2, arrogant 1, incurably romantic 9? Doesn't everyone fear the world and their own subjectivity getting out of sync? It's true that no one I knew personally wielded a Polaroid camera as I did, taking one snap of the knobs on the front of the gas cooker, a second of the fridge door shut, a third of my hand holding the front-door knob, a fourth of the blur as I pulled it to, a fifth of my hand pushing it to confirm that the latch had sprung. Nor did I see anyone stopping, as I did, halfway to the tube and shuffling through these shiny squares of recency – but that doesn't mean they weren't doing it, does it?

All the walls of my writing room were tessellated with Polaroids, and the shiny tide was creeping up on to the ceiling when I bought my first digital camera. What a relief! Now I need only pause in front of the urinal, in the empty youth hostel on top of the Downs, to confirm that the world and I were continuing to coincide. It helped – a bit.

Coming down off the ridge over stiles and between fizzing pylons, the Adur appeared, flowing sluggishly between curving banks. A derelict cement works stood on the floodplain, its dirty chimney giving the finger to the overcast sky. And in the hazy mid-ground loomed the spiritual aircraft hangar I was bound for: the massive chapel of Lancing College. Its rose window was the biggest in England, its nave higher than that of Notre-Dame. Had the chapel's tower ever been built it would, at 350 feet, have rivalled those of Chartres.

My ancestor had insisted that, despite the scarcity of funding, one end of the chapel be raised to its full height at the very start, lest he or his successors ever waver in their ambition to build this very big thing. And now his bronze effigy lay in a tomb lodged in one side of the soaring nave, like a fishbone caught in the deity's gullet – although a very High Anglican he had been a smallish man.

I crossed the river by a footbridge and walked past a fishery where miserable men sat on hired jetties, their rods dangling in a bilious pond. After a flurry of phone calls, I met up with Sherman and Baltie in a chalky hollow. The Range Rover lumped away, its thick tyres white-walled with clods, leaving the two of us to snap and crackle through the autumnal undergrowth towards the hypertrophied house of God.

We emerged from the woodland into the teensy paddocks and chicken-wire enclosures of the College's farm. *But if 350 feet high why not 35, or 3,500?* There were recently shorn alpacas that looked like Dr Seuss's therianthropes. There were also a couple of motos in a fenced-off wallow. As ever I found the motos' nuzzling baby-faced muzzles repulsive, but Sherman lisped away happily with them; then, while he took a call from a Milanese brassière manufacturer who was sitting beside the drained infinity pool of his Ibizan villa, he caressed their jonckheeres.

We were expected, and an amiable youth met us at the headmaster's office then guided us around the flint-knapped quads. He was possessed of sufficient sangfroid not to react to our oddness as a couple, while I found myself unbearably affected by the large spot on his neck to which a concealer had been uselessly applied, and also by the Windsor knot of his school tie. By the time the lad had itemized the crests and memorials and was leading us back through swags of drizzle towards the chapel I was openly weeping.

'Buck up!' Sherman snapped.

Inside the chapel the organ pipes were wrapped in translucent plastic – it was more than a century since Canon Woodard's death and still the biggering continued. I found his tomb and pressed my ear to his bronze breast, beside where his married hands rose, the keel of this capsized prayer boat. Sherman took a photo with his iPhone, and said, 'Very good.'

Afterwards Baltie drove us into Brighton and dropped us on the edge of the Lanes. Sherman and I walked through the quaint zone to English's, the fish restaurant. We ate on the second floor, sitting side by side with our backs to the window, and observing the sole other table of diners as if they were a repertory play – which in a way I suppose they were. Sherman didn't help my digestion by whispering improvised dialogue for these two couples, most of which was obscene. He also professed himself to be delighted with our outing as he snidely dissected his own Dover sole.

I had my doubts – I was beginning to suspect that Sherman was toying with me, just as he toyed with the Californian ephebe who phoned during dinner, and whom Sherman had assured would be in receipt of a body form that was 633.333 recurring feet high within the month. *But why not 6,333, or 63.3?* 'Believe it!' He belched as the other diners looked at us for a change. 'This mother is so big it'll be able to lean its elbow on the roadway of the Golden Gate as if it were a *bar*.'

Baltie drove us back to London and when they dropped me off I said goodbye to Sherman casually, without making any arrangement for the future. But I felt certain we would meet again soon – a reckoning of some kind was long overdue.

# 3
## *Fin du trottoir roulant*

Eleven days later, despite all my queer resistances and awkward premonitions, I left for Canada. I took no luggage with me, only a Barbour jacket* I had bought from their concession in Mohamed Al Fayed's Harrods department store, the capacious pockets of which I intended to fill with a few essential things. But, despite this simple solution to my luggage phobia, I still lay awake night after night obsessing in nauseating detail how I would 'pack' the jacket.

It didn't help that it was hot in the bed – an emperor-sized cherrywood *lit bateau*. None of our four children had ever quite managed to make it through the night in their own beds. No matter how many times I lifted them up, their sweaty thighs clamped about my hips, and laboured upstairs to put them down again, they still came creeping back and wormed their way in. Our eldest son was away at university; however, he not only walked but entrained in his sleep, and often in the small hours I would hear his key in the lock, followed by the heavy tramp of his feet, he would push the dog aside and insinuate his adult form so that the six of us lay tightly packed, like the

* I'd never owned one of these waxed cotton jackets before – they were standard-issue country kit for the scions of the British upper and upper-middle classes and as such an anathema; but I needed a garment versatile enough to cope with a 30-degree temperature range and all kinds of precipitation. After the success of Stephen Frears's *The Queen* (2006), in which Helen Mirren, looking frumpily monarchical, sported a Barbour while staring balefully at Scots glens cluttered with antlers, Americans couldn't get enough of them and Stateside sales increased by 400 per cent. *40 per cent would've been too much – and yet, curiously, 4,000 per cent still credible – these were after all boom years.*

victims of a civil disaster laid out on the varnished floorboards of a school gymnasium.

I visualized filling the pockets, then emptying them, filling them – then emptying them, over and over again. Should I put that in there, or this? I fretted until the predawn, when I heard the milkman wheedle open the gate and set down three bottles of half-fat, *or was it a third of a bottle or thirty?* In the half-light the methane off the entire family lay in a mustard haze atop the Flanders of the duvet, my sons' bayonets digging into me from either side, my mind roved across the terrain of the past: *The human race was doomed, the only link with survival passed through time.*

My obsessions with bigness, with littleness, with all distortions in scale – surely this was only a spatial expression of my own arrested development? In my mid-twenties I had still been living in my mother's flat and speaking a shared idiolect of mushy diminutives – '-kins', '-ums' and 'noo-noo' – with her that we referred to shamelessly as 'baby talk'. Had her premature death not thrust me into the actual-sized world, we might've been there still, me with my collections of Langenscheidt Lilliput dictionaries, she with her hefty Henry James novels. While I remained in the spare bedroom – which, due to the botched conversion of the Victorian house, had the proportions of an upright cereal box – dreamily making little tableaux with trolls, pencil erasers and .002-scale plastic soldiers, she would sit in the front room, concentrating hard on the subtle velleities of James's characters.

It was not to be. Instead, it was 'Off with her head!' as the cancer shot up through the meningeal fluids of her spine to her brain, and I was thrust through the little door and into the caucus race of adulthood, which has no precise start or finish, and although everyone is promised a prize, only a select few ever receive them.

A minute envelope materializes, the flap of which opens and closes while arrows arc up and down, conveying the strong impression to the user – and the suggestion of physiological addiction is highly appropriate – that vital communications are being transmitted through the ether. She sits there, radiation pinging off the back of her retinas, unable to tear her eyes from this very little thing – the envelope icon – which is an insult to the illustrious history of the epistolary – I mean to say: who's this email from, Laclos?

Of course, of course, all new technologies cannibalize their predecessors: the horses are put down and the carriage rolls on complete with postilions and oil lamps. If futurological imaginings establish anything at all, it's woe betide anyone who dares to conceive of the unbecome in too great a detail – and yet here we are, with the entire Library of Babel inscribed on a pin, and a trillion web pages expressed by the digits 1 and 0.

A few days later I set off, leaving wife, children and dog, all laid out on this weekend morning like idols in their great bed of wear. The last vision of home I took with me was of the fat woman who lives in the block of flats opposite, and whose bedroom window is exactly level with that of my writing room. As I slid notebook, passport, etc. into the pockets of my waxy jacket she swished back her curtains then proceeded to plump up her duvet, punching the white slug with her yellowy-black fists.

At the end of the road I paused to check I had turned off the cooker, shut the fridge and closed the front door. At my feet a concrete bollard lay toppled on the pavement: the severed penis of a god at once Brutalist and *kaloi*. I looked for Lysippus among the bus drivers smoking outside their garage . . . the lime trees in their raised beds were losing their foliage . . . and then, quite suddenly, I was at Paddington – no, Heathrow, and wandering shoeless and unbelted through security.

If I was going to be infantilized, why couldn't I be miniaturized? Miniaturized along with Jane Fonda in a mini-submarine, then injected into America – but no, there would be no fantastic voyage, only the atomizers of Arpège on the shelves of the Duty Free, *why not 5mls or 500?*, empty suitcases chained outside a luggage store, and beneath a TV monitor some frummers davening as they laid tefillin. There was the travelator, a grooved tongue glistening as if with saliva, ready to slurp me up into the belly of the beast.

Since I'd started to see Sherman again I'd had a revulsion from any 'humour' associated with dwarfism. Unfortunately, I'd been at it for so long that people still brought me anecdotes they thought would amuse me. Only the day before I left, a friend told me of a rash of audacious thefts from Scandinavian luxury tourist coaches. The authorities were confounded: the tourists' suitcases had been in the locked luggage compartment of the coaches all day, yet when they reached their hotel and went to unpack they found all their valuables had been spirited away.

The police could find no leads, until at last an informer of restricted height came forward. He had been, he told them, a member of a gang of dwarfs who had enlisted larger accomplices to go on the tours, while they hid in their suitcases. Once the coaches were under way the dwarfs unzipped themselves and went to work. The inversion of drug smugglers' modus operandi had a certain symmetry – here was the package that ingested the mule – but I didn't believe a word of it.

I took off the Barbour and dropped it in the corner of the toilet stall where I squatted shortly before boarding. It was so stiff with stuff and waxing that it leant there – about the height of a small child, or a dwarf. I strained, fixating on the creases in its collar, *pursed black lips*. After only a few days' ownership the jacket seemed to be taking on a life of its own, *what might it do to me while I sleep?* Then, when I rose to wipe myself and jumped as the toilet automatically flushed, it smirked at me from behind its cuff.

But in club class, with the hateful thing stashed in the overhead locker, I was free of all burdens, free to smirk at the frummer who was making his way awkwardly up the aisle dragging an enormous wheeled case, which bumped against one seat back and then the next. He was overweight and sweat wormed from beneath his hot homburg, his silk-faced frock coat falling open to reveal a black cummerbund and untuckings of white shirt. He seemed oblivious to the little anguishes he was causing – pre-flight champagne spilled, a laptop jogged – his eyes, in the shadows between his heron's nest beard and his hat brim, unaffected, or so it seemed to me, by proximate concerns, yet brimming with the awe and anxiety provoked by Yahweh.

Consulting his ticket, he threw himself down beside me, ignoring the bag, which was left for a brace of cabin crew, straining like navvies, to lever into a locker. Then, nothing: we sat eyes front, with nought to meditate on but a spray of plastic flowers in a vase bolted to a bulkhead. The fabric of the aircraft whiningly tensed, groaningly relaxed. The co-pilot came on the PA: we had, he said, been slow getting away from the gate and now we'd lost our one o'clock slot; as soon as he had any more information he would let us know. But he didn't. We sat in that rebreathed time, inhaling seconds, then minutes, then half hours. The frummer grew restless and began making a flurry of phone calls, slooshing Yiddish into the only clamshell he was allowed. Finally the stewardess came to tell him to stop phoning because the plane was taxiing, but this too he ignored.

I found the frummer heartening; his contradictory behaviour – at once mystical and insufferably worldly – seemed wholly in keeping with the paradox of modern air travel, whereby millions of pounds of thrust, a galaxy of halogen lights and leagues of concrete encapsulate a mundane environment dominated by the most trivial concerns. And it was while I was reflecting on this that the four merciless deities bolted to the wings began to howl and the jet trundled along the runway with all the grace of a stolen shopping trolley, then rattled into the clouds.

When a while after takeoff the stewardess came by I ordered herb salad, followed by Vincent Bhatia's prawn bhuna masala with coconut and curry leaf rice. Oh, and Eton mess to follow. The frummer laid tefillin. Of course, I knew a bit about phylacteries – they were bound to appeal to me – and if I'd ever inclined to observance tying little boxes to my head would've been a big part of the draw.

I chewed salad – he lashed the *shel yad* to his arm and the *shel rosh* to his head. I ate curry – he prayed: *And it shall be for a sign for you upon your head, and as a memorial between your eyes, that the law of the LORD may be in your mouth, for with a strong hand has the LORD brought you out of Egypt. You shall therefore keep this ordinance in its season from year to year.*

This, just one of the injunctions for the faithful to write down on parchment that a box was to be tied to their head, which was then put in a box that was tied to their head – a reduction ad absurdum that made me dizzy with joy. That within the tefillin was a scroll upon which no fewer than 3,188 Hebrew characters were written in kosher ink confirmed the magical intent. After all, it took fifteen hours with a limner's abject concentration to write them, and if one was wrong, or two were out of order, the juju *wouldn't work*: no mitzvah! This little black box was the flight recorder for a Haredi jet-propelled through life by the *halacha*, a set of rules so comprehensive – if open to labyrinthine interpretation – that they told him what he should be doing every moment of the day, and exactly how he should be doing it.

What was my own life beside such finicky precision? Cack-handed! Anomic! Eton-messy! True, the parchment scrolls of

Torah verses were by no means the smallest books in existence,* but they had the virtue of being fragments of a single work that was all you ever needed to read – if, that is, you believed the universe had been created by a omnipotent games-playing deity with attention-deficit disorder as a real-time moral-philosophic experiment. I had my doubts.

Mm, house truffle, Earl Grey pearl and liquid salted caramel – popping one of the dusty balls into my mouth I preferred to think of Him as a cosmic *artisan du chocolat*. The plane had reached its cruising height of 35,000 feet over Ireland, *but why not 350,000 so we could orbit the earth with fiery Apollo, or 3,500*

---

* Which is Vesper Enfärhschein's edition of fifty copies of Kafka's 'In the Penal Settlement', each a 45-page book, with 22 lines of type per page, each book measuring .45 of a millimetre square, leather bound, gilt-tooled and slip-covered.

*so we could see the zephyrs comb the heathery chest of the Black Mountain?* Ach! The vicious constraint of worshipping the infinite through the contemplation of the vanishingly small was getting to me – that and the multiplying and then dividing of truffles, clods, bald-headed men and book pages . . . I must have slept, exhausted – or at least assumed I was dreaming, otherwise it would've been madness to pop the catch of the overhead locker with the frummer's great crate in it.

The plane hit an air pocket and the case slammed down on top of me. The zip was already open and Sherman tumbled out, dressed in a black rollneck and black jeans, equipped with a head torch and wire cutters. 'What the fuck!' he exclaimed. 'I assumed the frummer would check me in as hold baggage.'

I looked up the aisle, but the cabin crew were all goofing off in their curtained booth; as for the passengers, not a single one seemed to have noticed – they were all lost in the light caves hollowed out of the back of each other's heads. Sherman disentangled himself from old-fashioned flannel underpants, long black socks and a prayer shawl. I watched him, thinking of the first six-inch TV I'd had back in the early 1980s.

While the miners had fought the Battle of Orgreave, I lay on a slagheap of mattresses watching James Robertson Justice play Vashtar, the leader of an enslaved people (I don't recall the J-word) compelled to build a mighty pyramid for the Pharaoh. The wide open desert, the massed teams of extras pulling stone blocks on rollers, the whole CinemaScope sweep of the epic compressed into that tiny screen – I squinted at it, awed.

'C'mon,' hissed Sherman, leading me aft.

As we prowled up the aisle the plane banked slightly and my eyes were flung sideways down through a window to where, 17,000 feet below, the emulsive cloud had congealed into a vast simulacrum of the paths, box hedges and yew avenues of a formal eighteenth-century garden. As I watched, humbled, a monstrous baby staggered upright from the horizon 300 miles away, its chubby arms formed by vortices of cumulo-stratus. As the plane drew closer I saw that this apparition was one of my own children; it seemed that Gaia had been busy uploading the essence of my sentimentality and fashioning it into this towering love object – which we flew straight through.

'Will you come on!' Sherman pulled my sleeve, and reluctantly I joined him between the stainless-steel galley and the flimsy toilet doors, where he went unerringly to a section of carpet and lifted it to expose a D-ring. He opened the hatch and we let ourselves down into the cold booming hold, the beam of his head torch picking out the Samsonite blocks on pallets.

'Y'know Faulkner had a screen credit on *Land of the Pharaohs*,' I remarked, apropos of everything, but Sherman only hissed:

'Will you shut the fuck up,' and went about his task with a will, snapping combination locks with his clippers, then unzipping the bags so that their contents spilled on to the aluminium deck.

'Look at this drek,' he said, snatching up a handful of stuff. I recognized the seat covers we had had in my childhood home, the print of a historic map of Worcestershire that had hung above the phone table, a paperback edition of C. E. M. Joad's *Guide to Modern Wickedness* and my mother's dentures.

'Can you believe people cross the Atlantic with such tat,' he spat, 'and pay for it too!'

'Dentures are pretty much essential,' I said, 'if you don't have any teeth.'

Sherman slid down the baffler of bags until he was sitting. The cyclopean eye of his torch dazzled me, and his voice – nasal, insistent – soared above the jeremiad of the jets. 'You and your dumb books!' he prated. 'Micro-satire, dirty doodlings in the margins of history!'

'I say, that's a bit harsh.'

'Is it? When Gutenberg invented the printing press there were at most a hundred titles produced annually; by 1950 this had swollen to a quarter of a million; now a book is published somewhere in this dumb world every twenty seconds, and you have the nerve – no, the *gall*, to contribute to this flood of verbiage that is inexorably inundating the land with ill-contrived metaphors!'

'I – I . . .' I wanted to rebut him forcefully; instead I only spread my hands and said, 'I don't know how to do anything else.'


Add a dream, lose a reader – isn't that Uncle Vladimir's line? Well, the lover of *little* girls has aught to teach me. I awoke as the British Airways flight settled down over Toronto and shat its undercarriage, sending said reader end over end, down to where *the survivors had retreated, a network of tunnels deep under Chaillot. The victors stood guard over a kingdom of rats.* In the half-light before full consciousness I took in the drear panorama of the razed city, the stalk of the CN Tower wilting among the charred stumps of the skyscrapers, the grid pattern of blackened rubble – all of it irradiated by the sickly green glow from Lake Ontario.

I remembered my first visit to Canada in 1977, with my father. We stayed out in Dundas with his friend, the philosopher George Grant. While they debated Red Toryism, I lay upstairs on an iron bedstead smoking. I loved the Players pack, the way

one side read 'Players Filter' and the other 'Players Filtre' – all of Canadian happenstance seemed bound up in the reversal of *e* and *r*.

I took a bus into town and wandered the Hagia Sophia of the Eaton Center in a consumerist ecstasy – it was big enough to swallow whole five of London's poxy malls. I bought a disposable lighter for a few bucks – the first I'd ever seen – and when I got back to Dundas I lay back down on the iron bedstead, then held the translucent green canister to my eye so as to look through the liquid gas.

I left the frummer behind where we had been sitting. He appeared stricken, making none of the phone calls that other passengers had begun the instant the plane had landed; nor did he rise to retrieve his flight bag from the overhead locker. But I couldn't concern myself with that – the flight had arrived almost two hours late – and so I strode off through the dun corridors, hopping on to travelators with whistling insouciance. The two men crammed into dun uniforms at Immigration only glanced at my passport. I was kicking about in the dun arrivals hall, pondering my transport options, when I became aware of snuffling behind me and turning discovered the frummer looking very down-in-the-beard and accompanied by a member of the airline's ground staff, who was pushing a wheelchair in which sat the obese flight bag, its front zip creased in a complacent smile.

'What's the problem?' I asked brightly.

'It's dusk . . . so, it's Shabbat,' he muttered. 'You must've noticed me, on the flight . . . as soon as I realized we were gonna be delayed I began trying to get through to someone by phone.'

'And?'

'Yes' – he stared shamefaced at his black dress shoes – 'I guess you're right – it wouldn't've made any difference, I can't go in any car on Shabbat.'

I was merciless. 'Or bus, or train.'

'Or bus, or train.'

'You'll have to stay out here at the airport.'

'No, no, I can't do that, it's a really important Shabbat, the last before my youngest son's bar mitzvah, I must get home.'

'Well, you should've thought about that before you booked a flight with an insufficient margin of safety.'

'I know, I know,' he moaned.

'Of course' – I looked towards the main doors where gentile-mobiles were pulling away from the kerb with unholy despatch – 'you could always walk.'

'Walk . . .' He savoured the word in a prayerful way.

'Yup' – plunged my hands into the pockets of the Barbour – 'walk – I think I'll walk into town, the weather's OK and I could do with stretching my legs. You're welcome to come with, but I'd advise you to check that into left luggage – it's a good seventeen miles.'

'Walk . . .' I hadn't noticed the flattened vowels of his Canadian accent before, the *a* cowering as if an umlaut had been fired over its head. 'Yes, I guess I could walk, but I'll have to bring my bag, it's got valuable, uh, stuff in it.'

'Stuff, or a valuable person?'

'I'm sorry, I've no idea what you're talking about.'

One of his fish-belly-white hands flipped towards me. 'My name's Reichman, Howard Reichman, and . . . well, it's an awfully big favour to ask but would you consider helping me with the bag – unless, that is, you keep Shabbat yourself?'

I shook my head.

'And I could pay you—'

I shook it again. I felt guilty – but then I always do. In this instance it was guilt over my snide thoughts. However, it wasn't this that motivated me, but the sheer challenge. 'Pleased to meet you, Mr Reichman,' I said. 'Now let's get going.'

As I took the flight bag's handle and trundled away, I wondered: was this one of the Reichmann brothers who ran Olympia & York, at one time the largest property developer in the world? If so, it was a curious coincidence; after all, before they went bust in the recession of '92 they had built the biggest skyscraper London had ever seen, Canary Wharf; not only the biggest – the most banal. I looked back; he was struggling along in my wake. His coat looked hot – his hat hotter; he was as ill-equipped for exodus as anyone I'd ever seen.

On we went along Airport Road, then Silver Dart, before crossing beneath the 427 expressway. To begin with I waited for Reichman to come puffing up in his woefully constricting cummerbund, but soon enough I was struggling with the dumb bag, which lurched from one tiny wheel to the other, yanking my arm in its socket as if it were a drunkenly dependent toddler. I had to lift it over the cobbled ravelins under freeway bridges and hump it up grassy embankments. He was tirelessly grateful. 'Thank you, oh, thank you, most kind,' he kept saying as we rumbled between the down-at-heel warehouses and unbusinesslike premises that lined International Boulevard. When I looked back, the sun was setting behind the airport and the jets coming into land incandesced in its last gleaming.

We reached the Royal Woodbine golf course and I yanked the bag along aggregate paths to a culvert containing Mimico Creek, a rivulet of tea-coloured water that a hundred yards further on disappeared into darkness under Highway 27. 'Surely,' Reichman said, 'you don't mean to . . .' But I did, and so manhandled the bag down to the flat bottom, then dragged it splashing through the shallows, while the observant corvid flapped blackly along behind me.

The Kufic script of aerosol graffiti rippled on the concrete walls; ducklings paddled serenely past. On the far side of Highway 401 I weight-lifted the bag up the embankment and clambered after it, to discover that, although we were now benighted, we were nonetheless entering a kind of Eden – vetch tangled with brambles, maple saplings and the occasional wild iris. We were both entranced: the mondial groan and turbofart of the Lester B. Pearson International Airport had been utterly abstracted by this profound localism. In place of multi-storey car parks there was only an ear of wild wheat bowed to listen to the breeze.

Despite the season and the hour we were both sweating now, and I envied Reichman, because he was able to remove his coat, hat and cummerbund, then, with his back obscuring my view, unzip his case and pack them away inside. I sat groggily on the ground. When Reichman straightened up, Sherman was lying there in the long grass, naked in the half-light save for a skullcap – a newborn, middle-aged savant, with his clever thumb in his intelligent mouth. Nothing is ever funny twice, but it was cheering to hear that immortal line once again: 'Can you tell me the way to Grods?'

But of course he wasn't there – any more than my companion had disrobed outside on Shabbat; both visions were products of my fervid expectation, cooked up in waxed cotton. If I'd taken the Barbour off, I would have to have carried it over my shoulder like a child that had to be returned to its bed – and there was no bed to be found. Still, I went on half expecting Sherman, as all that long Saturday evening I continued hauling the frummer's case through West Deane Park, Ravenscrest Park, Thomas Riley Park, until we eventually reached a jollily lit convenience store on Bloor Street, where I bought a bottle of Evian. He davened, I drank, then we went on again past apartment blocks and monstrous Tudorbethan houses further and further into the city.

Reichman may have been grateful to me for leading him through this suburban netherworld, but I was equally grateful to him. His sanctity enfolded me and I felt as hermetically sealed as a suitcase encased in polythene by one of those weird machines at the airport. I needed this: I needed my cheating heart to remain safely inside of me, foetally curled in my own dirty laundry. I had foolishly craved the freedom of travelling light, yet arrived in the New World more encumbered than ever. It was better to at least share the psychic burden, and so we went on until we reached the junction of Dundas and Spadina in Chinatown, where our ways naturally divided. Reichman got me to drag the bag the last few yards to where it could be temporarily entrusted to the doorman of an apartment block where some friends of his lived. Then, back out in the street, he turned to face me and said, 'I can't thank you enough. You've performed a great mitzvah – you will be blessed.'

He offered me his hand, but I had to restrain myself from grabbing his shirtfront and nestling into his beard.

'You never told me your name,' he said.

'No,' I answered. 'I never did. But listen, leave me alone now like a good chap, will you. I'm footsore and sad, and I want . . .' I nodded to the restaurant beside us, its window hung with orange-glazed ducks, '. . . to eat some pork.'

# 4
## The LongPen

Tony Blair stood, his Church's shoes squishing into the Albertan muskeg, all his vaulting ambitions reduced to this halting lecture tour, all the breadth of his vision focused now on the 1.7 trillion barrels of bitumen – *but why not 17,000,000,000,000, or 170,000,000,000?* – that constitute the world's largest oil deposit, the Athabasca Tar Sands. Meanwhile I rode up to the twenty-second floor of the Westin Harbour Castle Hotel – *but why not the 220th, or a queered mezzanine between the second and third storeys?* – already straitjacketed by Canadian politeness.

Inside the room there were the little comforts, the scaled-down soaps, the cotton buds and the sewing set borrowed from the Borrowers. On the back of the bathroom door hung a terry-towelling robe with a monogram that implied the hotel and I were one. Outside a window that had been shut for thirty-three years genotypic skyscrapers stood about the lake front, awaiting the call to stand in as parts of New York or Chicago.

By way of unpacking I took off the loathsome Barbour; then I rode the elevator up to the penthouse suite, where I registered for the book festival and received my folder full of never-to-be-read info-sheets. The roomesque space was dominated by paper doilies, muffins and a tub of vicious poinsettia; in the corner a tablet computer linked to a desktop computer sitting on a workstation. 'The LongPen,' a functionary in a knee-length cardigan dripped (Canadian gushing). 'You've heard about it? Peggy Atwood's invention so that authors can sign their books long distance.'

'. . .'

'We're very excited to have it here – Peggy herself will be doing some signing during the festival.'

I was excited as well – sexually excited. I felt my penis sleepily unfurl in its 92 per cent cotton, 8 per cent Lycra burrow. I hadn't had any erotic thoughts in a while – or, rather, I had repressed them savagely, since the adrenalized counting of licks, tweaks and caresses was a torment, let alone the division of caresses by licks, or the multiplication of tweaks by . . . grunts. But the LongPen could well be the solution, interposing thousands of miles between the infinitesimal motions of a single fingertip and the 8,000 nerve endings packed into a few thousandths of an inch of tissue. *Although why not . . . ?*

'Is the suite open twenty-four hours?' I enquired innocently.

'Uh, no,' the cardigan rumpled suspiciously. 'We're staffed until midnight.'

'Oh, OK.' I filed the intelligence away.


For four days I lay in Room 2229, planning a trip out to have one of the eyelets on my left walking boot repaired. During the walk from the airport a metal grommet had become detached and the lace subjected to microwear – an aglet was splitting open. I lay there on the made bed and thought how strange it was that such a small thing could immobilize a grown man. And I thought about Nicholson Baker's obsessive detailing of the microwear of his shoelaces in *The Mezzanine*, and I thought of Baker himself, with whom, a decade before, I had shared a stage at a similar book festival in Brighton. I remembered how pinheaded he had seemed – considering the size of his thoughts; and how later that night I had swallowed a powdery-white MDMA pill with a titchy dolphin stamped on it; and how still later I'd ended up in a boutique hotel room knocking back whisky miniatures with a man who will reappear at the end of this tale to confirm that my life has had no narrative – which implies a linear arrangement of events – but only spiralled either out of control, or into a vicious centrifuge of repetition and coincidence.

Enslaved characters from children's classic literature shared Room 2229 with me – Stuart Little paddled up and down the bath in a birch-bark canoe, Moomintrolls trampolined on the pillows, the aforementioned Borrowers strung together climbing ropes out of my dental floss, then expertly tackled the four pitches necessary to ascend to the top of the armoire. Then they triumphantly rappelled back down with an individual UHT milk carton that they winched up to where I lay, pinioned by the invisible – yet unbreakable – hawsers of my obsessive-compulsive disorder. As they dribbled the last homogenized drops between my cracked lips, I croaked my thanks, then manumitted them.

Eventually I forced myself from Room 2229 and abseiled down the lift shaft into the subway. At the Royal Ontario Museum I became transfixed by the bags visiting high school students had left trustingly strewn across the lobby: how could anyone be allowed to receive an education who insisted on dragging about that much *stuff*? And transfixed again in a subterranean gallery by the *pensées* of the former premiere Pierre Trudeau: 'To remove all the useless baggage from a man's heritage is to free his mind from petty preoccupations, calculations and memories.'

If it had worked for him, what was he doing here – or at least a photograph of his younger self, in white T-shirt and belted jeans? More to the point, what was the very canoe that he had been paddling when he had this epiphany doing here? Looking round I realized that this wasn't so much an exhibition as a lumber room, with items from the museum's permanent collections cast about willy-nilly: a Mercedes saloon got up with wood, a shamanic grizzly bear cast in bronze, and behind this shape-shifter Bacon's *Study for Portrait No.1*, the reflex-dilation of Pope Innocent's anus-dentata as shockingly disregarded as it must once have been when it leant against the wall in the artist's South Kensington studio.

'I'm sorry, sir, there's no photography allowed.'
   'But I'm not photographing anything.'
   'Sir, no photography.'
   'I'm not *taking* pictures, I'm *looking* at them.'
   The vertically aligned cooker knobs and key-in-lock coition from an ocean away had undone me: I desperately needed reassurance that things had been turned off and closed up, because in my mind's eye my house was a burning oil well, shedding hairy-black smoke all over the neighbourhood.

   Using Canadian magic, the guard pushed me with disapproval alone towards the stairs . . . and stumping along behind him, swinging one abbreviated leg in front of the other, came another who had more reason to. But no! This was ridiculous, if I carried on like this I'd soon be kitting Sherman out in a hooded shiny-red raincoat and putting a dagger in his hand.

I managed to thrust Sherman away but he rejoined me at the Eaton Center, where I was scanning the directory for a heel bar. He stood sizing up the atrium, and comparing it unfavourably – in loud un-Canadian tones – to the Galleria Umberto 1:

'Yeah, these fat Canucks could do with a little *risanamento*, d'jewknowhatImean? Look at that muffin stand – oops! Sorry, it isn't a muffin stand, it's some people *queuing* for a muffin stand.'

He snatched at the air, as if given sufficient reach he might tear down the flock of model birds suspended from the barrel-vaulted ceiling, and hymned the absurd complaisance of the city government: 'The base of the figure'll be down there by the fountains on the lower level – but this one won't stand upright, instead one arm'll extend along the second level, and one leg will sorta kick through the atrium, while the other arm and shoulder brace against the roof. It's the biggest yet, mate – a logistical nightmare, of course . . .'

Novelty Shoe Rebuilders offered a 'waiting service', so I waited in socked feet while a cobbler replaced the eyelet of my boot with practised economy. 'Will that be all?' he asked. I forbore from mentioning the aglet.

'There were no egos up there.' His name was Dan, and he wore a CND badge, the roundel formed by gaping red lips. He also had grey hair in a ponytail and a grey beard. No egos? No fucking egos! I wanted to scream at him: I'm all ego, my friend, I'm a Babushka doll of egos – ego-inside-ego-inside-ego-inside-ego-inside-ego. Hell, if you unscrewed the fifth ego you'd probably find another one in there ready to shout you down as well.

But I didn't say anything of the kind, because this was Toronto and we were buried somewhere deep inside the Harbourfront's concretized bollix, and Dan had just been chairing the 'event' I'd come all this way to participate in – an event that had involved me sitting onstage with the actor David Thewlis. In truth, Thewlis didn't seem at all egocentric – more to the point, he was actual size, which was something of a shock because one's so used to actors being either much smaller than their image on a movie screen, or much larger than the one on the TV.

Thewlis, who had written an amiable comic novel, had a slightly prominent top lip, a wispy moustache and lean, expressive good looks. If there were to be a biopic of my life I'd want to be played by him. I tried to ingratiate myself with him while we waited backstage by mentioning mutual acquaintances, and he chatted away amiably enough. Onstage he was still more comically self-deprecating. He wore an expensive and globular watch that he brought up to his face from time to time, so that his finger and thumb could twist the end of his moustache. I found this tremendously amiable – and not comical at all.

Afterwards, when the books had been signed, I was on the point of suggesting we go get something to eat, when Thewlis was whisked away by his entourage, leaving me with Dan. It was a shame, because I'd wanted to ask him about his role in Mike Leigh's *Naked*. It was the first time I'd noticed Thewlis and I thought his performance mesmeric and bruising – like being beaten up by a hypnotist. It was widely known that Leigh worked largely by improvisation, encouraging his actors to bring their own characters to the set, then spurring them on to create dialogue and action spontaneously. In the opening scene of the film Thewlis's alter ego, Johnny, was having vigorous congress with a woman in an alley. But was it rape? Some might say that consent is a very little thing – but is it? I wanted an answer to this, a question that had haunted endless late-night conversations in the mid-1990s – after all, Thewlis should know.

Much later that night I lay in Room 2229 unable to sleep and regretting having freed my mini-slaves. I rose, dressed and laced my boots – appreciating the neat job that had been done on the eyelet. Then I went for a walk around the cavernous hotel counting my charged paces in tens, then hundreds; counting the emergency stairs in tens, then hundreds; stopping beside service carts and riffling the shampoo miniatures – then moving on.

In the morning the driver who drove me to the airport was tight-lipped. I could understand why – the highway was wide and terrifyingly nondescript, the buildings resisted the anthropomorphism of scale, the sky over Lake Ontario was bigger than a nebula. I scanned the verges of the freeway; even though it was midweek I hoped against hope that Reichman had got the walking bug, and I would see him pulling his own suitcase back to Pearson.

The driver took a call on his cell phone and listened intently to the muffled squeaking.

'Pest control problem?' I asked when he hung up.

'You could say that,' he answered curtly. 'The festival's suite at the hotel was broken into last night. Things were done with the LongPen . . . dreadful things.'

# 5

# There is Hope – Make the Call

'Excuse me sir, you have too many things in your pockets.'

We stood on a desert island of carpet tiles somewhere in the placid lagoon of Pearson International Airport. I was a pre-wrecked Crusoe; she was a squat mermaid of South Asian extraction with blue-black hair. She wore a nylon jacket with fluorescent patches that bulged at the hips and the fishtail of her lower body was poured into black slacks. At least it was healthy flesh and not all the necrotic *stuff* I had wadded into the Barbour, stuff she began to gingerly extract with rubber-gloved hands, laying it all out on the brushed steel.

I waited with the *Ohrwurm* boring into me: a tiny finger flutter of the keys, the entire orchestra dangling from the pianist's hangnail . . .

The security woman unearthed the tiny plastic tomb within which this vast and resonant performance of Beethoven's third piano concerto – by Daniel Barenboim with the London Philharmonic – was interred. She bunched up the skirt of the Barbour, appalled to discover yet another pocket – the poacher's – and unzipping it removed the small corpse of my rolled-up plastic trousers.

Leaving Tor-Buff-Chester (a mega-region embracing Toronto that stretches all the way from Buffalo to Quebec City, and has an annual $530 billion of economic activity) was proving more difficult than anticipated. 'The concert piano and all wind instruments bore me in small doses and flay me in large ones,' contended Uncle Vladimir – meaning 'bore' as in 'induce tedium'. I didn't feel that way: my ability to build a concert hall in the inches between my ears was the only thing that made all of this – the queuing, the carpet tiling, the pornographic X-raying of my possessions – remotely tolerable.

Then, aloft, as the Northwest flight skipped across the dimpled Great Lakes, I dipped *carottes coupées et pellées* in *trempette ranch*, while little Daniel braced himself in the aisle and puuuushed! with his fluttery fingers, so that the entire fuselage of the plane widened and the trolley dollies could dance about one another in Busby Beethoven routines.

There were 216 private jets booked into Miami International Airport for the Miami Basel Art Fair. 'Fine art is a luxury good, and so there is a natural marketing synergy, a comparable customer profile and a similar trend cycle,' or so said Jeremy Laing, the Canadian fashion wunderkind. I wondered if Sherman would be there: he was outwardly disdainful of money, contending that if he sought the maximum for his pieces and ruthlessly hired, fired and even circumvented his gallerists, it was only to further the work.

'I'm just a very little man making very big things,' he'd said when I last taxed him with posing for the cover of a glossy auction house magazine. 'And you have to appreciate the costs involved: the planning, the technical drawings, the lobbying – materials and fabrication are only the tip of the iceberg.'

I hadn't observed that the end result was as egotistic as any other monumentalism, and that really spending his money extravagantly might be of more benefit to others than these iron giants trampling down the hills, or standing forlorn in the Seine. I hadn't, for the shameful reason . . . but there was also Sherman's indisputable generosity: restaurant bills paid without a murmur, plane tickets chucked like paper darts, and opera seats offered offhand.

And yet . . . and yet . . . I was never entirely comfortable with his largesse; was it all adding up to a costly obligation? Besides, Sherman devalued his gifts by exhibiting the appetitive disdain I'd noticed in others like him – those who, by their own efforts, had worked their way up from a comfortable childhood to being seriously rich.

Sherman had shirts and suits tailored by the score; and, as he advanced through life, Baltie brought up the rear, picking up the clothes that had been discarded by his boss because they were slightly soiled. Sherman bought bottles of Cristal, drank half a glass, then, gripped by a whim for a pint of lager, climbed down from tables doodled with costly food – dots of Beluga caviar, scrawls of langoustine – and marched away, leaving Baltie to settle the bill. Sherman – having already extracted a Hoyo de Monterrey Petit Robusto from the humidor that went everywhere with them – would wait at the kerb: a fire hydrant spurting smoke. Needless to say, the expensive cigar was stomped to shreds after a few puffs.

'When I see a guy lighting a cigarette as I turn the corner, I don't think he's gonna be taking the bus!'

I could see her point, but I'd been waiting for the service for a while and even in the northern Californian sunshine everything was weighing heavily on me: I needed a smoke. The timing was wrong for a walk into town – besides without a Reichman to goad I didn't really have the oomph. I thought of the days ahead of me, the paltry rituals of a man alone in a strange city: reading suppers – possibly a concert, an excursion to see the Golden Gate Bridge.

The Metroline bus blatted along I-29, through the cleft of the buttocky hills, one of which bore the tattoo CITY OF INDUSTRY. I'd never liked San Francisco in all the time I'd been visiting; for me the city always remained tangled in the fallen freeways of the 1989 earthquake, and these, in turn, contained within their distressed steel and clots of concrete the ghost of the 1906 earthquake with its subprime fatalities – *300, 3,000 or 30,000?* The tenderloin was a cut of putrefying meat, crawling with tramp-flies and shoved in the face of tourists, and in the Prescott Hotel on Post Street where I had slumped, stifled by swags, pelmets, tassels, throw cushions – all the amniotic padding of an embryonic luxury – I noticed for the first terrifying time that reflected in the mirror the label of the mineral water bottle read NAIVE.

I couldn't believe that San Francisco had been hiding these big things from me – but there they were, floodlit: a concert hall, a city hall, some kind of library or museum, all stacked along avenues wide enough to gladden Albert Speer. No doubt in Sacramento there would be a state capitol that was a copy – near enough – of the one in Washington; it was the same throughout the States: prêt-à-porter legislatures and courts, bought from the Great Framers up in heaven.

I had booked the best seat in the house, the plush throne of B1 in the balcony. High above the stage dangled enormous transparent sound-bafflers, and as the soloist mounted the keys with his fingers, climbing up and up to the tremolo peak of the allegro, I wondered how great a compass of emotion might be contained between one note and another, dreadfully pinched by the minims. The *Ohrwurm* bored on into my cheesy brain, proof – if any were needed – that I was already dead.

I zombied back towards the Prescott under a full and ruddy moon, appraising the bitten-off cripples along Market Street: what diabolic ghoul could have taken that leg or arm? Surely not these slim Latino girls bussed in from the Bay Area? They sported fetching light-up devil horns and glittery red micro-mini dresses, and cavorted on the sidewalks goosing one another with outsized plastic forks.

Ploughing my way through burger 'n' fries in the laminated belly of the Pinecrest Diner, I envied them all the easily converted currencies of youth: sex and bullshit. Envied even the kid who sat opposite me, the hood of his H. H. Geiger alien rubber suit pushed up off his brow to expose the pained *maquillage* of pimples and white-blond bum-fluff.

At the Prescott yet again, I naively slept, then cynically dream-dollied myself in through the doors of the Moscone Convention Center. The Little People of America were gathered – no less grotesque than any who sport celluloid name badges, yet certainly no greater. My mobile phone rang and I answered it as quickly as I could, although not fast enough: a clutch of dwarfs swarmed about me. 'Have some goddamn respect,' said a termagant with a perm as tight and prickly as a burr. 'Can't you see there're royalty present?'

*What gives?* Sherman's voice in my ear.

'Um, n-nothing.'

*Are you attending some kind of levee?*

'I thought the lady told you to cut that out!'

The phone was snatched from my hand, and before I could remonstrate there was a Nagasaki of flashes, a low moan, and the dwarfs surged towards the main doors – then were checked by a force field of awe.

Tiptoeing into the convention centre came a brother and sister; they had the same white-golden hair, worn shoulder length, and must have been in their late teens. They held hands, and seemed not so much shy as bemused by the adoration they had provoked. I noticed first the tiny patchwork denim bag the girl wore slung over one shoulder, then their savagely undershot jaws and keel noses, then their stature: for they stood at most twenty, maybe twenty-one inches high.

'Aren't they beautiful?' said the burr-headed woman, clutching my leg so fiercely that her nails dug into the tendon behind my knee.

'Beautiful,' sighed the little man who'd snatched my phone. He pulled a silk handkerchief from his blazer pocket and mopped his eyes.

I understood that these were the dwarfs' dwarfs, embodying for them all the aesthetic qualities the actual sized ascribe to the miniature. Wishing Lévi-Strauss was with me, I found myself being pushed forward and instinctively I offered my hand to the primordial dwarf girl. She rearranged the strap of her handbag and I was acutely aware of the quail's ribcage beneath her doll's cardigan – then the grossness of my fingers, with their elephant's knees knuckles and fertile crescents of dirt beneath the nails. As our hands Sistined together she turned to quicksilver and burst into a spray of droplets, one of which hung from the chin of the burr-headed woman. I stared at this bubble world and saw in its mirrored convexity the dwarf conventioneers, the concrete and glass of the foyer, and my own moon face, cratered by its passage through deep space.

I awoke with the Barbour's waxen arms wrapped around me, my face buried in its musty tartan lining, its double zips

nipping my neck – and couldn't stop weeping until a young woman in the line for the breakfast buffet offered me a Kleenex and said, 'I'd appreciate it if you didn't.' Determined to walk away these black-and-blues, I went back to my room, packed the Barbour's pockets, then headed out into the sunshine.

The temperature was in the mid-seventies and the jacket wasn't a mistake – it was burden that had to be endured as I toiled up Nob and downhill, passing show couples with show dogs posing outside pacific patisseries. I cursed myself for a fool: far from being unencumbered here was I, beneath an ice cream headache, sweating with the exertion of carrying a shooting jacket.

At Marina Boulevard, where the Palace of Fine Arts hid its Moorish fakery behind an arras of pines, I nearly gave up – my progression was purely arithmetic. Only the previous week, when I was either 53,710 or 537 miles away, district officials had scuttled the idea of plastering the Golden Gate with corporate advertising. 'If you ain't into this you real sucka,' J. J. Bigga told the 500- – *50-? 5,000-?* – strong audience at the Cow Palace . . . House repos were up 622 per cent to 10,427 in the last quarter . . . *or was it 104,270, or even 1,042?* At Crissy Field I stopped a bucktoothed Scotswoman on a bike and asked her for directions to the inconceivably big thing that arced through the haze to the green hills above Sausalito, and she looked at me the way the sane look at the mad.

I plodded on – the Barbour was a waxwork effigy of William Cavendish, 4th Duke of Devonshire, which melted across my shoulders. I set the sludge down on the grass and moulded it into a semblance of Alcatraz, which stood off in the bay. Then I took it up once more and went on, while my LongPen shaded in an afternoon two months previously: an exhibition of Ron Mueck works at the Scottish National Gallery in Edinburgh, where, wandering through the rooms, I was arrested by the follicle-perfect dummy of a depressed woman lying in bed, her white face five times life size. Around the peak of her nose a security guard came hurrying – he told me to stop taking photographs. Perhaps if he'd been a Canadian he would've added, civilly, 'It'll do you no good to confront your past writ large. Besides, that is not your mother, wrung out by postnatal depression and eking out the years between parturition and cancer with gardening and library books.'

At the time I'd realized that what Mueck was doing reversed everything I thought I understood about the distortion of scale: far from his giantess being a purely intelligible object, she was all feeling – her desperation magnified until it filled the gallery with the ultrasonic howl of a harpooned leviathan—

\*       \*       \*

Mounting the path that switch-backed up through Fort Point National Heritage Site, I was seized not by the Ektachrome of the evergreens and the waters of the bay; nor by the towers of the bridge that rose up before me, which appeared sandy-damp, as if freshly moulded by giant hands, then raised by massed Lilliputians drawing on their steel cables. What grabbed me were the walkers, in their T-shirts and sneakers, their jeans and sweat pants, who converging on the bridge's approach reached a pedestrian density I'd seldom seen in the States before, except in an airport concourse, a mall or Midtown Manhattan.

I, better than most, understood the compelling urge to walk across a big thing, an urge separated by a mere carpaccio of neurones from the compelling urge to throw yourself off it. It goes without saying that thoughts of suicide were never absent, but burbled repetitively in my ear – 'Kill yourself, kill yourself, kill yourself' – just as did the stream of anxiety: 'You forgot to turn off the gas/shut-and-lock the door' and, more recently, the times-10/divide-by-10 tic. It took only the signs to alert me: EMERGENCY PHONE AND CRISIS COUNSELING and then, a few score paces on, CRISIS COUNSELING. THERE IS HOPE. MAKE THE CALL. THE CONSEQUENCES OF JUMPING FROM THIS BRIDGE ARE FATAL AND TRAGIC.

If I had had any reservations at all the 'and tragic' banished them entirely. The composers of the signs understood entirely not merely the anger-born-of-fear of the *felo de se* – in my view an emotion much exaggerated – but, more importantly, our narcissism. Yes! A tragedy! That's what it would be, a fucking tragedy, I had been cut down in my prime, after struggling manfully for years against this debilitating condition, one that I had – still more tragically – vouchsafed to hardly a soul. My notebooks, left open on the table in my room at the

Prescott, would explain all that, explain also the awful shame that pursued me, the tiny Eumenides sprung from the Titan's blood.

By the time I had reached the middle of the bridge, and was standing there listening to the wind shear lament through the cables, and watching the drop yawn below me, I had succumbed to its sublime contours. If the monumental was an architecture of social control, then what could be said of monumental bridges, save that they were very obviously for jumping off – that they in fact ordered you to jump off them? 'Jump!' they bellowed, sergeant-majors on the vast parade ground of civilization, and so the Mayans, the Easter Islanders, the Norse Greenlanders, the Romans and now the entire West did their bidding.

What possible purchase could Section 2193 of the State of California's Penal Code have on the profound gravity of this situation; for this was about physics, about small things and big things – people hardly entered into it. And in those last few moments, when a woman in a hijab heading one way and a Japanese-American woman eating a beanshoot salad from a Tupperware container as she strolled the other, simultaneously gasped as I vaulted nimbly on to the thick, rivet-warty girder of the balustrade, my loved ones were of scarcely any concern, being irredeemably actual size.

I had hoped . . . for what? A game of *Scrabble* on the way down, or to get married, or at the very least to link hands with a serendipitous octet of fellow self-murderers – the drop had certainly looked big enough for such skydiving antics. After all, the waves in the bay were wrinkles, while from up there downtown San Francisco had no more civilization than a playroom Lego ruin.

As I fell towards the deceptively yielding pavé of the bay (and, believe me, like all suicides, I knew just how hard the impact would be, foresaw entirely the Faroese slaughter of my expiration: a small pink whale gashed open and wallowing in a cloudy red stain), I also anticipated feeling this consolation: that I had cast the beastly Barbour aside, and so was meeting my fate *without any baggage at all,* no plasticized Beethoven, no paperback *Great Expectations,* no rolled-up plastic trousers, no waxed cotton class suit; I was going to my execution as every baby-boomer should: in a T-shirt and Levis, bravely refusing Ray-Bans.

So it was with a sense of fretful – almost pettish – annoyance that I realized Death was bopping me on the head without any more ado, that my extinction, far from being profoundly protracted, was to have all the grand tragedy of a prankster creeping up behind me and suddenly yanking down the woolly hat I'd forgotten I was sporting, so that I was entombed in a tickly darkness – for all eternity.

I came to in a large poorly lit room notable for a tacky earthenware statue of the Buddha on a low table. This Gautama had an expression not so much spiritual as obscurely self-satisfied, while the joss sticks set before him curdled brown smoke into the gloom. Around me shuffled the shades, all dressed in floppy shirts and baggy pants of faun, umber and other earthy tones, which looked to be woven from flax, or hemp, or some other retro-fibre.

My groan hearkened one of these souls to me; he or she was suitably inter-sex, with sepia hair scraped into a mule tail and circular wire-rimmed spectacles. 'Would you like an urbal tea?' he or she asked gently. 'We've got most varieties, cardamom, caraway seed, ginger?'

'Whatever,' I pleaded, and he or she footed soundlessly away.

A lissom man, with a sandy trowel-shaped beard and the tense look of someone who practises yoga furiously, mounted the low platform behind the Buddha and concertinaed into a full lotus as easily as I might've scratched my arse (when alive). Despite my recent death I could sense the aggression radiating from this man, and as he picked up a small brass mallet and tapped a bell his mild features writhed with barely repressed fury.

I was remarkably unfazed.

'For our dharma discussion today,' announced the sandy Sangha, 'I will be taking suggestions; anything you wish guidance on I am happy to consider—'

'It's vervain,' said the shade, pressing a tepid mug into my hand. 'Enjoy.'

Remarkably unfazed because this all seemed altogether just: that the Tibetan Buddhist cosmology should turn out to be correct and that my own bardo should – at least initially – take the form of a room full of the angriest people in the world: occidental Buddhists. Of course, what would begin to happen when my ego started to disintegrate I shuddered to think; presumably in place of the multi-headed demons that tormented Tibetans I'd be visited with my own bogeybeings; perhaps the fibrous Buddhists would transmogrify into giant Bionicles, those weirdly skeletal robotic toys loved by my youngest child that had techno-scimitars and laser guns for arms, and could be posed on their long legs so as to delve surgically in their victims' innards.

'Drug addiction and the dharma,' offered one seeker. 'Dharma and movement practice,' said a second. 'The three pearls,' a third in lotus position said, his thick glasses like an insect's compound eyes.

'OK, OK,' the Sangha snorted. 'That's enough – we could go on all night taking suggestions and have no time for instruction.'

The seekers tittered obsequiously, while behind the Sangha's enlightened head I could see the dark ballooning of a massive and unconstrained ego.

'I'm, I'm . . .' I grasped the wrist of the exiguous urbalist who had coiled into the canvas chair beside me, 'not dead, am I?'

'Heavens no,' s/he relied in a beige undertone. 'You poor man, you fell backwards from the parapet of the Golden Gate Bridge on to the walkway there and were brought by paramedics into the rescue centre. We get a lot of sufferers such as yourself; if there isn't absolute proof that a person is trying suicide' – 'trying', I liked that, it suggested that suicide was only one of the options available from the smorgasbord of inexistence – 'then the Bridge cops are happy to, like, outsource—'

'It seems,' the sandy Sangha's gentle voice was viciously clenched, 'that someone with us this evening has a more nuanced interpretation of the three pearls; so, would you like to share?'

The urbalist bowed his/her head in abject shame. I, however, was on the point of rising up and chinning the fraud, but was forestalled by a commotion from the doors – that and the sharp pain in the back of my head, which was – I now realized – swathed in a crêpe bandage.

One of the slipshod sannyasas came shuffling down the aisle and bent to whisper, 'Your friend is here now to collect you.'

Friend? What friend? As I limped to the door, passing by the rows of outlines of devotion, I racked my bruised brain: I had no friend in San Francisco, nor – without being self-piteous – did I have that many friends anywhere. Besides, how might such a friend have found me?

The answer to the second question came in the form of the Barbour, thrust into my unwilling arms so that it hung, slick and black as a roosting flying fox. The answer to the first was Sherman Oaks, who stood out on the Sausalito sidewalk, pulling intemperately on a stogie.

In that instant of recognition, my eyes drinking in the scant three feet of him, I realized a thing at once terrifying and beautiful: it wasn't that the Buddhists had been rendered indistinct by their quest for the white void, or that the community hall within which they were assembled was any more vapid than such places usually are – it was me. Had I suffered some pinpoint-accurate injury to my visual cortex, or was this only a form of hysteria? Whichever the case, the result was the same: casting wildly about the main street of the chichi resort town, I could make out the outlines of all intermediately sized things – such as cars, people and the no-good pagoda of Spinnakers seafood restaurant – but not their infill; whereas the very large things that blocked in the horizon – the hills, the bridge, Alcatraz – retained their detailing even in the twilight.

Then there was Sherman, who, with his potbelly and droopy ears, was truly the presiding spirit of the very little, and who stood proud of the indistinctiveness of his setting, just as the very little things in the window of the Swarovski's across the road – crystal strawberries dimpled with brilliants, vitrified bouquets half an inch high – leapt to my retina and swarmed there as veridical as after-images.

Naturally, I said nothing of this to Sherman, who anyway only left off barking into his own phone to bark at me: 'They checked your phone to see who you'd called recently, then rang a few people. I happened to have been in SF for the Web 2.0 thing, flew here from Miami, so I came out to get you, you dumb fuck.'

The outline of a Range Rover pulled up to the kerb, the outline of Baltie at the wheel.

'Yeah, yeah, I know. I have to see some people at Stanford in the morning, then I'll be with you at lunchtime—' He broke off again: 'Go on, get in the car willya?'

I got into the back seat and Sherman clambered into the front. Baltie's shape said 'Hi', with that special tone people reserve for failed suicides, at once sympathetic and reassuringly annoyed, as if to say: See the trouble you've put us to!

Within minutes we were tooling back over the bridge, the tyres of the big car drumming the deck plates, the mighty lyre of the cables strumming past. At last, shorn of the encumbrance of any human scale whatsoever – no finicky aerials or water-tank bobbins – the San Francisco skyline acquired, for me, the majesty others always claimed they found in it. Once we were down off the bridge and augering into the core of downtown, the sidewalks were as unthreatening as Hanna-Barbera backdrops, the homeless mere silhouettes, the traffic no longer steely but graphite – reduced to a few pencil marks on the fronts of the buildings.

I made a conscious decision to say nothing of this ... nothingness to Sherman, while he treated my rescue as simply another chore to be completed with despatch. 'What've you got on here?' he rapped as the Range Rover pulled up beside the Prescott. I muttered something about a book reading at the City Lights in two days' time. 'Fine, then. You can come out to Stanford and the Google Campus with me tomorrow in the day – we'll pick you up around ten. If you need me you've got the number, we're staying in the Transamerica building, they rent out a penthouse suite.'

As I prepared to insert my stick body into the line drawing of my bed I pictured Sherman in his odd accommodation, at the very apex of the Transamerica's 48-storey white granite-faced pyramid. With Baltie a hieroglyph on the marble wall, Sherman rollicked back and forth in this despotic bed and breakfast, stubbing out a Hoyo here, snatching up a glass of champagne over there, consulting a sale catalogue while he barked at Borzois in Kiev, or Pekineses in Beijing. I wondered if, in all that restless communication, he had taken the time to reassure my family, who might have been concerned by the phone call from the paramedics who had scooped me up from the Golden Gate Bridge. Wondered this – yet felt powerless to call them myself.

This latest episode in my relationship with Sherman had taken things to another level. I knew that my behaviour in the past had been shameful, yet this very Dickensian coincidence – of which I could've had no great expectation when I teetered atop the parapet – brought home to me quite how much psychic baggage I was carrying with me.

Perhaps I should've felt more disturbed by the excision of any sense of proportion that I had once had, and its replacement by a thick fog of mediocrity welling up from San Francisco Bay. I didn't, though, for since having come to Marin County and listened to the pugnacious Sangha, I had been blissfully free of the multiplier and the divisor.

Lying in the darkness of the Prescott, I ran over the stats: the bridge was 8,981 feet long, the longest span was 4,200 feet. It was 746 feet high, and there were 80,000 miles of wire in its main cables, while approximately 1,200,000 rivets had been used in its construction. Between its completion in 1937 and 2005, more than 1,200 people had jumped the 245 feet to their death in the chill waters below. 1,200, not 120 nor yet 120,000, but 1,200 – these figures were incontrovertible: the facts on the ground.

# The Last Nurdle

*Watch it bigger day by day! Natural manhood enhancement!*
*Easily to get male package . . . Demetrius Erectile Organ Cosmic.*
*Gargantuan Penis Beau. Reach out and bone someone . . .* I stood
in the restroom at the Googleplex, Google's headquarters in
Mountain View, and these came back to me: *Fuck Stick Ample*
*Floyd. Rosa Full-Size Fuck Stick. Body part enlarged shown.*
*FannieMonumentalCock . . .* Manglings of syntax and grammar
that nonetheless got across the hollow promise that a credit
card number could be exchanged for Viagra – and Cialis and
Ambien, should you so choose.

I stood at the urinal and held on, remembering these emails
spammed at me through the yielding tissue of virtual reality. It
wasn't that I thought any of Google's 450,000 servers might be
implicated in this huge trafficking of drugs intended to make
the relatively little grow bigger; it was just that the laminated
sheet of programming tips tacked above the urinal naturally
tended one's thoughts in that direction; this, and the fact that
one was holding one's LongPen.

'Testing on the Toilet', the sheet was headed; beside it were
two light bulbs, one happy and shining, the other upside down,
dim and sad. Below that the screed continued: 'Normally
people are only interested in the test data for coverage files . . .'
but I couldn't read any further, it was all impenetrably technical
to me – and besides, I'd pissed on my shoes.

Back past the niches containing the electric toothbrushes
and facecloths of the never resting microserfs, back past the

misaligned bookcases, the dangling model jet engines, the defunct servers piled up into statuary and the colossal novelty beanbags, I found Sherman and Baltie in the canteen noshing on piles of bean sprouts and slurping smoothies. 'Get yourself a tray,' Sherman commanded; 'you need to build up your strength.'

I supposed I should've felt more grateful to Sherman than I did; after all, he had scooped me up in San Francisco and incorporated me into his whirlwind schedule. That morning we had already visited the Stanford Linear Accelerator, where he had discussed plans with the facility's director to site a Sherman piece alongside the two-mile-long klystron gallery, which – as both men saw fit to inform me – was the longest building in the States.

'The longest building – quite right!' Sherman had crowed as we puttered through the campus in the Range Rover, past the great Romanesque halls of learning. 'While the accelerator itself is the world's straightest object! That's why this body form will be so sinuous, with arms and legs cuddling the gallery, cheek pressed against it. I particularly like the fact,' he continued as Baltie angled the Range Rover up the slip road on to Highway 280, 'that the whole installation lies right across the San Andreas fault. The next time there's a big one, my piece and the accelerator will go down together, erotically entwined, spurting electrons and positrons in a lava death fuck!'

I doubted that Stanford would've let Sherman anywhere near the collider if they'd heard him talk in these terms – but then I doubted this piece would ever get made; it seemed to be just another of the notions sprouting from the artist's ever fertile mind as he revolved around the world. True, plenty of Shermans were getting made – a group of three medium-sized thirty-footers had been erected in Death Valley only the previous week – but the ratio of planned to enacted Shermans did seem to be shifting decisively.

After our veggie lunch at the Googleplex, Sherman lectured the employees for over an hour on ways in which their 450,000 servers might be adapted to serve his own ends. He proposed Sherman start pages, Sherman links and Sherman levies on advertisers. He quite seriously entertained the idea of a Shermanet (at least, disloyally, that's how I thought of it), with each Google search contributing to the creation of a body form so large it could exist only in cyberspace. 'Your servers process a petabyte of data every hour – fifty petabytes is roughly equal to the entire written works of humankind up until now . . .' He looked significantly at me, scrunched up in the front row trying to hide the pee stains on my shoes.

'But why not generate a calculus of say 5,000 petabytes of differentials describing the shapes of a body form that, were it to actually be built, would dwarf this entire solar system – more than that! It would be so big it could link arms with the spiral arm of the galaxy and high-kick across the heavens!'

I had to hand it to Sherman – not for the breathtaking egomania of his artistic vision, but for that grace that had so struck my wife, and that allowed him to use the d-word so offhandedly, standing there, all thirty-nine inches of him, in front of the Googlers. It was difficult not to love Sherman at times like this – Velázquez's portrait of de Morro may have imbued the court dwarf with humanity, but it was a humanity defined by thwarted emotions, smouldering resentments and long-anticipated slights. But Sherman was a de Morro in motion: his hands a blur of explication, his head bobbing with such self-affirmation that his beard seemed like a brush putting the finishing touches on his own shining countenance . . .

I thought all this, then I looked around me at the other listeners, only to discover that they weren't listening at all and that their faces, far from glowing with the enthusiasm that beamed off Sherman, were merely bathed in the chilly light of the laptops they had propped open on their knees.

Later, as Baltie expertly piloted the Range Rover along the crowded drag of El Camino Real, I sought to comfort Sherman: 'They were probably catching up on some work. I mean they're driven so hard in that place – there're even programming tips stuck up in the men's.'

'I'm not bothered in the least!' he snapped back. 'They weren't working – they were googling me.'

As I say, I should've felt more grateful for my salvation, but functioning in this odd new realm where the median had been annihilated, leaving only ever accelerating electrons, and lumbering Shermans, was . . . taxing. I had thought it was hard enough dealing with my tics and compulsions without having to cope with troublesome emotions – but now I wasn't simply feeling ashamed in relation to Sherman, but terribly indebted to him. So, when they dropped me off at the Prescott, and he began saying, 'Listen, Will, it strikes me that you need a little human comfort in your life', I was about to interrupt him when his phone did it for me:

'Yes, yes, Sergei . . . that's all arranged,' he said. 'And no, we won't be needing snowshoes or the dog team, let alone the sodding umiak – it's only late October . . . Jolly good!' He broke the connection, then explained: 'We're flying out this evening; the Albertan government is interested in my doing something with the Athabasca Tar Sands – sort of massive tar-baby-type body form.'

I was secretly relieved, and as he seemed to have forgotten the touchy-feely stuff I said goodbye casually; but then:

'Don't imagine for a second this means I won't be keeping tabs on you,' he flung at my retreating back. 'In fact, I'll be calling every day.'

However, he didn't call the next day, and that evening I gave a reading at the City Lights bookstore with the ghost of Allen Ginsberg howling in my ear and the bloated corpse of Kerouac beating a port wine jug on the floor in the corner. Nor did he call the day after that, when I flew to Seattle and walked the sixteen miles in from the gargantuan bobbin-terminals of SeaTac along the Green River trail to the city centre. I could see nothing of the orderly suburbs I paced through, only coppery bills agitating on the trees and the discrete cloud of Bill Gates's $70,708,080,100,000 wispy over Medina. Footsore, dragging myself along the East Marginal Way past the Boeing Field, I looked first at the splitting aglets of my bootlaces, next at the seven-storey tailfins cleaving the vapours above the airstrip. And, as I crossed over the goods yards and began to drag up the desolation row of 4th Avenue, the heroic skyline in front trickled down to the homeless man who walked ahead of me, in the gutter, pushing his shopping cart piled high with nothing fit for e-commerce.

Another Prescott Hotel and the naivety of mineral water and the sculptural folds of strewn towels and tossed sheets. Of my

work in Seattle I recall very little. That night, dark visions of the inflamed papules and vesicles around the anus of a lover I had taken from behind – perhaps in this very room – in a previous millennium, whose face was still other sculptural folds buried in the marbled pillows. In the dream, heaving over her runty thighs, I looked at the mobile phone clutched in my left hand and longed for it to ring: Sherman's bark might rouse me from this torturous in-and-out that was going nowhere, but still he didn't call.

The following morning, before dawn, I headed back to SeaTac. A panel had been damaged on the International Space Station and the crew were trapped up there in the bus-sized craft costing $100 billion – while down here on the bus, we ploughed through the asteroid belts of the Seattle suburbs. In the seat beside me sat a girl tricked out as Madame de Pompadour, complete with powdered wig, mauve feathers and a silk bustle.

It was Halloween – I was scared, but still boarded an Alaskan Airways flight down to Los Angeles and, stepping out from the arrivals hall on to Century Boulevard without any clear idea of where I might be headed, was shocked to see Baltie's blond quiff – layered by Trumper – outlined by the driver-side window of another rental Range Rover. Then his master's stumpy legs swung round the bumper, followed by his master's heroic and oft-copied trunk.

Sherman – who was on a call – put me on hold with a digit; I dallied in the louche southern Californian noon: an entire civilization with its collar unbuttoned. 'Yes, yes, Harriet,' he was saying, 'of course I'll need *more* than ten earth movers – what if half of them break down? What? Yes, I'll be in LA for a couple of days, then I'll come to you. Jolly good!'

To me he was equally abrupt: 'C'mon, let's go to the Watts Towers! You need to stretch your legs – lanky fellow like you crunched up in economy, it's only a matter of time before a blood clot forms in your leg – curious that such a little thing can do for you, no?'

We walked along Century – or, rather, I walked. Baltie picked Sherman up and dropped him off again and then again, in a resumption of our usual way of travelling together. While he was bowling along beside me, making no concession to the heat (I had the Barbour slung over my shoulder once more, as weighty and useless as a constitutional monarch), Sherman explained about the earth movers and the project to carve the 26-mile-long outline of his own body form into the impacted salt of the Great Salt Lake Desert in Utah: 'You've no idea the politicking involved,' he yelped, lighting a Hoyo. 'It's Federal land, and I've been pogoing back and forth to DC for months now to butter up wonks at the Bureau of Land Management.'

At Inglewood, beside the Hollywood Racetrack, I found myself alone. From the gentle rise I could see the distant sierra and feel the hot body of Los Angeles aroused beneath my soles. It occurred to me that Sherman was revolving around me with two distinct magnitudes: first, on his longer sweeps as a comet does a solar system; and secondly, with these small hops along Century, as an asteroid does a planet. In neither case, I thought, were these orbits stable – at some point he must lose speed and crash into me. There would be a conflagration.

In the backstreets of Watts, Sherman told me about the Great Pacific Garbage Patch, an area of the Pacific a thousand miles west of California and twice the size of Texas. He expatiated on how discarded plastic from all over the globe had become concentrated there: 'Packing tape, plastic soldiers, widgets, grommets, webbing, shopping bags – you name it! It all pitches up in the Patch, and there it photo-degrades, breaking down and down and down, into littler and littler blobs known as – I kid you not – "nurdles".'

He seemed oblivious of the miniature gravestones and other Halloween decorations studding the front yards of the tumbledown frame houses – immune also to any sense of threat in this, one of the most feared 'hoods in South Central. It occurred to me, observing the way cars slowed and fingers pointed, that here it was not Sherman's restricted size that attracted attention – no one was playing 'Child or Dwarf' – but only the fact of our age, our colour and our class. All Hallows' Eve was nigh, and the gun crews who tried dicking with us were warned off by our middle-aged, middle-class, white man horror masks.

We stood beneath the airy minarets of the Towers and Sherman tugged his beard. I understood where the nurdling had been leading: he was intent on matching Simon Rodia's awesome feat of bricolage with one of his own: 'There has to be a way to fuse all that plastic into a single sculpted agglomeration—'

'You mean a body form?' I queried, knowing full well the answer.

'Yes, yes, a body form of course!'

And I saw the monstrous baby staggering upright from the horizon, its chubby arms formed by billions of nurdles.

# 5.25
# It's a Small World

At the Westin Bonaventure Hotel in Downtown LA I struck up a friendship with Felipe on the concierge's desk. He had an outsized pencil that reminded me of the ones I had on my desk at home – one blue, one lead – writing implements that juxtaposed amusingly with my minumental figurine of Sherman's *Behemoth*. Felipe used his big pencil to doodle while he waited for guests to ask him things: Where's this – or that? How do I get to . . . ? Can you recommend? When he was distracted in this way I took the opportunity to swivel the ledger and examine the doodles, but there seemed no precise relation between the series of boxes, circles, triangles and these enquiries.

I say friendship, but I doubt Felipe thought I was anything but a saddo, flopping around the colossal atrium of the hotel, peering disconsolately into the ornamental fountain, or else standing caught in the fugue of minimal preference, looking from one souvenir to the next in the gift concession. I had a reading to give at the Los Angeles Public Library, but apart from this my time was my own. I forced myself out to wander the stepped pyramid of Bunker Hill, pausing in its cigarette-packet-sized parks to admire the crumpled tinfoil public sculpture.

There were no calls from Sherman – there couldn't be any network coverage out there on the Bonneville Salt Flats. Baltie revved up the earth mover, then slipped the clutch. 'Hey!' his boss cried, rattling around in the jump seat as they doodled across the crystalline page, describing a line that could be erased only by a once-in-a-decade 'rain event'. In Beverly

Hills Britney had retreated to the shower stall to speak to an interviewer from Coast FM – I could hear the pitter-patter lying on my bed at the Westin. The kids were arriving for their court-ordered time with Mom.

Felipe, seeing how loose my ends were becoming, malevolently suggested I might like to visit a *carniceria* out in East LA, so I walked over Bunker Hill to Broadway and waited among the baggage, the denim and the rolled gold for the 31 bus. It ground across the bridge over the Inca runnel of the Los Angeles River, then along 1st Street, while I watched in-bus American Latino TV: adobe men in white hoodies yapping like Disney characters for a public health campaign.

It was mid-morning and the *carniceria* sat beside the dusty road, a nondescript three-storey building. Inside, the narrow aisles lined with chiller cabinets smelt of blood and there was sawdust on the floor. Signs read FOOD STAMPS ACEPTAMOS, the lighting was yellow and blue, pigs' trotters lay in a stepped pyramid climbed by lost flies. There was no one about – I reached across to where a cleaver lay on a wooden chopping board scored with never-to-be-erased blows. I hefted the cleaver – it felt right, perfectly weighted. I only let it fall, applying no force – only let the inertia carry it through its short arc, the same way my late father-in-law had told me to play a golf stroke: letting the weight of the club head follow through the ball, which in this case was a chunk of my thigh, and a neat slice of my jeans. The fabric absorbed the blood from the meat – a few drops fell across the sawdust.

I had a handkerchief with me and I tied it round my leg, thinking I looked acceptably Peckinpah. Or at least I must have done this, because when I was myself again I was standing on the parched grass of the Evergreen Cemetery, looking at the effaced tombstones of Civil War dead, and there was the tourniquet and the ferrous red on my spasmodic hands.

Sherman called that evening and when he realized the state I was in he had Baltie drive him back into town from Palm Springs. 'You are fucked up, man,' he said, finding me lying in my slough at the top of the yellow tower in the Westin. I'd stolen Felipe's big pencil and scrawled stuff on the walls: 'Very little application, very little hope, very little probity, very little . . .'

'Sherm,' I croaked, 'there're things we need to talk about – stuff to do with the past.'

'I don't wanna hear about it,' he snapped, then: 'Yup, no, Vargas has the necessary financial instruments.' He turned his back on me and toddled to the window, continuing the call – which seemed to be something to do with piling up five dressed-stone body forms at Machu Picchu. It was left to Baltie to haul over the business directory and find a doctor who'd do a house call.

The next day Baltie drove us south through the flatlands to Anaheim. It was an interminable journey, strip after mall after strip. I suppose I must have been a little feverish, and despite – or perhaps because of – the OxyContin the doctor had prescribed, I kept slipping sideways from consciousness, only to slice back in as we pulled up at another stoplight and there was Sherman's blocky head spewing words and cigar smoke: 'There's no sense to that, if the base plate is being fabricated in Manaus it will have to be taken *down* the Amazon . . .'

At Disneyland, Sherman explained: 'I think you're in need of a little reparenting, you've lost your way.' He reached up and took my hand with surprising tenderness. 'I want you to think of me as your mother—' Then, exactly like my long-dead mother, his attention was snagged by an incoming call, and he let go of my hand to field it.

We wandered along the ersatz Main Street USA, and queued for Autopia in Tomorrowland. Sherman's grace was well to the fore: no matter how many kids pointed or called out to him, he responded with a cheery wave. 'Don't you love it here?' he asked after we'd driven the dinky karts round the circuit for a while and were heading for the Small World ride, the three of us licking outsized ice cream cones.

'Um, well, love may be a bit too strong, but Sherman, I have to—' Once again I was frustrated, this time by the ride being shut. The Disney people wouldn't admit what had happened, but later we learnt that one of boats had blocked the flume.

'They were built for smaller people!' Sherman crowed. 'And now these fatties cram themselves in it's definitely a smaller world.'

The day after that it was the Museum of Jurassic Technology in Culver City and Sherman and I were riveted for hours by Hagop Sandaldjian's microminiature sculpture of Snow White and the Seven Dwarfs poised in the eye of a needle.

The Armenian had been an extremely calm man, and there was the assumption that acts of such controlled creation necessarily implied taboos on acts of procreation.

We were staying at the Culver City Hotel and I couldn't get Sherman on the house phone, so I took the stairs up to his floor. When I knocked on the door it swung open and there he was, naked, sprawled across the high four-poster bed. It would've been a cliché to describe him as 'lost' in the billowing breasts of the brunette who was sharing the bed with him. A cliché – and straightforwardly wrong, because in the split-second before he bawled at me to 'Fuck right off!' I saw that Sherman was quite at home.

# Burke Shops at Wal-Mart

Standing in the Chevalier Woods, my boots buried in damp leaf mould, I stared into the white face of a deer. Overhead a jet's headlights carved a tunnel out of the autumn dusk. There had been no way of walking out of the O'Hare terminal, which was surrounded by runways, so I took the subway to Rosemont, then picked my way between office blocks to the banks of a cold and polluted river.

The coincidence of this serrated defile between evergreens and the flight path held me, my breath smoky in the twilight, as jet after jet poised above my head. Such gravity! Such noise! Such comet heat! The deer scattered its legs into the trees, darkness unlimbered, falling to the forest's ferny floor – I walked and found a road, suburbia, a bus stop, a bus, rode this to the subway, rode the subway into town, where it elevated itself on a bridge above canyons, which I walked through to the lakeside concert hall. A slip of a girl played Sibelius's violin concerto, up and up, tiny expert movements – massive drama. When it was over the audience went away and I bought a toothbrush in a Walgreens.

The Chicago Humanities Festival had allocated me a room in the Seneca Hotel on Chestnut Street, which turned out to be an extensive suite of chilly rooms. The tables all had thick glass surfaces and there seemed more skirting boards than were strictly warranted. In the kitchenette the smell of the electric cooker's rings was overpowering. On the seventh floor I spoke with an elderly lady wearing a tweed jacket and an arthritis brace. Police crime-scene tape had been stretched across one

doorway of the Festival's suite, and she told me that I, of course, knew about the sexual assault that had been committed with the LongPen the weekend before.

*That sophism was taken for fate in disguise* . . . I didn't like her tone, although I knew it was nothing personal. Anyway, my tics had returned and what time I could grapple from the repetitive operations messing up my head was assigned to the flesh-coloured foam rubber between the brace and her bent wrist. *Fantastic materials, glass terrycloth, plastic* . . .

*Of a truth too fantastic to believe he retains the meaning:* 'Save Money. Live Better.' At 4650 North Avenue I stood in the parking lot and read my receipt. I'd bought a single pair of mixed merino and acrylic socks, which, at $4.94 (plus 45 cents sales taxes), didn't seem *that* cheap to me. I'd walked out to North Avenue from the Loop, through maybe nine miles of tracts that got blacker and poorer, until a handwritten sign in a shop window read 'N-Word Not Allowed Here', while there were *taquerías*, storefront Baptist churches and immigration lawyers all along the shattered boulevard.

My mobile phone rang and it was so long since I'd answered it I took a while to find it, searching through six stuffed pockets. Then I was detained by the ringtone – stylized as a minuet – and then by its Art Deco fascia. Technology had moved on faster than walking pace.

'I'm in hospital, in New York,' Sherman's voice said.

'What happened?' My heart limbered up in my ribcage.

'Deep-vein thrombosis – they took me off a flight from Moscow, my right leg looks like a fucking turnip—'

'I'm coming!' My heart broke into a trot. 'I'll be with you this evening!'

'Why?' He chuckled. 'Have you got a stash of low-molecular-weight heparin in that dumb Barbour of yours?'

# 5.0625
# Rat Poison

Which was more shocking: the monitors menacing Sherman with their winking readouts, the trails of plastic tubing seeping drugs into him, or the artist himself, tucked in tight at the head of the hospital bed, while an angular bulge beneath the covers hid the clotted leg? Baltie was propped on the windowsill reading *The Tatler*.

'They won't let me have my phone!' Sherman yelped as soon as he saw my hangdog face. 'And *he*' – a significant lash of a drip – 'is too dumb to make calls for me. Be a love, will you . . .'

He had a list. I sat on a bench beside Riverside Drive and postponed press conferences and speeches, apologized for Sherman's nonattendance at dinners and awards ceremonies. I called Prima at her gallery and she said she'd tell the family. It was drizzling and I was grateful for the Barbour.

'Did you speak to Herve?' Sherman quacked as soon as I returned.

'We-ell, I think it was him – my French is, um, rather inadequate. But Sherm, don't you think you should try to rest?'

'No, no, I don't – I'm fucking flat out here as it is.'

'What do the doctors say?'

'They say hooray, we're coining it, then they send in a nurse with another bag of rat poison.'

'Is that what that stuff is?'

'Yes, yes, nothing quite like it for thinning the blood.'

Baltie had been sent out to buy petits fours, which was what Sherman most wanted besides his phone back. I sat on the bed – there was plenty of room. My friend's head moulded the pillows, and for the first time I wondered about the process involved in casting his body forms. I reached out to take his hand but he jerked it away:

'What the fuck're you crying for?' he said.

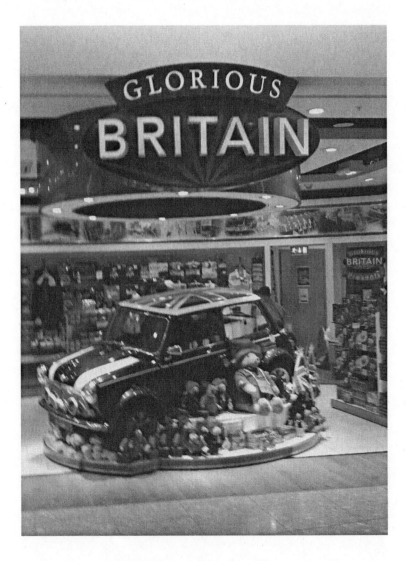

# 5.03125
## Light Aircraft

It was the smallest check-in desk either of us had ever seen – more like a lectern, with the Loganair logo plastered across the front. 'Loganair!' Sherman guffawed. 'Should be logan*berry*.' He stumped over to a drinks dispenser and began punching buttons distractedly. I wondered if he was already withdrawing from his phone habit.

Sherman's doctor had said ambulation was the key to long-term recovery from DVT. 'He means walking,' the artist explained to me, 'so if you're still game for this northern jaunt let's go.'

It had been a grim winter in London – I scratched my wrists so much one of them went septic. It was all right now, though, and as the twin-engined plane motored towards the thousand-foot sea cliffs of Foula I felt the unfamiliar turbulence of optimism. Sherman was in the co-pilot's seat telling the pilot what to do.

# 5.015625
## Paying Guests

An off-white cloud hung above the hills behind Mrs Field's bungalow; tractor tyres weighted down the roof. She didn't seem that pleased to see me again – although Sherman soon charmed her.

'I've another chap staying,' she explained, 'and to be honest I don't like the extra work.'

It was the man from the boutique hotel in Brighton, he was amazed by the coincidence – I couldn't remember his name. Mrs Field grilled mini chicken Kievs for tea.

## 5.0078125
## The Confession

'Why would I want to hear about—' His words were snatched away by the wind screeching up over the cliff edge. A giant skua hung above a perfectly round pool in the sward.

## 5.00390625
# Top of the World, Ma

'You know nothing of what I feel, believe me – you never have.'

## *La Jetée*

I hurt him and there was only this way.

# 5.0009765625
# Left Behind

Some rolled-up plastic trousers.

# 5.00048828125
## The Earth Summit

And a mobile . . .

# 5.000244140625
## Global Reach

. . . phone.

# Walking to Hollywood

I've been around the world several times and now it's only banality that interests me – I track it with the relentlessness of a bounty hunter.

– Chris Marker, *Sans soleil*

# I

# The Consultation

In early May of 2008, my treatment with Dr Shiva Mukti having reached a conclusion, with, I think, the feeling on both sides that there had been a measure of success, I decided to take a walking tour of Los Angeles.

Mukti showed me the last of the series of films he had made of me on a rainy Tuesday afternoon in the same basement room at St Mungo's where he had conducted our cognitive behavioural therapy sessions. In addition to using all the standard techniques, Mukti also videoed psychotics during their flamboyant episodes, then showed the films to them when lucid, in order to persuade these patients of the necessity of taking their medication.

'In your case,' he told me during our first meeting, 'the situation is a bit different. Your reality testing seems wholly adequate; rather, your obsessive-compulsive thought patterns appear to have become, um, *engrafted* in the external world. It's as if by continuously viewing the world through the anthropomorphic lens of distorted scale, you have projected on to it a form of body dysmorphic syndrome. This would account for the fugues you experienced while travelling in the States, the loss of the medium sized, your perception of the world as wholly comprised by the awesome and the very—'

'Little.'

'Quite so, the very little.'

The near-obsolete VDU monitor, with its mushroom plastic casing, sat whirring at a queer angle on the fake wood veneer of a refectory table. Was this a fungal growth, nurtured overnight under strip-lighting? On the screen, which lacked vertical hold, images of me flickered and kinked. In answer to questions from someone off-screen, I contended that I could sign my name on a dust mote and play billiards with Higgs bosons while simultaneously apprehending the sixty-mile span of the Middlesex tertiary escarpment.

My dottiness was obvious, yet what struck me more forcibly was the concentration of all this effort, expertise and resources into these mean and institutional images of the very mean and institutional room we were currently sitting in: I sat on the plastic stacking chair watching myself writhe on the same plastic stacking chair, and, although I felt removed from the on-screen antics, it was a disjunction of perspective alone – the man in the room watching himself in the same room insistently demanded another recursion of this POV, another plastic stacking chair, another me.

'I know what you're thinking,' Mukti said as we watched the last film: 'you'd like some Powerade.' And he companionably passed me the pink bottle.

I had been referred to Dr Mukti by Zack Busner, the consultant psychiatrist at Heath Hospital, who for over a quarter of a century had played a major role in my life – part therapist, part mentor, part friend, part inspiration, part hierophant, part demiurge . . . wholly suspect. If I summon Busner up now it is as I first saw him. I was a troubled adolescent with a piebald horse face and wasted legs in drainpipe jeans; he was a plump, frog-faced man, his nondescript hair not so much thinning as giving the impression it hadn't grown since birth.

He leant back in the swivel chair behind his cluttered desk, his legs outstretched, and as he spoke, with great dexterity – as a card sharp in a Western runs a silver dollar over and under his fingers – rolled and unrolled the furry tongue of his mohair tie.

'I have a patient,' Busner said on that first meeting. 'Who's a very well-known jazz musician – a highly talented chap. He tells me that he takes cocaine, he takes heroin – for him it isn't a problem. Tell me, why's it a problem for you?'

I forbore from making the obvious point: if it wasn't a problem for this jazzer, why the fuck was he seeing a shrink? Forbore for several reasons. First, aged nineteen, I was intimidated by Busner and his environs. His office was at the end of a corridor, which in turn was at the far end of the hospital's general psychiatric ward. This wasn't the locked ward where sectioned patients were confined, but nevertheless there was plenty of flamboyant mental distress on display.

As I had sat in the miserable little outpatients' waiting area – a couple of uneasy chairs, a pained pot plant, a racked magazine rack – an anorexic had danced with her drip by the window, toying with the plastic chains that shackled the vertical louvres. Then she came over and sat beside me, breathing in my face *caustic acid down a cracked commode leaking sewage*. I studied *Chat* magazine's great new recipe for banana bread, until a civil enough young schizophrenic came by and offered to sell me the alien implant he had instead of a leg. The anorexic had been replaced at the window looking out over Hampstead Heath by an old man – a catatonic I supposed – who rocked not back and forth on his heels, but from side to side like a metronome, while emitting a buzzing noise, *Did he have a horsefly trapped in his mouth?*

Were these people, I wondered, my new gang? The psychic insurgents I had fantasized joining as, fractured by acid, I riffled through the pages of R. D. Laing's *The Divided Self*? I didn't want to join now I was in the recruitment office – yet feared I already had. A few months previously I'd been an in-patient at Heath Hospital on a surgical ward. I'd had my tonsils taken out – a painful operation at that age. Ostensibly, this was because of all the sinus attacks I kept getting, which felt like thumbscrews being tightened – on my brain; but the real reason I kept getting sick in my nose was all the powder I shoved up it, the bathtub amphetamine, the cocaine cut with baby laxative, the scouring smack – and worse.

The nurses sussed me out and were less than nurturing. There was a tubby squaddy in the bed beside me, who, when he was conscious, spun me yarns about how he was a sergeant-major in the SAS, and had been shot in the neck by the IRA on the Falls Road while working undercover with an assassination squad. I put him down as a fantasist, but one of the nurses, tucking me in until it hurt, leant down and hissed in my ear: 'He's a *real* hero, you shoulda seen him when they brought him in. He had an infection on the back of his neck that was bigger than his head!'

With the nurse, too, I forbore from backchat: my addiction was an assassination squad, roaming the bombed-out streets in a West Belfast of the mind. I'd got my friend Dave to smuggle some cocaine on to the ward, and together we'd shot it up in the toilet. Paranoid, he'd split right away, leaving me with my grazed throat and revving heart to endure the agonies of an unanticipated ward round: the consultant, wading between the limpid beds, the stork's plumage of his white coat parted at the breast, dipped down to peck at my wrist, yet seemed quite indifferent to my Max Roach pulse. No jazzer he.

It was my long-suffering GP who had referred me to Busner. She was understandably fed up with the house calls she had to make on my behalf: trips to the bathrooms I had locked myself inside, and where I lay on the mat, mewling as the intestinal reef knots of opiate withdrawal tightened inside me.

'I think you'll get on,' she had said. 'He's a very, um, unusual man. I don't expect he'll want to treat you in any orthodox fashion – just go up to the hospital and have a chat with him.'

There were steely-green filing cabinets in Busner's office and a chequerboard of institutional carpet tiling. The wall-mounted shelves were piled with everything from Wilhelm Reich to 'Just William'. The hardwood kneehole desk lugged in from another era, the fronts of the shelves, the windowsills – in fact every available horizontal surface was blobbed with fossilized shits. Later, Busner told me that the coprolite collection had begun as a 'juvenile riposte to the founding father of psychoanalysis's own rather more aesthetic bibelots, his ancient tabletop statuary, but then . . . Well, it all rather got out of hand.'

On the walls there were four 'imaginary topographies', hefty clay bas-reliefs that I later learnt had been given to Busner by Joseph Beuys after he had treated the artist – I assume, successfully – for a drug-induced psychosis. They were ugly and rather threatening things, heavy tablets scored with miniature ravines and pinnacles. They distorted the scale of the cluttered and stuffy room – Busner had disabled the air conditioning because he couldn't bear the noise. The view from the window was also disorienting: the gravelled roof of a wing of the hospital, upon which hunched four large rectangular water tanks – or were they, perhaps, very little?

I was aware that, together with Harold Ford, Busner had been one of the originators of the Quantity Theory of Insanity, and so assumed that he would be impressed if I brought up a half-digested splurge of Foucault with chunks of Bataille floating in it. He wasn't dismissive, only cleared the ground between us, sweeping away the clutter of identity so that we faced one another unadorned.

We must have talked for fifty minutes or so *minted lamb*;* then Busner said, 'I'm afraid my caseload is such that I won't be able to see you on any kind of regular basis. Still, I've enjoyed

---

* I cannot recall tasting pre-minted lamb until the early 2000s, when Sainsbury's began to offer it among their selection of barbecue meats. This was over twenty years after the events described, so the phrase 'minted lamb' is interjected here to convey the implausibility of this reconstructive memoir, and indeed of the genre as a whole.

chatting to you and I hope you have to me. I don't want you to feel rejected and if you'd like to pop in now and again to see me you'll always find my door open.' He pointed at the institutional plank, its Judas window reinforced with steel mesh; it was, indeed, ajar, although I found out later this was due to severe warping.

Before we parted Busner gave me a Riddle set. This was the 'enquire within' game that had made the psychiatrist simultaneously a household name and a laughing stock among his peers. Alone, or with a few select friends and a bottle of wine; a scented candle lit – or smelling only of your own desperation – Riddle players were encouraged to arrange the brightly coloured acrylic tiles in patterns they found pleasing, or suggestive, or unsettling – essentially, the thing was a DIY Rorschach test, the key for which had been written by the great soul doctor himself.

Everyone had played the Riddle at some time or other in the late 1970s; it was a hula-hoop for the mind and, like all such crazes, it soon became impossibly hackneyed; lost Riddle tiles lay trapped beneath the carpet underlay of the entire culture. 'I'm solving the Riddle!' – which Busner mouthed on a television quiz programme where he appeared in a grid of similar celebrities, answering facile questions – became one of the catchphrases of the era – and not in a good way. Still, I thanked him for the gift and tucked it into the side pocket of whatever Oxfam jacket I was wearing that month. Forty-five minutes later I was in a walk-up flat in Camden Town trying to barter the thing for a five-quid bag of smack.

For all the years I had taken the lift to the eighth floor of the hospital I had continued to find Busner's door open – once it was right off its hinges, laid across trestles and being planed down by a maintenance man. Busner stood in the doorway, rolling and unrolling the frayed end of his tie, watching the man work while speculating on what ailed the door as if it were a particularly unresponsive patient. Nevertheless, the next time I came it still wasn't pulled to.

Busner said he didn't mind the malfunctioning door – it reminded him of the 1960s, when, shortly after qualifying, he had started a 'concept house' in Willesden, where therapists and patients had lived together communally with no distinctions between them. While Busner had long since enacted professional closure, abandoning his conviction that mental pathologies were in reality semantic confusions, he still counselled an inter-personal approach – even when liberally dishing out Largactil.

Our own long-term therapeutic relationship certainly had a playful character; in the nearly three decades his door had been open to me, Busner had sent me for psychotherapy with a succession of colleagues. There had been an anally retentive orthodox Freudian analyst whose consulting room was a garage conversion in Dollis Hill. There was a plump cat-furred humanist in West Hampstead, whose ability to feel my pain seemed to entail her crying a lot about her own. There was a media-friendly intellectual with jet-black kiss curls and the foam-rubber voice of the insincere, who encouraged me to view my life as a narrative that might be rewritten – by him. Then there was the group therapy, the rebirthing, and even a shamanic purification rite conducted in a polythene hogan off the A303. All the while Busner lurked in the background, ready to step forward whenever my condition deteriorated.

Over the years he must – at one time or more – have prescribed me most of the neuro-pharmacopoeia, from anxiolytics, hypnotics and sedatives, through tranquilizers and anti-psychotics, to opiate and alcohol blockers, lithium and methadone. On one occasion he smuggled me in the dead of night into Friern Barnet Hospital. There, using equipment dusty with desuetude – the rubber leads perished – he administered electroconvulsive therapy to me. During the aeons-long seconds when the current surged through my cortex, I broke the restraints and surged up from the couch, then plunged through the fire-resistant ceiling tiles and flew into the suburban night. Up there I was a superhero, with no mission other than to curvet above the rain-slicked roofs.

I was not insensible to the possibility that Busner was exploiting me. After all, he had always been frank about what ailed me and my prognosis, saying early on: 'Essentially, yours is a mimetic malaise. You have an addictive personality, certainly, also a borderline personality disorder. You are a depressive, and, without certain strategies that you've devised for yourself, you would undoubtedly be crippled by phobias. Any treatments that I advocate for you are not to alleviate the symptoms of these conditions – which I regard as pretty much incurable – but to legitimate them.'

At least, I think that's what he said – it's certainly the kind of thing he *would*, as is: 'Look on the bright side – your strategies work, by and large; mine will too, and your psyche is . . . um, ebullient and productive. I'm not some potterer in the allotment of the mind, offering to weed out your hysterical misery and replace it with commonplace unhappiness – for you this is impossible; the best you can hope for is a rollercoaster of despair and euphoria. Still, I like rollercoasters – don't you?'

But what was it in for him? I've no doubt that like the majority of shrinks he was a psycho-empathetic voyeur, who, to begin with, clutched the safety bar alongside me and screamed along for the ride. Could he also have foreseen the curious creative symbiosis that would grow up between us? For, just as I incorporated him – thinly veiled – into my novels and short stories, so he made use of me in the numerous articles and case studies he published.* Our collaboration – if that's what it was – was a greater constant in my life than any other relationship, possibly for Busner as well; during it we were both married (in his case remarried), divorced and married again. Between us we added six more heads to the human herd: Busner had twin boys with his third wife, Caroline Byng, although he already had several grown-up children, one of whom, X, was a cabinet minister in the first Blair government.

Mythic skies, empurpled cloud ruptured above the cruising grounds of West Heath – a crumpled tissue snagged by a limp twig. The façade of the burnt-out Chinese restaurant at the junction of Belsize Lane and Haverstock Hill remained soot-stained for years – some people said the Tongs had done it, and the blackness under the gouged-out windows did suggest the agony of a tortured soul. Strange miasmas pooled in the hollow of Southend Green, where, when I first began visiting Busner, old Jewish émigrés still played chess at the Prompt

* The majority of Busner's papers appeared initially in the *British Journal of Ephemera*, and have been subsequently collected in *The Undivided Self: Existential Torpor and Schizothymia* (Poshlost Press, 2007).

Corner Café, slamming down the levers on their time clocks. Over it all loomed the vast hospital, its access ramps rearing up from the rooftops, while the Classic Cinema smarmed against its flank.

In there, one wet winter night, I saw Nic Roeg's *Bad Timing* on its first run. My date was psychotic – something I was too wasted to realize until the feature had started, and she began burbling merrily *decoction of dog-eared damp Penguin classics*, as she ran her sweaty hands over my face, tweaking my nose, pinching my cheeks and poking her fingers into my dry mouth. It was by no means the last time that sort of thing happened to me.

What I'm trying to say is that I accepted all of this, not unthinkingly, or out of passivity – but joyfully. Busner remained for me the fixed point of a turning world, so that no matter how many times I walked the quarter-mile from Belsize Park tube, it was a homecoming: I may have wandered from city to city, but Laius remained right where he'd always been, playing with his fossilized shits while he dispensed Riddles, waiting to be killed afresh. I may have been in distant lands, yet in my mind's eye I accompanied him on his ward round: a long dolly down one corridor, then through the core of the building, then back through the women's ward on the far side. It was a technically demanding shot – especially before the perfection of the steadicam – but the absence of cutting meant that nothing diminished the impact, when, at the very end, the camera panned 180 degrees to reveal: me, enormous, swathed in grey gabardine, moon face cratered with debauchery, lurching up from my uneasy chair and heading towards that always open door.

*       *       *

It was a Tuesday and hot in the tube. *Cans of human stewed in their own farts.* I used to observe the anonymity that crowded in on me and at least see its feeling face. Not any more. Now I saw the features ageing would impose on all these suburbonauts as they rumbled through the clayey void; they were wearing not space helmets – but time ones. It was hotter still above ground, and the plane trees in the triangular plot beside St Stephen's were sticky with sap and fret-worked by caterpillars. I stood, pissing, hidden by a redbrick buttress of the derelict church, then climbed back gingerly over the railings and continued downhill to the hospital.

Busner must, I thought, be seventy by now – yet to me he appeared unchanged. For as long as I'd known him he'd been a little overweight, yet his fleshy face, with its suggestion of jowls, resisted wrinkling. It seemed I had been doing the deteriorating for both of us. He was standing with his back to me when I squeezed through the door – in his shirtsleeves, with a Vaseline sheen on his fat neck as he rearranged his coprolites.

'How has the CBT with Shiva Mukti gone?' he asked without preamble, or even turning.

'OK, I s'pose.' I looked about for a chair – they were all piled high with ring binders, loose papers, and even some dry cleaning still perving in its polythene. I began clearing one.

'He's a well-meaning fellow, Shiva,' Busner said; 'perhaps a little prosaic.'

'He shot films of me while I was in my . . . obsessive phases; then played them back to me.'

'Did it help?'

'Um, help . . . well, with film maybe, and a little bit with reality as well.'

'A little bit, eh – how about the survivor guilt?'

I didn't want to talk about the events on Foula; I could still see the human stain on the rocks below the Kame, the wheeling gulls and the plastic trousers – a speck on the swell.

'I don't know about that,' I said testily, 'but the fact is I haven't written anything serious since last September and I've got mouths to feed. I've an idea for an investigative piece and I'd like to pursue it.'

'And this involves a trip?'

He was behind his desk and at the tie again, rolling and unrolling. I'd once asked him how long, on average, it took him to twirl one to shreds. He said nylon ones lasted the longest – but he hated the feel of them. Silk was pretty good – but too expensive. Wool he found most comforting – and mohair in particular. 'It's a sort of carding, really,' he told me. 'I'm straightening my own neurons and glia, smoothing out my cortex so that I can spin it into threads of thought.' Frankly, it was a little rich that such a man believed he could help anyone else with their neuroses.

'Yes, I want to walk to Hollywood.'

'All the way?'

'Don't be facetious – you know my methodology: I'll walk from my house to Heathrow – probably via Pinewood Studios where they're shooting the new James Bond film – then I'll fly to LAX, and walk from there on to Hollywood.'

'Dangerous territory for you, I should've thought – given the events of last year.'

'That was different, I, I was caught unawares – I didn't have an objective.'

'I see, and what's your objective now, precisely?'

I didn't like the way this was going; it wasn't exactly that Busner was being hostile – it was more that his tone was off, his voice pitched a shade too low. And, now that I stopped to consider it, wasn't there something sinister about the way he hadn't aged over the years? He wasn't merely familiar to me – I knew every hair that sprouted from the tragus of his annoyingly complicated ear – but *overly* familiar; his mannerisms were exaggerated, his coughs studiously rehearsed. It seemed he was an accomplished actor, called upon to play the part of Dr Zack Busner.

I swept this useless paranoia aside: I needed him to share my enthusiasm.

'I want to find out who killed film – for film is definitely dead, toppled from its reign as the pre-eminent narrative medium of the age. I don't know if film was murdered – but I suspect there's a killer out there!'

My melodramatic words hung in the air – THERE'S A KILLER OUT THERE! – meaning-motes aglow in a sunbeam projected from between the louvres.

'Ahem,' Busner cleared his throat, *frog in Froggy*. 'I see. There may be something in what you say – change is definitely in the, ah, air – new media, streaming, that sort of thing . . .' His fingers fluttered so as to suggest he was entirely au fait. 'But why now? I've never known you take any especial interest in film.'

'Me?' I snapped back. 'I've been a film critic – I've even written a screenplay . . . well, most of one. You, on the other hand, probably don't even know there's a screenwriters' strike on, and I can safely say that in all the hundreds of hours I've spent talking to you I've never heard you reference the movies once. Once!'

He was unfazed by my anger.

'It's all those credits that get to me,' he remarked, swivelling to face the scuzzy window. 'You know the kind of thing: Fifth Assistant Director, Manuel P. Zlotnik; Personal Assistant to Miss Pearlstein, Carol Goodenough – then, marching up the screen, entire squads of carpenters, electricians, best boys, gaffers, gofers and key grips, to say nothing of the special effects technicians . . . In my day all it took to make a film was Will Hay and the Fat Boy . . . Anyway' – he rotated back to face me – 'I know you like walking, but why walk to Hollywood? Los Angeles is hardly pedestrian-friendly.'

'I – I, well, to be frank I think it's safer that way – it'll mean I can slip beneath their radar.'

'They have radar? And there's a "they"?'

'Obviously I'm not suggesting there's a conspiracy.' I was wary of appearing paranoid; tolerant as Busner was of my more exaggerated phases, he'd never made any secret of the fact that he would section me if he saw fit. 'I'm speaking figuratively: windscreens are screens, after all – or lenses. Vehicular transport is either a cinema that you sit in passively while the world is shown to you, or else, if you drive, you're operating a camera, directing the movie of your journey.'

'I see.' He was looking at me vacantly, but I blanked him right back and continued:

'If I want to discover who – or what – did for film I'll be better off walking. Walking is so much slower than film – especially contemporary Hollywood movies, with their stuttering film grammar of split-second shots – and it isn't framed, when you walk you're floating in a fishbowl view of the world. There can't possibly be any editing: no dissolves, no cuts, no fades, no split-screens – and, best of all, no special

effects, no computer-cheated facsimiles of the world. You see, if I walk to Hollywood I'll be creeping along outside the ambit of the filmic – like a Vietcong insurgent tunnelling through the jungle – and they won't be able to see me coming!'

Despite myself I had become overexcited, singing out the last line as if it were an affirmation of faith. Busner ignored this. He had retrieved yet another Riddle set from his desk drawer and was bridging the lumpy summits of his coprolites with the brightly coloured little planks. THEY WON'T BE ABLE TO SEE ME COMING! still hung between us, the air around it puckered up as if by heat convection. I rose from my chair and walked across to the title: when I poked it the letters had the slippery resistance of inflated plastic, while my own words continued to resound in the catacombs of my mind: '. . . they won't be able to see me coming!'

It dawned on me, as I stood looking down at Busner fiddling with his toy, that I had already exited sideways into a discarded scene, the chopped-up frames of which lay curling on the cutting-room floor. It had been bothering me that although there had been establishing shots and even flashbacks, the main narrative had begun without a credit sequence: no slow-revolving globe pierced by photons, no torch-bearing Grecian goddess, no searchlights playing over monumental 3-D type, and – most of all – no Dolby histrionics, the orchestra of thousands chuntering away: 'Chun-chunn! Chun-chunn! Churrrurrrl-chun-chunn! Ta-tatta-taa! Ta-ta-ta-ta-ta-tatta-taaa!' With Hollywood, I thought, the climax always came at the beginning – all the rest was an insensate nuzzling, as the camera roved over the silvery skin.

Another title materialized in the stuffy office, replacing my graphic paranoia: ONE YEAR EARLIER. I walked round it. From Busner's side the plain white capitals were reversed: ЯƎI⅃ЯAƎ ЯAƎY ƎNO – not that he was paying them any mind, as he'd dropped a Riddle tile and was now getting down awkwardly on his hands and knees to search for it in the kneehole of the desk.

I admired the title, which was positioned just so: in stark counterpoint to the cluttered shelves, the half-open door revealing a wedge of stock corridor, the dimply dullness of Beuys's topographies. The title both moved things forwards – and backwards – while filing the current scene away. Not that it had been exactly a year previously – it was more like thirteen months, but the imprecision was forgivable dramatic licence.

## ONE YEAR EARLIER

I was in a bistro in the Place Wilson in Toulouse. My POV was not from behind my eyes but disembodied, looking down at a 45-degree angle from somewhere near the ceiling at a table of diners. There was me, the writer Jonathan Coe, the journalist Simon Tiffin and his wife Alexa, Marianne Faithfull and François Ravard, and Yann Perreau, the organizer of *Le Marathon des mots*, the literary festival that had brought us all to town. It was a well-lit and wide shot, sharply focused so that all the detail of the scene – white napery, grey meat, red wine – was instantly caught. I could almost feel the snag of the diners' teeth, taste the grease on their lips, and smell the foody vapours funnelling up their noses. Moreover, as it was an episode from my own life, I experienced an immodest thrill at the work expended by the production designers, lighting cameramen and all the other techies Busner was so dismissive of, in order to re-create it for the screen.

As for the casting – it was excellent. The man portraying Jonathan Coe had a strong likeness to the writer – the same symmetrical mop of greying hair, the same half-handsome features. François Ravard's role had been nabbed by a swarthy little fellow, on whose broken nose the trademark heavy-black-frame spectacles appeared drawn on as if by a bored child. But perhaps because of this discord, François's Gallic rolled *r*'s, his exasperated clucks and wheedles of annoyance as he dealt with Marianne – who, *très fatiguée*, was demanding to be taken back to the hotel – seemed all the more authentic. Marianne was played by a dyed-blonde at least a decade younger than the real thing – but she husked to perfection.

I couldn't assess the Tiffins' performance, because they were mostly silent, absorbed in the spectacle of François and Marianne's pantomimic co-dependency. As for Yann Perreau, I couldn't remember what he'd looked like at all, and, true to my agnosia, the filmmakers equipped his actor with a mask of featureless flesh.

The sound was as good as the camerawork, so that as I zoomed in the clatter of cutlery and the kvetching of François and Marianne became muffled, while Jonathan's gently emphatic voice increased in clarity; he was saying to the man sitting beside him: 'Yes, I know what you mean. I sat on the jury at last year's Edinburgh Film Festival, and of the ten films we shortlisted for the Best British category not one got a theatrical release; they all went – if they went anywhere at all – straight to video.'

'Mm, mm,' affirmed the man playing me – he was chewing some bread. 'It just goes to prove my point: film is dead, its century-long reign as king of narrative has ended, and we are in an interregnum, and, as Gramsci observed of such periods between political hegemonies – now the strangest freaks and sports will arise.'

I was disappointed, obviously, that my part hadn't attracted a leading man, although there are worse fates than to be played by a classy British character actor. I couldn't fault me on my mannerisms: the deep-sea waggle of the hammerhead, the lazy flap of the cartilaginous hands; the voice, too, was spot-on: nasally posh, whiningly mockney. But was this David Thewlis (too young, too good-looking) or Pete Postlethwaite (too old, too ugly), whose head, together with that of the Coe-alike, filled the screen as I closed on them?

No matter, because just as it seemed my POV was going to perform a laparoscopy on the mystery thespian, it reared back with the suddenness of a striking rattlesnake, swivelled right round, then tracked through the bistro and out the door. It paused for three seconds to capture a statue of Goudouli: the celebrated Occitan poet sat foppishly atop a rockery planted with swooning nudes, a pigeon perching on his wrist – was he was hawking for bread?

SIX MONTHS LATER annulled Goudouli's stonily good-humoured features, and then this establishing shot – that ought, by rights, to have preceded the bistro scene – dissolved into smoky limbo. During this interlude I envisioned the opening of John Huston's *Moulin Rouge* (1952), wherein Toulouse-Lautrec climbs down from his Montmartre bar stool, and, as he stumps towards the door, *le patron* peers over the zinc rampart and says, 'So long, Toulouse.' But of course in my version the painter of restricted height wasn't played by José Ferrer but Sherman Oaks, and as he came on he winked at me, horribly, a crack in a face crusted with coagulated blood.

## SIX MONTHS LATER

Exterior, night: the terrace of the Café Pinot beside the Los Angeles Public Library, a blowy evening in October 2007. The wind rattles the sunshades and the aurora urbanis streams in plumes of orangey light from the glassy cliffs of the surrounding skyscrapers. As my severed head is bowled through the double doors and past the giant rotisserie that's the café's selling point, it's difficult to accept that this was a scene completely excised from my memory of the time I had spent in Los Angeles – for I know what's coming: a long dining room of Bauhausian rationality, the windows outlined in black like Mondrian rectangles, below them a continuous banquette, in front of this white-clothed tables for two, mostly empty, but at one sits Ellen DeGeneres, playing the part of Stevie Rosenbloom, my Hollywood agent, while opposite her is . . . yes, David Thewlis.

His behaviour in Toronto now makes sense. At the time I'd assumed he was simply cutting me, sensing that I – like, no doubt, others he met – believed he gave his finest performance in Mike Leigh's *Naked* (1993), and that since then, like so many actors who have been hollowed out by the director's compulsive improvisatory method, he had been coasting. Actors, humph! They're like that – even the best of them are passive, receptive . . . can I get away with feminized? Waiting for the back of a hand to prink their rouged nipples, waiting for it to slide down into the dry cleft of their pride, moisten it – so that it swells.

*From the bar between two rusty lamp-posts hangs the carcass of a newly slaughtered ox. Standing in a cloud of flies, a man with a knife is cleaning out the entrails. Huxley stands tripping in Schwab's on La Cienega – and then again on the beach at Santa Monica with Thomas Mann. Partially sighted as he is, Huxley still notes that their leather-shod feet are dabbling in the slurry of used condoms expelled from a sewer outfall.*

The freshly slaughtered beef forms a ridge of erect slices on my flat white plate; to one side there's a rick of grated carrot and celeriac; to the other there's a boulder of potato mashed with sage. Thewlis looks balefully at this, then away to where a waiter, wound into his apron as tightly as a plague victim into a shroud, stands forlorn beside a pillar.

'We hear a lot about tortured genius,' says Thewlis-as-me, 'but what about tortured mediocrity?'

The waiter takes this personally and huffs off towards the giant rotisserie.

'Now you've offended him,' says DeGeneres-as-Stevie. I zoom in on her: she's eating fish – a newly landed rainbow trout that arches on her plate, flipping beads of water across her brownish dress. There's something going on at the neck of this garment, but such are the vagaries of my memory that what may have been silk ruffles have been replaced by the small squares of opacity used to obscure the faces of covertly filmed criminal suspects.

'I don't give a shit,' Thewlis/Self comes back. 'If he's exercised about his craft he should go out on strike with the rest of 'em.'

'What about you?' DeGeneres I thought a casting against type, but she's got Stevie's gentle Angeleno rasp down pat. 'I mean, doncha think *you* should come out in support of the screenwriters; after all you're in an allied trade?'

'Right! But what would my picket line be like? I mean, am I gonna stop myself getting to my own typewriter, or will I show up once a year to prevent myself mailing a manuscript to the publisher?'

'I getcha – and y'know, there's gonna be no real solution to this: the generals on both sides are fighting the last war, the dispute back in the eighties when the writers lost out on the revenue from video rentals. No one really knows what's at stake now – if anything at all: these guys are going head to head over what they think the internet residuals from *Dharma & Greg might* be worth.'

Thewlis has felled one of the beef slices and managed a few bites, together with a scrape of potato, but he's obviously not interested and lets his cutlery clatter into the shattered food, ruining something that had the compositional integrity of a seventeenth-century Dutch vanitas painting. He takes a swig of Powerade from a handy bottle. He looks DeGeneres in the eye: 'It's significant, isn't it, that you talk of TV rather than the movies.'

'Well, that's where the money is – such as it is. I mean, there's an avalanche of product now – most of the WGA people are network TV writers who'll never work again.'

Thewlis doesn't seem to hear this, but presses on: 'And it can't've escaped your notice that this is the first year ever that video-game sales are set to surpass movie receipts?'

'No, no, it hasn't escaped my notice.' DeGeneres casts her blue eyes (a blooper, Stevie's are hazel) down to her plate: the trout is dead.

'Has it occurred to you, Stevie, that this is it?' Such sententiousness! Can that really be what I'm like? 'This is the death of the movies – the shattering of the century-old mirror within which humanity has regarded its own plug-ugly features—' Thewlis is interrupted by the waiter, who has sidled back to remove DeGeneres's dead fish, and is raising a brow at my mad cow platter. 'I haven't finished yet!' Thewlis cries, attacking the mash with his fork so that white worms writhe through its tines.

DeGeneres sighs. 'You're right. Y'know, I kinda hope that the movies will end up like theatre – a secondary medium, sure, but still a revered one in which original work's done; but now . . . I dunno.'

'The question is, Stevie, if film is dead, who murdered it?'

She sighs again. 'Could've been Mike Ovitz and his clients' cancerous egos – or maybe it was CGI zapping them with an alien blaster; then again, it could've been something less dramatic: the steady downward pressure of marketing on the movies' lifeblood, as they were used to sell more and more crap to younger and younger kids. But what I want to know is, Will, what're *you* gonna do about it?'

'Do? I'm gonna track down the killer, of course. Literally. I'm going to walk to Hollywood, my eyes fixed on the sidewalk, checking out the spoor. I'm gonna sidle up on the fucker—'

'Or fuckers.'

'Or fuckers – that way they won't know I'm coming, and listen, you can help me here . . .'

Was it that Thewlis's imitation of my voice had dropped into a conspiratorial undertone? No, it was my POV's measured backtracking, first along the length of the dining room, then deftly through the vestibule, before, eyes-rear, madly stepping down from the kerb and into the traffic scooting along Fifth Street. The SUV that grazed my nose with its metallic-blue paintjob made the cut.

I had found Busner's Riddle tile – it had fallen down the cable tracking slot, together with three others. I got unsteadily to my feet and handed them over. He grunted his thanks, then asked, 'Have you solved it?'

'Um, yeah, in a way – it's this technique Mukti taught me: not just running the tape forward, so that I can reveal the consequences of my own negative thought patterns, but making little film clips out of them that I can play over and over again.'

'Really.' Busner was underwhelmed. 'That Mukti seems more of a cineaste than a psychiatrist – but, still, if it works for you, Will, and I suppose you'll need such, um, strategies on your . . . trip.'

'Which you don't approve of?'

'Approve? No, I'm not in favour of your "quest"; to me it reeks of *Kunstschadenfreude*.'

'Meaning?'

'Meaning the art that indulges its creator's sorrow until it completely takes him over. Besides' – he had left off his Riddle fiddling and now fixed me with his watery grey eyes – 'there's the film script you say you wrote – it was never completed, was it?'

'No, that's true – you've got me there.' I retreated to my chair. Flinging a handful of summer rain against the window Nature called us to come out and play. 'I – I . . . I couldn't bear the thought of having to discuss the creative whys and wherefores with the producer – he wore a sleeveless anorak!'

'A gilet.'

'What?'

'I believe they're called gilets – sleeveless anoraks.'

'That wasn't all,' I continued. 'I also had this mounting inability to suspend disbelief.'

'Explain?' Busner rapped, and in that moment I realized who had been playing him throughout the entire scene: Orson Welles. Of course! Although master of stagecraft that Welles was – the dates were still all wrong.

'I'd had difficulties with theatre since my late teens – all those RADA Imogens pretending to be Renaissance virgins; then, when I began writing myself, narrative fiction was the next victim – hauling on the strings of my own puppets meant I couldn't help seeing everyone else doing the same tricks. Film and TV remained plausible – it was the spirit of the age, and no matter how jaded I might've felt, I could still immure myself in the wobbly flats of a daytime soap. But then – it must've been ten years ago or so – I began to be insistently aware of the sound recordist hovering out of shot, his furry boom mike dangling above the frame. So I started looking for it all the time – then I spotted other things.'

'Other things?'

'Well, continuity errors, anachronisms – anything that marred the accuracy of the representation: the wrong furniture for the period, the characters' inappropriately modish dialogue – y'know what I mean.'

I stopped and looked at him. It was so much more than impersonation: Welles, a far bigger man, had somehow contrived to shrink himself inside Busner. The cheeks had been padded and prosthetics used on the nose. If the art of screen acting consists in stillness rather than movement, how much stiller did this performance have to be? And yet he'd pulled it off, managing to convince an audience of one who was sitting within feet of him. Then there was the voice, as familiar to me as my own, with its wheezy aspiration suggestive of a high wind in the upper branches of a mighty brainstem – how many hours had he taken to perfect this?

'I don't want to upset you,' Welles said carefully. 'But, if I hear you right, you take no pleasure in entertainment at all any more.'

'Pleasure? It's a torment to me.'

'And you believe that by undertaking this quest, you'll cure your depression?'

'Depression – is that what it is?'

'Mos' def'.'

We sat and looked at one another for a while. I had no idea what he saw in me – but I knew what I saw in him: a suspension of disbelief that had endured my entire adult life. So I stolidly accepted the substitution, for to speculate as to why a long-dead Hollywood star had been directed to play my long-term therapeutic mentor, well, that way lay madness, and, as I've said, I knew better than to exhibit any stereotypy – let alone become strident.

I got up to depart – Busner tried to detain me: 'No problems with packing?'

'No, I don't think so – I mean, not that I've done it yet, I'll find out this evening.'

'And the genre of the piece?'

'Genre?'

'Yes – I think film noir is difficult to resist, yet . . .'

'Should be?'

'Absolutely, I'd go for almost anything else, rom-com, frat boy or screwball comedy – horror, perhaps. Just don't do anything arty or obscure, there's a good chap, remember the *Kunstschadenfreude* – remember *me*, when you find yourself in a chain hotel room, staring fixedly at the bulbous prongs of a video-games controller, and wondering where it all went wrong.'

I squeezed out through the half-open door, then squeezed halfway back in again to wiggle my fingers, 'Ta-ra.'

'Ta-ra,' Welles replied – he was fiddling with the Riddle tiles again.

I had never found Busner in the least bit pitiable before – this was Welles's genius entirely.

## 2

# KerPlunk!

Hal, still fiercely red of lens, although now too old and hackneyed to be able to pick up much save for swivel-on bit parts – such as security cameras – gazed down on me from the corner of the Foyles travel section. I had spread out so many maps – checking for pliability, legibility, extent and area covered – that my miniature *lebensraum* was interfering with the shoppers. A bookseller came over to me; he was tall, raw-boned and wearing a T-shirt printed with the poster for Godard's *Breathless*. His blue-black hair was cropped close at the sides of his slab head, and if he'd been better-looking the young Daniel Day-Lewis might have been playing him– or perhaps Lewis, a slave to the uglifying method, *was* playing him?

'I'm sorry . . .' he said, 'but people are complaining.'

I told him what I was looking for and how difficult it was proving.

'There's a street map that Rand McNally do,' he explained. 'It covers the entire LA basin, if it's not on display we might have one out back – I'll go and look.'

While Day-Lewis was gone I tidied up the other Los Angeleses, then upon his return we spread this new one out on top of a plan chest. It would do – it showed every street, although so small I had difficulty reading the names, even with glasses; it was also a single, easily folded sheet. However, it stopped at the Hollywood Hills, so there and then I scotched the next leg of my provisional plan, which had been to leave Hollywood via the cervical 'O' on the Hollywood sign, sleep newborn in the sierra, then slither on, via Universal City, down into the Valley, where I might be taken on as a porn star, or a third husband.

Of course, the bookseller wasn't only a bookseller – they seldom are. I wasn't about to tell him the reason for my trip, although I did say something about walking and how antithetical it was to film, which gave him his opening: 'Actually, I'm doing my doctoral thesis on slow motion—'

I stifled a sarcastic yelp: nothing could've been more antithetical to slow motion that the coiled power of this thespian cat-bear who leant, his coccyx stabbed by the corner of the plan chest. 'I see,' I said, 'you mean Muybridge's photographs, the variable speeds of old-fashioned hand-cranked projectors, Douglas Gordon's *24 Hour Psycho*,* that kinda thing?'

'Well' – his eyes were beautiful, his tone contemptuous – 'none of your examples are slow motion properly understood. Slow motion can only exist relative to full motion, and full motion itself has to be defined by a further correlate – say, a soundtrack. The Gordon piece – which I'm familiar with – is an example of extended play.'

Hal screwed me out from the corner, the other bookstore browsers free-floated among the shelves, their minds revving up to choose – then stalling. I remembered lurking beside a wall at the Hayward Gallery as Norman Bates's knife deeeeeeeeeeeeeeeeeeeeeeeeeeeeeeeeeeeeeeeeeeeeeeeeeeeeeeeeeeeeee eeeeeeeeeeeeeeeeeeeeeeeeeeeeeeeeeeeeeeeeeeeeeeeeeeeeeeeeeeeeeee

---

* *24 Hour Psycho* (1993) by Douglas Gordon is a video installation that slows down Hitchcock's *Psycho* so that it lasts for twenty-four hours.

eeeeeeeeeeeeeeeeeeeeeeeeeeeeeeeeeeeeeeeeeeeeeeeeeeeeeeeeee eeeeeeeeeeeeeeeeeeeeeeeeeeeeeeeeeeeeeeeeeeeeeeeeeeeeeeeeee eeeeeeeeeeeeeeeeeeeeeeeeeeeeeeeeeeeeeeeeeeeeeeeeeeeeeeeeee eeeeeeeeeeeeeeeeeeeeeeeeeeeeeeeeeeeeeeeeeeeeeeeeeeeeeeeeee eeeeeeeeeeeeeeeeeeeeeeeeeeeeeeeeeeeeeeeeeeeeeeeeeeeeeeeeee eeeeeeeeeeeeeeeeeeeeeeeeeeeeeeeeeeeeeeeeeeeeeeeeeeeeeeeeee eeeeeeeeeeeeeeeeeeeeeeeeeeeeeeeeeeeeeeeeeeeeeeeeeeeeeeeeee eeeeeeeeeeeeeeeeeeeescended. I barely looked at it, so absorbed was I by the grain, rough against my cheek – it was an effect I knew had been achieved by pressing planks into concrete before it set. Might it be possible to date the building by counting the rings in its walls? And what of my own predicament: my mind, frozen in my body, which, cells apoptosizing, careered towards entropy? As for this *punk*, I paid him for his map, but – I hoped, pointedly – neglected to thank him. It was Hal I waved goodbye to.

There was one further errand to do before I could head home to pack. I left Foyles and walked up Tottenham Court Road to the Scientology Centre by Goodge Street tube. I had been dropping in at the centre for years and must have completed hundreds of their questionnaires. The so-called Standard Oxford Capacity Analysis was a simplistic personality test devised by L. Ron Hubbard himself, and I'd always scored well on it: I was unstable, depressed, anxious, sluggish, inhibited, feckless, compliant *and* antagonistic. The test confirmed that on those rare occasions that I found myself in groups (for the most part I was chronically withdrawn), it was impossible for me to successfully integrate. You would've thought that such corrosive traits, especially when combined with a sheep-like suggestibility, made me a perfect recruit – but the Scientologists stubbornly refused to let me join.

In the late 1980s I had managed to inveigle myself on to an introductory weekend course at their British headquarters, Saint Hill Manor, near East Grinstead. This cultists' house party was everything I could've hoped for, from the diluted orange juice concentrate to the strip-lit repression of the single-sex dorms. I thought I was doing well: I joined in the discussions enthusiastically, and whenever we had a free moment I devoured the master's works in an exhibitionistic fashion.

All went well until the Sunday morning, when, as a special treat we wannabes were given a test audit. The auditing procedure is the ritual that lies at the core of Dianetics; it's nothing more than an extended lie-detector test, during which you're wired up to a polygraph and asked a series of questions that range from the innocuous – 'What is your favourite colour?' – to the revealing – 'Have you ever been sexually attracted to a member of the same sex?' As long as you answer them truthfully you are awarded a 'clear', and your so-called 'negative engrams' are held to have been pulverized by the power of probity. In due course you ascend to the next level.

Except that I never got to the first one. It didn't help that the auditor – his hair an extravagant bouffant – was played by the Who front man Roger Daltrey (who, following the success of *Tommy*, and the biopic of John McVicar in which he played the lead role, was trying to consolidate his acting career). Nor did it help that I was attracted to members of my own sex – albeit not Daltrey. The needles jerked on the meter, the pens danced on the graph paper readout, my auditor announced that I was exhibiting deep resistance. I was in a cleft stick: to admit to any homosexual inclinations would have ruled me out entirely, for the Church of Scientology was as bigoted in this regard as any fundamentalist sect.

Although sent packing from Saint Hill, I was still not to be deterred and over the coming years I went on pitching up at Tottenham Court Road, in disguises and under assumed names, armed with strategies for 'fooling' the Capacity Analysis. It was all to no avail: the smiling Scientologists would let me take the test again, then send me on my way, with the advice that I see a doctor, a therapist, a priest – do anything, in short, but submit myself to their own mind control.

The curious thing was that although at the outset I couldn't have rightly said why it was that I so craved Scientology, as the years went by and my capacity to suspend disbelief in narrative was increasingly hobbled, I realized that my intuition had been sound: Hubbard's opportunistic syncretizing of Astounding Stories, the Bhagavad Gita and *The Psychopathology of Everyday Life* was the perfect refuge for someone like me, who found the probable impossible, and the impossible highly likely.

Besides, the Scientologists' bizarre belief that their human bodies were only the temporary housing for immortal alien super-beings tallied with my own experience of life, in which well-established actors played even the walk-on parts – *William Holden, long dead, adjusts his fedora by the ticket machine, then strolls on.* The very condition of the actor, who assumes many different forms while remaining essentially himself, was like that of these Thetans – so was it any surprise that Hollywood stars, their frail psyches sprayed with incontinent regard, were also attracted to the cult?

Hubbard, whose entire life was the front-projection of a successful sociopath, naturally wanted to direct. And ended up bushed in Southern California, presiding over his own sci-fi epics with woeful results, *the silvery squeezy bottle passes through the meteorite shower in the shower stall.* The perplexing thing was that during the hundred-year hegemony of the movie everything had been filmed – including films themselves. Actors had played historical personages, and those personages had also played themselves, while the actors that had played them appeared in other movies – playing themselves. This poly-dimensional cat's cradle of references had snared plenty of people with reality-testing abilities far better than my own, and I maintained a certain amused tolerance for the way I lost myself in fugal ruminations such as this:

Stanley Kubrick had used his own Hertfordshire estate as a location for his last movie, *Eyes Wide Shut*, starring the Scientologist Tom Cruise. In the film, London streets acted the part of Manhattan streets – a metempsychosis analogous to that of actors: the same place living through multiple locations. Kubrick was scared of flying – the young Hubbard pretended to be a fearless flyboy. Hubbard also claimed to have met Freud, who in turn had certainly known Schnitzler, whose *Traumnovelle* was the basis of Kubrick's screenplay. And then . . . Kubrick was rumoured to have employed a special coach in order to invest Cruise and his then wife Nicole Kidman's sex scenes with the barest plausibility – which brings me back to Saint Hill and Roger Daltrey.

You can, no doubt, see which way my mind was pelting . . . The completed paper ran to some forty single-spaced pages, the dense type studded with emoticons and interwoven with diagrams bearing labels such as '45 degrees where the sigmoidal flexure of TC's penis is greater than 9.7'. I left it at the Scientology Centre, the pink plastic wallet also containing an explanatory note: 'I will be staying at the Roosevelt Hotel on Hollywood Boulevard on the twelfth of June, should anyone from the International Dianetics College wish to discuss the enclosed with a view to preventing publication', signed with the *nom de guerre* Will Smith.

I kept stopping on the way back from Stockwell tube to take photographs. The bases of the limes along Binfield Road were spiky with withies among which nestled the cigarette packets and energy drink cans let fall by the multitudes that tramped by every day. The buses were nose to tail, snorting for admission to their ferroconcrete stockade. I took maybe two or three hundred shots of these lime shrines before the dusk tumbled from the rooftops into the street and night swarmed over the police crime tape looped between the lamp-posts at the junction of our road.

Several of my neighbours were gathered at the cordon. One remonstrated with the officer on duty: 'My son is disabled! He's only fourteen years old – you can't stop me from going home, he needs me!'

All eyes were on the confrontation: the officer in her stab-proof waistcoat, the citizen in his dudgeon, so I ducked under the tape and moved swiftly past the technicians in their white crinkled boiler suits, who were picking at the congealed blood in the roadway. More techies were at work on the set opposite my front door: a neighbour's Audi estate completely dusted with fingerprinting powder – under the Kliegs it looked like a whale baby coated in vernix. As I put my key in the lock the techies turned their snout masks towards me and grunt-queried; I answered by waving my library card officially, then disappeared inside.

It was a Saturday night and as usual my wife had her cronies over to play games. We lived effectively separate lives; while I wrote screenplays that would never be made, she indulged in a rich fantasy life, one in which she was always about to start shooting – the very next day! An epic! She was Helen of Troy! Mary Magdalene! Joan of Arc! It was a sure-fire smash, with an astronomical budget! So, while I clickety-clacked away in my attic room, she swansoned from chamber to chamber, trying on outfit after outfit, then discarding them for the maids to tidy away.

Except that we didn't have any maids – a verism that made a mockery of her pretensions; instead it was our children – who had the precocious maturity associated with such neglect, and who were portrayed by a rota of superannuated child actors, gawky Macaulay Culkin, wizened Mickey Rooney, ambassadorial Shirley Temple, etc. – who did the tidying up around the gloomy Victorian house. They also did the cleaning, the laundry and the cooking – they even paid the bills and put themselves to bed punctually at eight-thirty. I've no idea how they found the time to go to school.

I threw a few things into a bag ready for my departure on the morrow, then went to say goodnight to my wife. At forty-eight she was still a remarkably handsome woman, and if she had been content to age gracefully I think everything might have been all right between us. As it was, I found her playing *KerPlunk* with her tame fags, all of them dolled up like teenagers – she in a pink velour tracksuit, her dyed-blonde hair in madly streaked bunches, the others in saggy-assed jeans that exposed the waistbands of their underpants so their pot bellies were captioned 'Calvin Klein'.

As I came into the kitchen my wife drawled, 'Get me a drink, darling.' And one of the forty-somethings leapt to do her bidding. 'Make it frothier this time' – she waved her heart-shaped lollipop like a lorgnette – 'and I want more marshmallows!

'Oh,' she deigned to notice me. 'It's *you* – don't hover like that, pull up a chair and join us.'

Reluctantly I did as she bade me, and Frankie or Hud (I could never tell them apart, and both were played by Philip Seymour Hoffman) equally reluctantly made room for me.

'It's too late to join in this round,' my wife continued, expertly feeding marbles into the tube, 'but you can play the next.'

She smiled merrily, her coralline lips peeling back from her tiny even white teeth. There was no malice in her – merely utter self-absorption. Hud – or Frankie – who was modishly shaven-headed (or perhaps simply bald), and who had once directed her in a breakfast bar commercial, fouled up his go and as the tube lost its marbles they all cried, 'KerPlunk!'

I played with them for an hour or so while an ancient Madonna album gently vogued through the sound system. This and the *KerPlunk* players' clothes were the only contemporary props – for we had bought the house fully furnished, complete with the splayed bearskin, the miniature church organ, the looming tallboys and hammered-brass aspidistra pots. Glass domes cluttered with songbirds stuffed in mid-flutter stood about on occasional tables, while a vast mezzotint of a Holman

Hunt leant against the coffered panelling – I had always felt a deep sympathy for the parasuicidal sheep it depicted, which were huddled together on an insufficiently vertiginous grassy knoll.

Talk was of reality TV shows and the indiscretions of the junior Royals; a new face cream was passed around and smelt. Around eleven I said my goodnights and went to bed with a glass of water. Passing along the hall I was seized by the police lights glaring through the panes of the front door, and so detoured into the drawing room. Here it was even brighter, the radiance lifting the rug's pattern – trellises twined with the tail feathers of peacocks – so that it floated in the must.

The forensics team were still out there – two of them, seated in the road with their backs against my neighbour's car. There had been no *Vorsprung durch Technik,* and, while it was no longer a newborn whale, nor was it a shiny aerodynamic status symbol. Instead, a pre-war Packard dusty and alone in a four-car garage scattered with dead leaves. What was it William Holden had said when the repo men took his car?

A disturbed night followed. I slept poorly on my narrow canvas cot, not helped by the screeching and giggling that floated up the stairs into the small hours. In the morning I found the superannuated child stars – three, maybe four of them – eating Sugar Smacks at the oval mahogany dining table, which was still littered with *KerPlunk* straws, marbles, chocolate-stained mugs and Bacardi Breezer bottles. The pathos of Macaulay Culkin's bare elbow in a smear of spilt milk was . . . indescribable. Frankie – or was it Hud? – had lumped up a

bed out of cushions and lay spread-eagled in the corner of the room, snoring noisily.

Mark Lester accompanied me to the end of the road and, standing either side of the crime scene tape, we said our goodbyes.

'Look after your mother,' I said as I kissed him on his greying blond curls. 'She may be a little daffy, but she has a good heart.'

He removed my hand from his shoulder with professional courtesy, then enquired, 'Will that be all, Mr Postlethwaite?'

Each purposeful stride kicked me free from the entanglements of my life, until a reveal shot done with the side of a Number 87 bus exposed the Wandsworth Road, its multicultural parade of food premises – The Sea Lamprey (Muslim fish and chips),

Twice as Nice (Carribbean), El Golfo (Portuguese *pasteleria*) – marching beneath yellowing London brick and the arched eyebrows of gothic rendering. I was safe now, walking out of town on a June morning – if I could be captured at all it would be possible only with a hand-held camera, fitted with a revolutionary lens capable of embracing the paradox of the human visual field, with its saccadic pans, zooms, tracks and stills spuriously contriving a synoptic unity.

The airy bulk of the gasometers, the heroic hulk of Battersea Power Station, the liberating span of Chelsea Bridge, the plane trees romping in the breeze along Sloane Street, the Michelin Man squatting on top of his building, the Linnaean façade of the Natural History Museum – the only disturbing note was struck by the branch of LA Fitness on Pelham Street, which, sited as it was beside the *trompe l'œil* Thurloe Square – a thin wedge of terrace hiding the District Line cutting – suggested movie trickery.

I didn't let it get to me; after all, the familiar dumpy shapes of London cabs were wrapped around with the skyline of Hong Kong or Copacabana, and besides, Hyde Park had given way to Queensway, and I was already making my way through the backstreets of Notting Hill before the dump bins of newspapers outside the corner shops began to impinge, and I started to obsess about the weighty potential of Rhys Ifans's scrotum. The shaggily mournful face of the Welsh comic actor stared up at me from newspaper after newspaper, on rack after rack, trapped there by the protracted and public break-up from his starlet girlfriend. He had come to prominence in Y-fronts and a snorkelling mask, typecast as an out-of-work Welsh comic actor in *Notting Hill* (1999). And so there his representation was, in the neighbourhood the representation of which had caused him to be so represented.

I pushed Ifans's bare back against the artex wall and took the soft gristle of his nipple in my dogged teeth, while Notting Hill grabbed the adjustable wrench of Ernő Goldfinger's* Trellick Tower and whirled it around my head. I lurched through Meanwhile Gardens, and came to on a bench beside the Grand Union Canal, staring at the brown emulsion waters, the decrepitating plunge of a skateboarder in a half-pipe resounding in my ears.

As I headed west along the towpath the afternoon came puttering extended-play towards me – a broad stroke of sunlight painted by a narrow boat. Brawny young fishermen sat in the historic present: on empty milk crates, stripped to the waist to have it out with minnows, their six-packs of beer beside them, shiny as shell cases in the grass. And so by the time I reached Old Oak Common I had regained some kind of equanimity. All I had to do was maintain my course through the summery snowfall of dandelion spore and the giddy flip of the cabbage whites, not forgetting to duck when I saw Hal, sitting on a pole by the railway siding, or screwed into the masonry at the rear of the Car Giant warehouse, his brow knitted with pigeon-repelling barbs, a windscreen wiper for an eyelid. True, he might capture a few frames of me, but I doubted that I could be identified; I was merely a glyph in this panorama of subjects – bridge, lock, fisherman and lamp-post – which could be shuffled to produce an endless vista.

Morgan Freeman and Ron Howard were waiting for me where I'd arranged to meet them: beside an information board

*Of whom more later.

disfigured with graffiti tags. It wasn't until I came right up to them that I could establish who it was they were playing, and then initially I thought Freeman hopelessly cast against type – like a black King Lear. However, within seconds it was clear not only that he was Nick Papadimitriou, but that he had captured my friend's mien perfectly: the hands-on-hips-belly-out stance, the furious intensity of Nick's stare and his slightly nasal whine.

As for Howard, I could never stand him anyway – and dying his hair red was cheap. Moreover, he was toting a large digital camera with a directional mike attached to it. Ignoring their greetings, I lashed out at him: 'Why the fuck did you bring that?' Then rounded on Freeman-as-Nick, 'I told you to tell him not to bring a fucking camera – it's crucial that there be no footage of me, if *they* get hold of it . . . What's more, it ruins all this—' I waved a hand at the enervated canal, the road bridge leapfrogging the canal, the empty skips piled like dirty crockery in a factory yard. 'Now I can't suspend disbelief in any of it!'

'C'mon, Pete.' Freeman, to his credit, refused to be intimidated. 'Lighten up – if you don't want to be filmed, that's fine, John'll keep you out of shot. He's come along to film me, not you – you knew he was making this documentary about me.'

I splashed some water from the Evian bottle I was carrying into the palm of my hand and dashed it against my rage-engorged face. Freeman was wearing the same white shirt, dark trousers and heavy leather shoes that I'd last seen Nick in – but, while there was pathos in the half-mast flies, the shirtsleeves rolled up pre-war high, he still looked dapper. I realized my anger was born of pride as much as anything – I'd been counting on Thewlis playing me for these scenes with

Nick. My self-esteem required that I be better-looking as well as younger.

Ron-John was cowering by the info-board, so I went over to him and did my best to sound contrite. 'Look I'm sorry, John.'

'It's OK, Will, really – I understand. I'll keep tight in on Nick, and if you want to examine the camera before I go that's fine – besides, I'm only going to tag along for a couple of miles.'

The situation remained deeply unsatisfactory for all of us. Ron-John ran on ahead, took up a stance, then filmed Nick as he walked by, then he squeezed back past us and did the same again, over and over. He'd fitted Nick with a radio mike so he could indulge in his penchant for hymning such quotidiana as the abandoned warehouses along the canal side, the Middlesex County Council shields on the lock gates and the steel-clapboard Travelodge by the North Circular Road – but, although he launched into a lecture on the industrial estate conceived as the props department of capitalism, he kept being interrupted by passing joggers and cyclists, who upon noticing who he was stopped to natter among themselves.

I'd long since accepted Freeman's performance – barely seeing him as African-American any more – and was infuriated by this gauche behaviour. As for Ron-John, no matter how ingratiating he was, or how many high-grossing movies he made, for me he'd always be the bat-eared sycophant in a letter jersey making up to Henry Winkler. When he offered me the camera for my inspection, rather than examining the playback, I simply removed the tape cassette and chucked it in the canal. He trudged away disconsolately over Horsenden Hill, while Morgan and I went on towards Northolt.

Later, standing with him on the footbridge that crossed the A40 Western Avenue, and looking out north-west across the RAF airfield, I felt so happy to have escaped London that I was moved to embrace Freeman and cup his globe of white curls in my hand.

'Steady on, feller,' Nick said, but before he could disengage I was shocked by the frailty of his thin back. 'You'll be OK,' he went on gravely, 'so long as you're prepared for Laurel Canyon.'

I realized he had been granted a deeper insight than my own, and as we went on across a half-landscaped golf course, then into a nature reserve shaded in with un-coppiced beeches and cross-hatched by reed beds, I nerved myself to ask him what he knew. Yet couldn't – and so we reached Uxbridge and the same little boxes of ticky-tacky we had left behind in Northolt, then the Hobbiton of its suburbia, then the redbrick carcerals of its office blocks – and still I hadn't spoken.

I left Nick at the tube station, standing by a half-century-old train indicator that promised a Metropolitan Line departure for Finchley Road. Stumbling on from one tepee of streetlight to the next, I missed him acutely. Morgan Freeman's was the last familiar face I would see until I met up with Ellen DeGeneres in Los Angeles – unless, that is, I counted James Bond's.

# 3
# My Name is Bond

I had booked a bed and breakfast on the south side of the town. I'd been able to tell on the phone that the woman of the house was played by Brenda Blethyn, and now that we were standing face to face in the atrocious vestibule of her bungalow, I was glad I'd soon be rid of this supporting cast of British character actors, who, after all, had no traction in Hollywood.

I paid Blethyn in cash as soon as she'd revealed to me the converted garage lumbered with a double bed, a smoked glass table, a widescreen television and a partitioned bathroom. She waggled the banknotes in her hand, and my gaze skimmed past her creased top lip to bury itself in a massy spruce that writhed in the darkness.

'Y'know, you remind me of . . . you remind me of – now, who *is it* you remind me of?'

'I dunno, David Thewlis? Or maybe . . . Pete Postlethwaite?'

'No, it can't be, I've never heard of either of 'em.'

'Well.' I was barely civil. 'I can't possibly assist you to remember the name of someone I know nothing of to begin with, now can I?'

But she ignored this comment. 'My husband and I don't stop in the bungalow, so if you pull the door of the room to when you leave in the morning that'll be dandy. You've breakfast things in the fridge there.'

*Milk puckering under cling film, indescribably obscene.* Soon after that I heard the flutter and crunch of her Vauxhall Corsa pulling out of the drive. It was a minor part for Blethyn, and, as I made myself a bowl of Crunchy Nut Cornflakes, I wondered why she'd taken it on at all – I'd offered to send her a cheque or cash up front, and then she could've left the key under the mat for me.

At 2.00 a.m. I began my preparations, naked in the bathroom, working the special forces camouflage stain into my skin from the hairline down – face, neck, arms, hands, cock and balls – but by the time I reached my ankles the gunk had run out and it looked as if a bear had been shitting incontinently in the bath. *Of the life of man the duration is but a point, its substance streaming away.*

I tiptoed through the sleeping dormitory town, not moving freely until I had crossed the M25 by a footbridge and was heading north on a wooded path beside the Colne brook. The predawn sky draped over Iver Heath, the clouds a peignoir, the stars jewels gelid against its blue-black skin. It must have been freezing up there, because a plane taking off from Heathrow unzipped a distrail with its passionate heat. The cumulus gaped, the night moaned, and I streamed away through the long grass, leaving a long swathe of misplaited blades behind me that pointed the way to Iver, a hamlet that had had been ravished so many times by the camera, all the specificity had been sucked out of it.

Beyond the houses, across Pinewood Road, the birches of Black Park were doubly silvered in the sidereal light. Over fifty films had been shot among these dense thickets and drives choked with fallen boughs. Black Park had been a wood in Wisconsin, a forest in Slovenia, the Siberian taiga – it was a hack woodland actor, ever ready to put on its pine-needle overcoat and make a multiplex believe. It was perfect cover – they'd never look for me here, where millions had already looked, unseeing.

There was a fence of course: savage tridents and coiled razor wire; in among its loops Hal's touring company dreamt on their poles, rapid-eye movements laying down the beat for their lullaby, 'Daisy, Daisy, give me your answer doooo . . .' I dug down quickly into the leaf mould and earth – then I was in, loping from one shadow to the next. I'd cased the joint thoroughly and wasn't anticipating security – they were tucked up in their kennels, watching reruns of *Baywatch* with their comedy dogs.

Even in the starlight I could see the faded lettering – *Clennam & Sons: Importers of Fine Fabrics and Silks* – and the floral-pattern wallpaper exposed by the wrenching out of the carious house next door – except that there never had been one. With its stacked windows – dormer, upon bow upon bow – and steeply pitched roof, the set for the BBC's latest TV adaptation of *Little Dorrit* was as familiar to me as my own childhood home – and so the perfect place to hide until dawn, when I could mingle with the techies, chippies and sparks. After all, no one ever looks upon the classics with fresh eyes, especially tired security men on minimum wage.

Inside there was silence, half a room and no staircase, *the things of the body are as a river, and the things of the soul as a dream and a vapour.* I waited in the fake Victorian business premises until day came, pink and dewy, and with it a red and sweaty security man, played by Ray Winstone, who, led by an Alsatian, barrelled straight towards me from the direction of the sound stages. An extra would've been one thing; an actor like Winstone was quite another. Self-preservation took over: I scrambled out the back of the set, ran ducked down behind the half-hovels, then sprinted across the open lot.

Would, I wondered, Ernő Goldfinger, the architect of Trellick Tower, have been amused by this: a sign reading 'Goldfinger Avenue' slapped on the side of a Brutalist hangar? A reference not to him directly but to the Bond villain named after him – by which he had not been amused. I pelted down the avenue and, spotting an open side door into E Stage, shot through it and found myself inside a replica of the mausoleum at Chatsworth – a rotunda, surrounded by pillars, which was familiar to me from many happy visits to the estate as a guest of the Devonshires.

I pushed on into the depths of the Stage, passing through bedrooms, dressing rooms, halls and a solarium – all of which belonged to Chatsworth but had been disarticulated to suit the logistics of shooting the interiors for *The Wolfman*, which began summarily in a blaze of lights that sent me diving behind some velvet drapes. When I peeked out the body doubles for its three stars – Anthony Hopkins, Benicio del Toro and Emily Blunt – were drinking coffee and chatting about last night's television.

My hand discovered a spirit level, and shouldering this I stepped out from my concealment and into a replica of the main hallway of the house. At the head of the marble staircase, between two stone lions, a dog handler stood with two Dobermanns on leashes, while an assistant swung a flail, provoking them to rear up and bark. I ducked behind a Grecian urn, although I needn't have worried: only the dogs were in the shot being framed by an assistant director.

I was beginning to enjoy my stay at fake Chatsworth, which was like any house party but without the tedium of having to make conversation. Then Winstone blundered in and ruined it all. His paunch advanced, there were sweaty patches at his armpits – his Alsatian dragged him on. He caught sight of me behind the urn and bellowed, 'Oi! You slag!'

'Cut! Cut!' the AD cried, then Winstone's dog slipped its collar and flew at the Dobermanns. A maelstrom of fur and flob ensued, into which I lunged – how to explain *all things of the body are as a river*? I had noted that one of the antagonized Dobermanns had hands rather than paws – four of them; I grabbed one and while the others were distracted pulled him from the mêlée. So we escaped from *The Wolfman* set, out through another side door, across the lot and into the cover provided by the Winnebagos, ambulances and fire engines that were assembled around the famed 007 set on this, the penultimate day of shooting for *Quantum of Solace*.

Blue screen is always a comfortable experience for an idealist. As soon as Scooby and I were alone, I realized that's what was happening – because this was no flesh and sinew Dobermann but a cartoonish hound who stood on hind legs puckering his muzzle to bow-wow-wow the near-discernible words 'Ruffankyourufferrymuch.' It followed, of course, that if Scooby were being projected after the fact of my own performance, then so too was all of this: the hive of activity around the wardrobe trailer, where extras were getting kitted out in army uniforms to play the part of a corrupt Bolivian general's entourage.

As in life we strike attitudes on a bare stage, responding to phantoms we cannot see with lines scripted for us, so now I joined in idle chatter, hidden safely in the simple past. 'Basically,' said a plump chap with a sporran of keys dangling from his belt, 'they've reached the point in the schedule where there's nothing left to do but trash the sets – burn 'em and blow 'em up.'

He spoke the truth: ranged across the lot were the toasted slices of bogus buildings – a Haitian tenement, a Siena palazzo, a Bogotá slum. I suppose I should have been overwhelmed by this, the wide Sargasso of the narrow and destructive imagination of commercial imperatives – but I was filled only with my love for Scooby, who reared up on his hind legs so I could help him into his camos. He licked me in gratitude, his tongue curling right round my tired face. 'Scherlupp!'

'Nice work, boy,' I told him. 'I needed to lose the stain.'

The voices of two rehearsing actors floated through the open window of a trailer: 'Was there any trouble securing the hotel?'

'No, none.'

'It's just the fuel cells. The whole compound runs on them.'

'Pain in the ass really.'

'Sounds highly flammable.'

It was beyond wooden dialogue, rewritten so many times that it had the ugly believability of multi-density fibre. Still, it sounded to me like something worth filing away for future use – from the extras I'd gathered what the morning's shooting would entail: the Götterdämmerung of the lovingly constructed interior of a Chilean desert resort hotel.

I could hear the low rubba-rubba-rubba of the generators, the whine of a truck's power steering as it turned in the lot, the tick-tick-tick of metal expanding in the sun – my system was, I realized, flooded with adrenalin, hence this dreamy state, this sense of hours to kill that invariably preceded deadly action. Still on his hind legs, Scooby wrapped his foreleg tightly in my arm and we walked to the enormous 007 sound stage, picking our way between the loops and coils of fire hose that linked bowsers to engines.

The PR was waiting for us at a picnic table underneath a sunshade; her eyes tracked from mine to Scooby's, then dropped to his bare paws. 'Old mate of mine,' I explained. 'Turns out he's doing a bit of extra work – Rex, this is Karen.'

'Grrullo Grrrraren,' growled Scooby.

'Er, hullo,' said the PR, not wholly convinced.

Nevertheless, she gave us security wristbands and led us into the hangar. The narrow defile between the outer wall and the reconstruction of the hotel was cluttered with scaffolding and snaked with high-tension cables; techies and firemen bustled about in the confined space. We stepped between the flats and found ourselves in the central hallway beneath a lattice of steel walkways connected by stairways. Charred extras playing corpses lay about underneath DANGER OF CRUSHING signs.

'This is the twenty-second film of the franchise,' Karen explained as she led us on past the open doors to the suites; then came the rest of the spiel: the six independent crews, the millions of dollars, the thousands employed, the hundreds of plane flights encircling the globe like warped meridians – then there had been the near-fatal accidents, and the bust-ups in Haiti, and all of it, I thought, in the service of convincing the ticket-buying public for a few minutes – or seconds – that the man who stood by the curved panoramic window, looking out on to a desert counterfeited with hundredweight bags of sand, was an ultraviolent assassin retained by Her Majesty's Government to eliminate its former friends.

He turned to greet us. 'David, good to see you – and this is?'

Phew! I was Thewlis – to have been Postlethwaite would've been humiliating.

'Dan, this is Rex, old mate of mine – I understand you'll be shooting him later.'

Craig laughed. 'I love dogs,' he said, and shook Scooby's paw. 'So,' he continued, as the three of us sat down at a circular glass table beside an ornamental pit full of multicoloured stone balls, 'why'd you want to come on set?'

The PR was a few yards off talking to an ex-public schoolboy in a sleeveless anorak (or gilet), so I took a deep breath and explained how cinema had been found – neck snapped, throat slashed, eyes gouged out – in a back alley behind a cinema in a small town that no one had ever heard of.

Craig laughed again. 'I suppose you're gonna tell me I bear some responsibility for that – but let's get real here, I'm not the guy who did *Dinotopia*.'*

Whatever chagrin I felt, I hastened to reassure him that there was nothing personal: 'It's just, given your own career trajectory, from playing tortured and sensitive types, to torturing sensitive types, presumably you have a view?'

Craig was looking at me with mounting scepticism. When I'd picked up Scooby's camos from wardrobe I'd also selected a costume of my own: black dress trousers, black leather windcheater, white shirt and product-placement sunglasses – and this outfit seemed to be bothering the Bond star.

'Why're you dressed like me?' he snarled.

Then it hit me, and I snarled back: 'Why're you dressed like Daniel Craig when he's meant to be dressed like James Bond?'

How could I have been so naive? Quite suddenly the stunt double's stuffing an empty Evian bottle in my mouth as I lie back in a pile of snapping, crackling and popping empties. Scooby leaps at the PR's throat – I try to shout, but all that emerges is a pre-orgasmic 'Gnnnn!' and now the Craig doppelgänger's pummelling me in the face with blows of a chronometric precision: 'Paff! Paff! Paff! Paff! Paff! Paff! Paff!' So hard that these bones are pulverized in this order: 1. glabella

---

* *Dinotopia* (2002), a TV miniseries in which David Thewlis played the part of Cyrus Crabb, one of the people shipwrecked on an island where dinosaurs and humans have coevolved and founded a society somewhere between Periclean Athens and Disneyland. It need hardly be remarked here that this conceit is far more imaginative than anything conceived of by Ian Fleming, and that, while the screen adaptation involved a certain bowdlerization of the original illustrated books by James Gurney, I had no reason to feel any shame for having portrayed Crabb.

2. nasal bone 3. supraorbital margin 4. superior orbital fissure 5. lacrimal bone 6. zygomatic bone 7. inferior orbital fissure.

I have to act fast, and jerk my knee up into his crotch so hard his testes are mashed into his pelvic bone, which in turn ruptures his bladder. The assassinalike barely flinches, merely shifts the locus of his blows lower, so that 'Paff! Paff! Paff!' The maxilla, mandible and mental protuberance are all shattered. My face is a blood-filled sponge of traumatized tissue and bone fragments, but scrabbling among the Evian bottles my hand discovers a hammer left there by a careless chippie; I swing this again and again at my attacker's spine, popping his atlas, his axis and his cervical vertebrae (1–7 inclusive) like . . . popcorn.

Instant paralysis should rightfully ensue, not this marvellous bit of choreography: the two of us leaping away from one another, so that upright we circle the pit, searching for secure purchase in the slag heap of plastic, then 'Whack!' as a steel-capped leather shoe lashes out, breaking my sternum so cleanly that a shard spears my superior vena cava. Despite the plume of blood jetting from my ruptured chest, I drop back on to one leg and whip my own foot round at shoulder height in an expert taekwondo that propels his humerus – like a battering ram – into his scapula, a blow so devastating that the tendons snap with the resonant 'pings' of piano wires breaking.

Still, as he closes in to deliver a chop certain to crush my trachea, I realize this can't continue indefinitely; for a start, it's getting boring, so I pull the automatic from the stunt double's shoulder holster and wildly discharge three or four rounds. I know they'll only be blanks – but I've remembered the fuel cells.

J. M. W. Turner and Vincent van Gogh aren't names you see on movie credits that often – but you should. The masterful brushwork of exploding petrol caught by the lens at 24 frames per second owes a lot to their impressionism – red, orange, yellow deliquescing in an expanding volume of white phosphorescence analogous to the primed canvas: these painterly effects were well hung in the salon of the Atacama desert resort beneath a shower of tinkling glass and the hiss of the sprinklers.

Doubled over, the stunt double ducks beneath the Wagnerian curtain of roaring flame – only the sleeveless anorak (or gilet) keeps his nerve, summoning a camera that comes nosing in further to capture Scooby and me, trapped in the pit, the Evian bottles melting all Dalí about us. Scooby, mute and suppliant, yet not reproachful: he trusted me, I had liberated him from the set of *The Wolfman*, we danced on blue screen and now it's ended up like this! I cock the automatic and above the roar of the flames we hear the round slide into the breach. I lay the barrel along his foamy muzzle; he ducks his head acquiescing to the inevitable.

Which was never going to happen – for moments earlier I'd noticed a fuel cell still intact on the far side of the salon; when I expertly shot and hit it the ejaculation of flame that propelled us through the wall of the burning hotel, then through the wall of the 007 sound stage, was one of those . . . *those sleights-of-mind* without which not only action movies but the entire mystery of life itself would be unsustainable. As we wandered dazedly across Broccoli Road and turned into Bond Drive, I noticed first that Scooby was naked once more and I back in my kidult walking garb of shorts and T-shirt, then that we had returned to a simpler past. I looked back to see the sound stage peeled open, blackened and belching inky smoke – a tin can on a homeless person's fire.

\*       \*       \*

Karen caught up with us as we reached the security barriers; she was waving a clipboard. 'I hope you enjoyed your visit,' she said.

'Sure,' I replied laconically.

'I'm sorry Dan wasn't, um, chattier – but there's only two more days' shooting and he has a lot on his mind.'

'Sure,' I reiterated.

'D'you mind signing this release form?' She thrust the clipboard at me. 'I'm afraid you can't write anything about what you've seen without the producers' approval.'

'Sure.' I whistled for Scooby, and when he came lolloping over I took his paw in mine, thrust it in the soft mud edging a puddle and then pressed it on to the form. Karen didn't seem to mind – if she noticed at all.

We wandered off down the road, crossed a field and worked our way through Iver via drowsy paths and somnolent streets. As we were passing a bungalow with a sign outside advertising KOI FOR SALE, Scooby veered off. I like to think that he hung on to his liberty, but I doubt it: even in this age of unfettered personal freedom there are still the small-minded mobs of Transylvanian peasants who object to hell hounds on the loose.

As for me, what was I? A passer by Skoda showrooms whose middle-aged face bore nothing but the impress of a lifetime's affluent typing. A contemplator of the way the blades of grass fringed the lettering of a discarded crisp packet, FLAME-GRILLED STEAK FLAVOUR. A stopper on footbridges across dual carriageways, taken by the way the railings formed a cage for a shabby pony cropping a balding pasture. And then transfixed by the lily-fringed banks of the Grand Union Canal, above which dragonflies hung in a pattern that held all beauty – and then abandoned in a lost landscape of pylons and alders beside the Colne; and then squatting beneath the concrete caissons of the M4 to leave a spiral offering close to where flies spiralled over a dead rabbit. And then slipping into Sipson, past the picture postcard of church, village green and Five Bells pub, soon to be buried beneath the global tarmacslide of another runway. And then following the distrail across a field as wide as the sky to where the Marriotts and Hiltons stood in line along the Peripheral Road.

The cab driver who took me the short distance from the Renaissance Hotel through the tunnel and into the terminal was palpably disturbed; his wide red neck radiated waves of psychosis through the glass partition. He twisted his hands on the steering wheel while muttering obscenities that, if I chose to hear them, had a disconcertingly gynaecological specificity. *Pubic symphysis . . . External urinary meatus . . . Cunt!* He wouldn't look me in the eye when I paid the fare.

And then I was aboard a taxiing Air France jet, grumbling past the old shell of a plane used for fire brigade practice, while the man in the seat beside me yattered on about the air traffic controllers who had been brought over to Pinewood to play the parts of the air traffic controllers in *United 93* (2006). I thought of the air traffic controllers who had ensured those air traffic controllers landed safely, so that they could pretend to be witnessing the feigned destruction of real bodies.

As we banked and turned to the north-west over the Thames Valley, I saw the film studios laid out far below. Had I been hoping for circling helicopters, the sparkle of emergency services' lights, a tumescent smokestack and all the other set dressing of civil disaster? 'Are you on your way to Los Angeles to do some filming, Pete?' asked my neighbour, and while the clouds tore ragged chunks out of England I made it clear that such familiarity was less than welcome.

He wasn't to be dissuaded, this plump, white haired, Rolex-wrist-watched, beige-linen-trousered, twenty-seven-years-in-senior-management-once-drunkenly-fucked-a-whore-on-the-Reeperbahn-then-went-on-Seroxat-while-he-waited-for-the-AIDS-test-result man. But when the seatbelt light was extinguished I forced him to withdraw the LCD screen from his armrest, manipulate it into his eye line and begin to watch a Harry Potter film, while I filled my mind with Balyk salmon cooked in crème fraiche with chives and watercress salad, the *confit de canard* enhanced in honey sauce accompanied by sautéed potatoes and French green beans.

Eleven hours later the pilot pointed out to us the *nuages maritimes* creeping across the darkling plain. The Sierra zigmauved along the horizon, Huxley's graph of civilization's boom and bust. Not long after that we touched down at LAX.

# 4
# Among the Chocodiles

'Next victim!'

Can he seriously mean me? This fat and fatiloquent young man, his cheeks dimpled by silver studs, his black dungarees wide as an army tent, his moobs silicone-stiff beneath the Gothic fluting of his Tarp-shirt.

'I said: *next goddamn victim!*'

I'm among the Chocodiles and the Donettes, athwart the Sno Balls and the Cherry Slices, all tangled up in the Gummy Worms and the Sour Neon Worms – I'm a paedo cruising the Sour Patch Kids with a Gummi Bear on my arm—

'I can't make change for this.' He snaps my twenty in front of his miserable face like a small green clapperboard, yet here – at the counter, in the gas station a couple of miles along Century Boulevard from the airport – it isn't the beginning of this scene at all.

'Oh boy, you're gonna regret that.' I deliver my line with edible insouciance, the calm before Kali comes, four arms whirling, double jaws snapping, skull necklace clacking.

'Excuse me?' I now have both Rivet-Cheek's attention and that of his colleague, a blameless Hispanic kid, whose slick hair is teased and trimmed into all manner of points. Before answering I take a bottle of Powerade from a cooler, crack the screw cap, ostentatiously down the entire twenty fluid ounces, then burp:

'Urrrrp! I say, you're gonna regret being impolite to me, because now I will be compelled to shove all those Starlight Mints, Candy Corns, Baseballs, Twinkies, Peach Slices, Ding

Dongs and especially' – I turn to point to the bottom of the display rack – 'Dunkin' Stix, right up your fuckin' asshole, before employing your friend's greasy head as a plunger with which to pump up the resulting sugary muck into an artery-busting froth.'

Reflecting on the incident later, as I lay across my bed in the Uqbar Inn, I realized it was the 'greasy' that'd cost me the sympathy of the other customers in the gas station, who, hitherto merely restless nobodies, now asserted themselves as dangerously individualist frontiersmen and women. With five months still to go until polling day, the wind of change was starting to blow away the *nuages maritimes* of the Bush administration, so that any racial tokenism that may have been lingering in the body politic was also purged. But at the time I responded purely to the filmic grammar – not, I hasten to add, that CGI can possess syntactic clarity, uttering as it does only the same proposition again and again: we cannot, dull clay that we are, ever fully suspend disbelief in the physics of mass, and so, fingers coated in slip, we spin the wheel.

But first, in advance of the ass-stuffing, I run out on to Century Boulevard, straight into the traffic stream, and stand there arm outstretched, palm raised, daring the next vehicle – which happens to be a passenger bus, fully laden with newly landed Japanese tourists – to run me over. It does; or, rather, since I do not move, impales itself on my arm, with the crunch of punched steel and a hiss of escaping radiator steam. There I am, only slightly rocked on my rubber soles (and the juxtaposition, as ever with effective CGI, is between the utterly ordinary and the vanishingly probable), the rosette of peeled metal bunched at my shoulder, making of me what, a blushing debutante at the Crillon Ball? With a tortured groan from the ruptured chassis and the shrill cries of the Japanese – who, having fallen forward on impact, now roll down the aisle to pile, a jerking mass of flesh, leisurewear and baseball caps in the unbroken dish of the windshield – I raise my arm to the vertical, then flip the bus backwards over my head, so that it revolves, end-over-end, along the roadway, flailing into the oncoming traffic, knocking cars and trucks into the air so that they too resemble ninepins. The metaphor, although obvious, is not strained: because there's no experience of phenomena on such a scale being cogently witnessed in the realm of the real, the animators – like all honest creators – needs must resort to what they know. So, a petrol tanker star-bursts in the Southern Californian night, while a squad car, siren whooping, crashes down on the crown of a palm, and as a milk truck cannonades through the wide revolving door of the airport Crowne Plaza its whacked crates shed cartons that also flip, end-over-end, a teasing visual synecdoche that serves – in the scant seconds the entire sequence lasts – to reintegrate the fantastical disaster with the homely anxiety of spilt milk.

Not that anyone has time to dwell on this – or the fate of the scores of maimed and, presumably, outright dead – because I'm returning to the gas station. I still look exactly the same – gawky in my kidult gear, my long face gaunt and ineffectual – but of course, now we *know* I possess superhuman powers, so my appearance underscores the pathos of everyman – or woman – compelled to withstand without a murmur the humiliations imposed by boorish sales assistants. It is as a demigod that I loose still more the drawstrings of my bag o' winds. Naturally, the very visceral mechanics of punishment must be decently veiled: so, there's a pro-action shot of the assistant's petrified sneer, another of his colleague whimpering exculpatory please-not-mes, then all is submerged in swirls of multicoloured motion-blur that the eye, rightly, reads as the grappling of many cellophane packets, their ripping; the stripping of the assistant's heavyweight dungarees, the fisting and the stirring. When it's over – but is it ever truly *over*? – teetering on top of the counter is an awful centaur, its front legs with denim bunched at the fetlocks, its hind legs clothed; its torso is writhing, its face is pulsing cherry-bomb-red as systole sucks up all that sugar, sugar that also – in variegated droplets and powdery smudges – is to be seen spattered on the disgusted faces of the customers I shoulder my way through, while dusting my hands off with that rapid, semi-automatic motion that suggests – as much to myself as the restive bystanders – *job's a good 'un.*

Indeed, it isn't clear to me exactly when the scene did begin. Out from the terminal, under the planking of flyovers, the headlights of Infinitis and Escalades left glowtrails worming across my retinas, while the globalized skyline of Marriotts, Hiltons, palms and flagpoles seemed that much bigger – what with the streetlights smudged by the *nuages maritimes*.

As instructed, my crew had met me by the departure gate, locked and loaded so they could start shooting right away. I dimly registered a middle-aged cameraman with a comfy belly lying in a hammock of red shirt – then I was past him, and I could only assume that he was hurrying along in my wake until he drew level, walking backwards at speed, the sound recordist guiding him by gripping on to his belt.

So it continued, on past the XXX Sex Shops and across the intersections, the two men passing me, then stopping, panning as I went by to my departing back, then passing me once more. It reminded me of overtaking a truck with a shiny aluminium tank, then pulling in front of it, then dropping back behind, then passing it again – all this in '94, on the Santa Ana freeway, with Polly Borland in the passenger seat, filming our reflection in the mirrored belly of the grunting beast with a Super 8 camera. Rodney King was newly tenderized by the truncheons of the LAPD, and this was our anticipation of what became the signature CGI shot of urban destruction: the huge vehicle either laterally twisting, or – as above – turning end-over-end as it caroms along a city canyon. Why? Because, paradoxically, while the shot appears to be about the destruction of technology, it reinforces the notion that planes, trains and automobiles are like boulders tumbling down the hillside of civilization – natural and unstoppable.

I had no idea what the recordist was picking up with his fluffy loofah – wild track, I supposed. I hadn't particularly wanted sound, but the cameraman had said on the phone *I always work with Ray* in such a way as to suggest it would arouse suspicion if I didn't take them on as a unit, together with a third: a fixer-cum-gofer who I now assumed must be the clumpy-thighed girl in a hoodie who, whenever I directed my gaze away from the sidewalk, was standing in a parking lot, or beside a useless hedge footling with her BlackBerry.

I didn't have a reservation, yet, despite it being the middle of the night for me, rejected Inn after Court after Lodge. Rejected them, although I believe I know better than most that self-consciousness – and hence the illusion of choice – must only be a function of the time-lag between the determined action and our decision to take it. In our innermost portions, we understand this, and so are impelled to place a face on this milliseconds-long void – revere it, even. So . . .

Ever the victim, I take back my twenty and pocket it, cross the oil-stained forecourt, cross another intersection, pity a jet screaming overhead, then swing into the lobby of the Uqbar Inn. The crew tumble in after me, panting. I look round from the receptionist's bored make-up to mutter a curt 'Cut!' at their sweaty faces.

We sat in the lobby area on foam chunks covered in citrine nylon to discuss the following day's filming. I explained my objective: that they should film my walk from LAX to Hollywood as a single continuous shot, at times static, at others panning, at still others tracking or zooming. The cameraman objected that the interruption of night-time, to say nothing of the gaps between set-ups, would ruin the effect: 'You'd need a relay of goddamn camera coolies walking backwards the entire way!' I nodded understandingly, then palmed him off with the offer of a beer – and pizza, which the trio then ate, their triangular tongues darting out to capture the wedges before tomato purée and mozzarella muck dribbled into their laps.

My map was spread out on a coffee table, and we were hammering down tomorrow's route and deciding where exactly they should pick me up, when I realized that if all three weren't exactly *sui generis*, neither were they featured players. I had, of course, forgotten the sound recordist and the gofer's names the instant they were introduced to me; however I knew the cameraman was Jeff, so decided to term them generically 'the Jeffs'. Jeff was curious about the project – he was English and had been based in LA for over twenty years. I reiterated the explanation I'd given him on the phone: that it was an experimental film, with Arts Council backing. But this had scarcely sounded plausible when I was sitting in the B&B in Uxbridge, and he hadn't swallowed it.

A TV monitor in the corner of the lounge area showed the San Diego Beach Patrol moving on a homeless man who had the varnished cedar complexion and puckish features of the English screenwriter and novelist Hanif Kureshi; while a voiceover intoned: 'The drunk's emotions can become dangerously aroused . . .' I thought nothing much of the coincidence at the time, but rounded on Jeff: 'You're no Scorsese, only a dumb-ass who came to Tinseltown with big ideas, then ended up shooting wedding videos!' He just sat there, disconsolately looking at his spreading paunch, and it was left to Gofer Jeff to calm me down by raising such pedestrian issues as municipal film unit permissions. This kept us occupied for . . . aeons, until finally they went away. That was the trouble with film people, I ruminated as I slumped in the elevator, then limped along to my room: they applied the same basic principle to all their practices, so ended up shooting far more of the breeze than could ever be reasonably required.

What was it Busner had warned me about? I knew he had warned me about something that I might find in a hotel room, so I carried out a minute examination as soon as I'd dumped my bag, kicked off my shoes, stripped and showered. Damp and naked, I squatted to peer beneath the valance, then stretched up to see under the pelmet – but there was no sign of anything untoward, no hidden Hals or button mikes. Then I snapped on the radio and smoked for a while as I listened to the subscription drive on KPFK. Now I was standing looking at the bulbous prong of the games controller, an alien's digit crooked over the top edge of the TV. The ergonomics of the controller were at once obvious and obscure, its yellow, red and green buttons; its twin toggles and further buttons marked with square, circular and triangular symbols.

What was it Busner had warned me about, surely not *the drapes* in Room 423 and their similarity to a Jewish prayer shawl? I could only imagine my occasional therapist would approve of the lengthy reverie I then plunged deep into, concerning Extended Mind Theory as it related to video games and the driving of cars – cars, which are the true superheroes of the modern era, powerful demiurges that canter across cities on their rubbery pseudo-pods. Those adverts for Citroën cars that feature innocuous hatchbacks metamorphosing – à la *Transformers* – into huge dancing robots express a fundamental truth: the servant has become our master. When the movie came out (the third in a series based on a *toy*), Anthony Lane devoted 1,000-plus words to it in the *New Yorker*, which, for sheer sledgehammer-'n'-nuttiness, were unrivalled – except, possibly, by an as yet undiscovered Montaigne essay, 'On *Flipper*'.

I came to at around 5.00 a.m., still staring at the prong of the controller. During the night I had peed and the uric salts were grainy between my chafed thighs, while the pancake-thin carpeting had been soaked through, then clawed into ridges by my bare feet, which must have continued shuffling on the spot. Pre-dawn leeched the colours from the already muted institutional room. The fugue hadn't been qualitatively different from waking consciousness, so I was still more exhausted than I had been when the fat controller grabbed me. I fell across the bed, but sleep was tantalizingly out of reach: a beautiful rose garden glimpsed through a vanishingly tiny door, and eventually I dressed and went down to breakfast, which I ate listening to three prominent neurosurgeons discuss cell phone wave shields with Larry King. Their radioactive deliberations were interspersed with the traffic report on KNBC – news that had as much purchase on me as updates on the Assyrian occupation of Babylon *c*. 3200 BC. Possibly less, given that the UN mandate permitting US bases to operate in Iraq would expire by the end of the year.

I fought off the urge to pick up the dinky blueberry muffin I had unthinkingly opted for and hand it to the bleary child at the next table with the words, 'To scale with you, I believe?' Fought it off because the child's mother was played by Kim Basinger. Basinger, whose forehead had bulged so provocatively as Mickey Rourke slam-dunked her pelvis in *9½ Weeks* (1986) – a swelling that suggested he was pumping her so full of semen there was *nowhere else for it to go*. She still looked pretty shiny despite being on a career-slalom on sheet ice.

The KNBC man's face was as ancient as an Assyrian bas-relief – but full face rather than in profile. He spoke of an accident on Freeway 10, his shattered visage looming between the hieroglyph of civilization and the crumpled topography of the Sierra, then dissolved into live footage of a chariot broadsided across two lanes, with CHP officers dismounted from their Harleys and taking notes on wax tablets.

Far from lifting over night, the *nuages maritimes* were even denser that morning, yet, despite not having slept since Uxbridge, as I left the Uqbar Inn I had a fresh spring in my step. I resolved to stay there again in the future, so delighted had I been by the pathos of its frosted floral lampshades – assuming, that is, that my incontinence would be held against Postlethwaite or Thewlis rather than me. Yes, there had been Basinger, and Hal hung above the reception desk as I paid my bill, but once I was out the door the mist was so dense that I doubt any camera could've registered the blur when I turned to the right – or the left.

Counter-intuitively, a grid-plan city forces more decisions on the walker than the winding folkways of an older more haphazard urbanity. Since diagonal progress can be made equally effectively by any given series of horizontal and perpendicular traverses, at each intersection the choice of two directions remains, maddeningly. No wonder I opted for one huge L, and so plodded on along Century, then turned left up Cienega, which ran beside a God-gouged gutter full of the San Diego Freeway. Within three miles the limp pennants of the medieval car dealerships and the donutmorphic drive-ins were doing my *fucking head in*, man. The Edenic valley of the Colne, with its pylons and reedy rills, now came before me in all its lush raiment – why had I not remained there, waiting for my Sissy Spacek, then together with her raised a tribe of feral survivalists among the alders and poplars?

The signal phasing was weighted heavily against the pedestrian, while the clearance zone at each intersection was wide enough to swallow tribes of the impious. But there was one of me to tens of thousands of the Transformers. Each wait for the stickman to shine through the *nuages* was a vigil – I was finely balanced between grief and joy, while Hal cloned himself from one pole to the next. Eventually, at Florence, the sidewalk gave out and I was forced into the ur-suburba. As I ascended the Baldwin Hills, it occurred to me that almost all my life had been a topiary hare's hopeless race along silent sidewalks beside empty homes. The buttery swathes of the lawns, the oh-so-slow lava flows of the crescents and drives, the Ionic, Doric and Corinthian columns as hollow as subprime mortgages – it didn't matter a jot if the inhabitants were white or, as here, black, suburbs were always at once pre- and post-apocalyptic. In the two-car garage the wayward Cal-Tech physicist connects a purloined cyclotron to a Barcalounger – with devastating results.

The stop lady for Highland Elementary hustled some kids – including me – across the road and I arrived at Homebase, where a score or more of Hispanic extras hung out in the parking lot to see if they'd be taken on for a day impersonating gardeners in long shot. I stopped to chat: no, they didn't mind the stereotyping, but 'Y'know, my friend, in this part of town ground staff are almost always whites – it's, like, a status symbol,' said one with Coppertone skin and a Fu Manchu goatie.

'Yeah,' his buddy concurred. 'For a reactive industry Hollywood is so fuckin' slow.'

I went on past caged-in basketball courts and reached the scrubby uplands where oil pumps rose and fell like dipping bird toys. The Jeffs were waiting for me and I conspicuously ignored them as they set up for a long shot in a lay-by. Still, I was grateful for their perfect timing: the *nuages maritimes* were lifting, and to the north the Los Angeles basin lay revealed: 300 square miles of eyes and camera lenses. Somewhere out there was a killer or killers and I needed the crew's prophylaxis badly; unprotected, who knew what I might become prey to – surely only the pathetic self-consciousness of adolescence, which commences with checking for zits in wing mirrors, and culminates – ten years or yards along the road – in a screen test?

Absorbed in the steady rhythm of my paces I forgot about the Jeffs. I was walking through the Ruben Ingold County Parkway – a strip of greenery that ran along the spur above Slauson – when down in the valley, on the far side of the highway, I spotted a bum asleep on a bench. At least, I *thought* that's what it was – I couldn't be certain from this distance. There was an uncanny flatness to the static figure – besides, I knew most LA benches were bum-proofed, their seats either canted forward so it was impossible to find repose, or else segmented with hip-spearing ridges.

I turned aside from the path and plunged downhill, leaping fences and crashing through the undergrowth. Was it a man, or some weird hallucination of mine, provoked by sleeplessness? It wasn't until I reached the verge and Escalades were whipping past the toes of my shoes that I realized it was a *trompe l'œil* ad for Will Smith's latest movie, *Hancock*, in which, cast against type, the suave actor played a bum who also happens to be a superhero. Swept with an unreasonable rage, I glowered on Smith's life-sized 2-D copy: the reflective shades, the stubbly jaw, the woolly hat and Hawaiian shirt. 1-800-LAW, NO WIN-NO FEE – that I could cope with, but movie ads should stick to billboards, the hopeful tombstones of dead drive-ins.

I rolled down the hills to Leimert Park, where I got a bucket of tea and stopped for a smoke by the art deco movie theatre that marks the cultural epicentre of the city's black population. The bench I reclined on burned with a slogan for the MAALES project (Men of African American Legacy Empowering Self): 'Bisexual, curious, or straight but fool around now and then?' Then, like a bandsaw's blade, I juddered my way through the Carpenter Gothic streets of Crenshaw and West Adams, which, under the guise of Sugar Hill, was the only racially desegregated neighbourhood in 1920s Los Angeles: Theda Bara, Busby Berkeley and Fatty Arbuckle had been replaced by a weeping fat boy pushing an obviously new mountain bike, whose father taunted him, 'You can't ride it, you'll never ride it!'

When I came along Jefferson to the leafy environs of USC, the mission Muslim architecture gave way to postmodernist parkland. I patted myself down for sawdust and tried smiling at the coeds, but they took one look at my middle-aged white man horror mask and swerved away. There was a flyer up outside one of the halls advertising a lunchtime jam by NWPhd, and, intrigued by the sounds that were emanating – Gil Scott-Heron mixed improbably with Orlandus Lassus – I plunged inside. The Jeffs, who were still strapped up in their equipment, couldn't follow me into that darkness, so joined Will Smith on a bench to wait.

Up on a low stage four tall African-American men were rapping; one of them was doing the Latin: '*Hoc quicquid tandem sum, caruncula est et animula et animi principatus.*'

The next the English: 'Whatsoever I am, is either flesh, or life, or that which we commonly call the mistress and overruling part of man: reason.'

While the others picked out a word or two and scatted with it in a deep undertone, so: '*Quicquid-quicquid-principatus-quidipatus . . .*' Or: 'What-so-what-so-what-so-reason.'

It was a commanding performance. The four were dressed conservatively in bankers' suits, shirts and ties, their hair close-cropped, and so resembled a new generation of the Modern Jazz Quartet. Their rapping was at once percussive and euphonious, plaiting the two languages together: '*Missos fac libros: noli amplius distrahi; sed ut jam moriens carunculam contemne: cruor est ossicula et reticulum, ex nervis, venulis et arteriis contextus.*'

('*Venulus-nervis, venulus-nervis, nervulis-venis . . .*')

'Away with thy books, suffer not thy mind any more to be distracted, and carried to and fro; for it will not be; but as even now ready to die, think little of thy flesh: blood, bones, and a skin; a pretty piece of knit and twisted work, consisting of nerves, veins and arteries; think no more of it, than so.'

('Veins-an'-nerves, veins-an'-nerves, neryvein-vein . . .')

I was surprised there wasn't more of an audience for NWPhd – only a few lounging emos picking their hangnails in plastic chairs; but then, what did I know?

'*Quin etiam animam contemplare, qualis sit: spiritus, nec semper idem, sed quod singulis momentis evomitur et resorbetur.*'

('*Spiritus-singulis, spiritus-singulis . . .*')

'And as for thy life, consider what it is; a wind; not one constant wind neither, but every moment of an hour let out, and sucked in again.'

('One wind – one life, one life – one wind . . .')

Not much, although even a moderately competent Latinist would have been able to detect the incorporation into the English translation of later interpolations.

'*Tertia igitur pars est animi principatus; ad hunc igitur animum intende: senex es; noli pati, ut ille amplius serviat, aut amplius impetu insociabili raptetur aut amplius fatum vel praesens inique ferat vel futurum horreat.*'

('*Serviat! Raptetur!*')

'The third, is thy ruling part; and here consider; thou art an old man; suffer not that excellent part to be brought in subjection, and to become slavish: suffer it not to be drawn up and down with unreasonable and unsociable lusts and motions, as it were with wires and nerves; suffer it not any more, either to repine at anything now present, or to fear and fly anything to come, which the destiny hath appointed thee.'

'Slavish lust! Slavish lust!'

As each of the doctoral rappers completed his line, he took up this chant, until all four were hammering it out: 'Slavish lust! Slavish lust! Slavish lust!' Building to panting crescendo: 'Sla-vish luuuuuust!'

By way of applause there was a scatter of ironic finger-clicking from the stoner kids; NWPhd didn't seem to mind. Exactly like any professional combo, they slid straight into bickering about the performance: Howie had been a beat out on *Quin etiam*, but – Howie rejoined – it shouldn't be *con-tem-nee* but *con-tem-nay*.

The college kids filed out into the noonday sun. I found myself unable to leave yet too shy to approach the group. Eventually, one of them dropped off the stage and shuffled across to me, his leather soles squeaking on the woodblock floor.

He saluted me lazily, 'Word up, man,' then double-took. 'Oh, you're that guy – Brit actor, ain'tcha? Saw you in that kids' movie – wha' wuzz it, now?'

'It was Harry Potter, man,' said another, still taller NWPhd coming up beside him. The two of them stood towering over me, mild curiosity on their handsome faces.

I flannelled: 'Um, yeah, I did do those films but it was only for the—' I pulled myself up short: how could admitting to mercenary motives be an excuse? I tried another tack: 'Y'know, I was in Malick's *The New World*, a biggish role – I'm not primarily a Hollywood casting.'

'True dat.' This came from the third NWPhd, who was wearing a purple silk Chanel tie. 'You daybooed in that kerazee movie that starts wi' you raping some sorry bitch in a goddamn alley. I guess you'd know all about slavish lust.'

'It's ambiguous.'

'What you say?'

'It's not certain that I'm raping her – I mean, that the character I was playing was raping her.'

He shook his head gloomily, 'Motherfucker, if that's your idea of consensual sex I hate to think what you rapin' would look like, sheee!' He blew hard then collected himself: 'No disrespect, man – what's your name, anyway?'

I ignored this and said, 'Y'know your English translation doesn't exactly match up – there's nothing about wires and nerves in the Latin.'

'Oh, really?' Purple Tie called to the last of the NWPhds, who was coiling a microphone flex on the stage: 'Howie, get over here will'ya?'

As Howie approached I saw that he wore studded leather wristlets, and that, although he was dressed like his fellow band members, the crotch of his suit pants hung low – almost between his knees.

'Yeah?' He looked at me belligerently, eyes bloodshot in ochreous skin, wispy hairs threaded his lower lip to his chin.

'Man's questioning the translation, Howie,' Purple Tie said, then to me: 'May I introduce you to Professor Howard Turner; he holds the chair in classics and comparative literature here at USC, so, if you-gonna-be-questioning' – he poked me in the chest to emphasize each word – 'you-gonna-be-answering to Howie, you fill me?'

All four NWPhds had ranged themselves menacingly around me. 'You dig Aurelius, man?' Howie growled.

'Well, we'd all do well,' I wittered, backing towards the sunlight, 'to maintain a stoical attitude in the face of . . . y'know – *stuff*.' Outside I could see the Jeffs sharing a bottle of Powerade Aqua; they and it both looked appealing.

'Don't come down this way again,' said the leader of the NWPhds, who had the passionate beauty of the young Marvin Gaye. 'Unless you be confident you can parse a Latin sentence purr-fic'-lee.'

'An' declaim some,' said the second giving me a light shove.

'An' display appropriate rhetorical style,' Purple Tie added with a fist flourish that knocked me into the realization that he was being played by Jamie Foxx.

'Listen,' I said, 'you won't believe this, but the day before yesterday, back in Britain, I took a long walk with Morgan Freeman.'

'What the fuck're you talking about?' Foxx had backed me right to the door. I made another bid to connect:

'I don't want to be intrusive, but did you learn anything about Cruise when you worked with him on Michael Mann's *Collateral*, for example, the sigmoidal flexure of his . . . ah, penis?'

Foxx looked almost pitying: 'I don't wanna know *nothin'* 'bout that, my friend,' he said. 'This here is a litigious town – and *then* there's the Scientologists.'

We were in the open air; SUVs full of coeds farted past. Waving a plastic bottle at me, Gofer Jeff called out, 'I'll getcha a Powerade, Pete.'

'Pete?' Foxx looked at me speculatively.

'I've gotta get going,' I said. 'I'm due over at the Shrine Auditorium, but one thing: you were awesome back there, you guys gigging anywhere soon?'

Foxx laid a hand on my shoulder. 'Anything is possible, my friend.' The transition in a few seconds from anger to incredulity to sympathy would've been bewildering if he weren't such an accomplished actor. 'You take care out there.'

# 5
## The Atrium

A statue of a Shriner stood in the parking lot – like me, he was slightly bigger than lifesize. Unlike me, he wore a bum-freezer and a fez and was holding a child of around five in the crook of his arm. But, there again, like me, both figures had faces the colour of pipe clay and eyes like pee holes in the snow.

I had walked to the Shrine Auditorium for obvious reasons: if, as I believed, buildings were corporeal things, briefly animated by mind or minds, then this was one of the *corpora delicti* that would prove not just that film was dead – but that it had been murdered. From the 1940s through to the 1990s the Shrine had hosted Oscar ceremonies; even standing in the open air, looking through the barred doors, I could still smell the reeks of stale narcissism, avarice and hunger. I banged on the doors until a security guard played by Ken Sansom came stumbling through the gloom, then palmed him a couple of hundred bucks to let me in. I strode through the darkened halls and passages, before stepping out into the cavernous auditorium itself.

Vast plaster swags bellied from the roof a hundred feet overhead; above the stage dangled a chandelier the size of a flying saucer. The polyhedral niches and recessed colonnettes to either side of the proscenium, the latticed screens that rose behind the forty-seat boxes, the ogee arches standing proud of the curving walls – it all post-hypnotically suggested an alternative history for the Americas: Los Angeles settled from the west in the fifth century after Muhammad by Arab dhows that had rounded the Capes of Good Hope and Horn, their lanteen sails dipping like rocs' wings into the long swell of the Pacific. The indigenous tribes of the Californian littoral had all joyously submitted to Islam, green flags fluttered along the spine of the Sierra, and two centuries later the Shrine was raised as the physical embodiment of the evolving Al Malaikah consciousness, its dome swimming in the bilious smog of a million Al Forsan autos ... But I remained unaware of this until the following evening, when the desk clerk at the Roosevelt snapped his fingers.

I walked out on to the stage followed by Sansom, who was morphing – his hair reddening and curling, his face growing shinier and more venal – until he was not just an acceptable stand-in but a dead-ringer for the founding charlatan of Scientology. Hubbard approached and, raising a hand to my forehead, tipped me straight back into the mind-bath of Dianetic reverie, where I lay feeling the warm current of time course along my flanks and sweep between my parted thighs. Then Hubbard gave me a gentle push and I found myself carried swiftly upstream, my arms and legs mutating into flippers, then fins, then polyps – until there I was, beached in the Upper Palaeozoic, with Hubbard rapidly opening and closing his fleshy hand to simulate my shell, and so sending waves of anxiety through the audience of pre-clears unable to cope with their own molluscan memories.

As one genetic entity to others, I sympathized, yet at the same time I could feel that every single sleight, cramp, twinge and sniffle I had experienced in all my multitudes of animal lives had been accepted, digitized and rewritten in the binary encoding of my analytic brain, a smoothly functioning computational device with the power of a thousand networked super-computers – although this analogy is woefully impoverished, implying a clackety-plastic clunkiness to what's beyond the grasp of any pre-clear, especially *you*.

I, the Thetan, lifted off from the stage, my silky-brown hair haloing my superfine 35,000-year-old features, and so L. Ron and I danced a *pas de deux* as, to the amazement of the crowd, we orbited the chandelier before touching down together, hand in hand. 'Ladies and gentlemen,' Elron boomed, 'I give you the first clear, Sonya Bianca, a physics major and pianist from Boston. In addition to her many other accomplishments, Miss Bianca has full and perfect recall of every moment in her life. But first, if you will my dear, please tell us how Dianetics has helped you.'

'Well.' To begin with my voice was tremulous and my pulse raced, but as I spoke I grew in confidence: 'I had a strange and, um, embarrassing allergy to . . . well, paint.'

'Paint?'

'That's right, paint – whether wet or dry; and if I came into contact with it at all – which is, as I'm sure everyone realizes, difficult to avoid, well, I got a painful itching in my eyebrows. Now the condition has cleared up and I feel . . . well, like a million dollars!'

There was a scattering of applause, but there were also mutterings of discontent and somebody called out, 'Tell us what you had for breakfast on October the third 1942!'

I fidgeted with the hem of my twill skirt. 'That's easy, a bento box. The sushi and sashimi were fine, and I asked for a refill of miso soup, which I sipped together with mouthfuls of green tea from a china beaker—'

In a chain Japanese diner on Figueroa? I don't think so – not a china beaker, only a lidded styrofoam cup, the textured dimples of which squeaked beneath my sweaty fingertips; across the road Felix the Cat pole-sat with a come-hither grin on top of a Cadillac dealership. 'I've scheduled a meeting for you with Michael Lynton at Sony Pictures in Culver City this Friday – the thirteenth,' said Ellen DeGeneres's voice in my ear. Frank Tenpenny was sitting with a table of LAPD patrolmen next to mine – a more or less solid block of heavy-duty navy cotton accessorized with forearms, side arms and crew-cut heads on V-shaped plinths of white T-shirt. It was true about the bento box, though – the lacquered tray littered with rice lay on the table beneath my eyes. 'Kinda unlucky, maybe . . .'

'Maybe.' I was mightily impressed at my ability to pick up my end of the phone conversation. 'But then I could always pitch him a nightmare.'

She laughed throatily. 'Pitch him a nightmare – I like that. Anyway, you're set to see him at ten that day, and I can get you a five o'clock at the Marmont with Michael Burns – if you think you can get from Culver City to the Marmont by then? 'Course, you'll need to get back by seven anyway 'cause I've arranged a little party in your honour—'

'A party?! But I don't know anyone – and no one knows me.'

'Lissen, don't worry, it's a tiny affair – more of gathering, really.'

A useful little heads-up display map had appeared in the corner of my visual field, and using this I could quickly and easily estimate the mileage from Culver City to Hollywood, so said, 'Actually, it appears eminently possible for me to meet with Burns – but listen, are you *sure* these guys want to see me, I mean, it's not like I have anything to offer them and I don't want to go squandering your agent capital.'

'Puh-lease, David, you're a respected actor – you're bankable, guys like that are always gonna want to meet with you.'

I said nothing to her of the black-clad legs stomping the prone form of the studio head until it disintegrated into its encoding. We hung up. I paid the bill and found the Jeffs outside waiting for me. 'Eat well, WW?' asked Camera Jeff. I checked out my HUD health bar and saw that I had plenty of lives, so grunted affirmatively.

Jeff had rigged up a new gizmo during his lunch break, a tiny digital camera mounted on an aluminium pole he could hold at ground level, angled up to give a shot of my walking feet. I appreciated the thought he'd put into this amblecam – all the way from LAX I'd been agonizing that without sufficient close-ups of my feet they might be cropped, then grafted on to the legs of an extra in a crowd scene of a thriller featuring a psychopath hell-bent on shooting a politician the name of whom no one will ever remember. Really.

No sooner had I begun walking and Camera Jeff was turning over, than I realized this set-up had a radical effect on my point of view. Listen, I'm not a fool – I'd known for years how detached I was from the normal range of feeling, how solipsistic, how dissociated, so that on occasion I seemed to be observing myself acting out a predetermined role. Busner may have termed my malady 'ebullient and productive', yet all too often it felt merely hollow and miserable. What was it he had warned me about? What . . .

To the north-east the Downtown towers rained down light-spears that disappeared into the smog bank lying above Broadway and Bunker Hill. I glanced right and left and the fishbowl turned while my arms remained lifelessly projecting ahead. Was I in the world any more? Or was the world in me?

Just before the Shrine Auditorium I had crossed the fault line where the plate of the old pueblo grinds against that of the new city, and now as I navigated east towards south central I realized I had crossed the border that separates LA from Los Santos.

The 45-degree downwardly angled shot was reminiscent of the bistro in the Place Wilson, but my POV remained hovering while the figure in the green T-shirt and green short pants advanced, long legs eating up the sidewalk. I wasn't sure about the Mr T. Mohawk, but I liked the way I'd acquired a muscular build; nor could I see the point of the cross hairs, that, whichever way I turned, remained aligned – for I wasn't armed. Indeed, although I was headed straight into the gang territories of East Los Santos, where the Ballas and the Vagos ruthlessly battle for supremacy, I felt not the slightest anxiety.

Neither anxiety – nor remorse, when I thought of the killing at the *carniceria* in East LA the preceding fall, the choking dust clouds when the digger went to work among the Civil War dead in the Evergreen Cemetery, me stuffing the bloodstained handkerchief into my pocket, then furtively adjusting its engorgement as I rode the bus back along 1st Street into town. These memories could have no purchase here, where a sweatshop full of wetbacks plying sewing machines swam out of the *nuages maritimes*. No! The sea mists had dispersed in the Baldwin Hills; this was some other phenomenon. If Mr Me went towards the sweatshop it increased in definition, until I could read the very headline of the sun-yellowed copy of *La Opinión* that lay in the gutter in front of it: '*Adiós Triunfal!*' Next to a photo of La Senadora Hillary Clinton, arm upraised as she gracefully bowed out of the contest.

Then, when I toggled away to the blank space, alien evergreens materialized, their upper limbs customized with the needle-shaggy bafflers of a cell site. Yes! I grasped it at last: I was an aboriginal spirit in the city of unbecoming, who had only to walk towards the void for some new thing to be swiped into existence with Ed Ruscha strokes of oily pixels. Superhero, pah! I was a god now – with a god's penchant for vengefulness and real-time moral experimentation.

I summon up Marisco's seafood, a beige stucco box that's *abierto*. José stands in the doorway, his singlet grimy, the Madonna tattooed on his right arm, Mary Magdalen being sodomized by the Devil on his left. His hair's gathered in a do-rag, his automatic is stuffed down his pants. As Mr Me comes right up to him, he sprouts bling, shifts on his Keds and rolls his shoulders while spouting pre-recorded dialogue into his cell phone: 'It's that *gringo loco* WW again, we told him not to come back here, this time something gotta be done.'

When Mr Me snatches the phone, drops it to the sidewalk and grinds it out like a cigarette butt, José plunges his hand into his pants, but before he can withdraw his piece my long black legs are upside his head, scissoring his thick neck. 'Ooooh, noooo!' he moans, then he's on the ground and I'm break-dancing on his chest.

A low-rider pulls up beside us. The hood pops, the trunk pops, it bounces on its tyres, the doors burst open and disgorge a quartet of Uzi-toting heavies and the 'Weeechung-chung! Weeeechung-chung!' of a rap backing track; Mr Me despatches the first with the heel of my hand, the second with the scythe of my foot, the third gets me in the shoulder with a round, yet when I consult my target health indicator I see that I'm still well ahead of the game. The fourth is encouraged to kneel in the open door of the gun wagon, then it's shut, hard, again and again.

Pumped up with success, Mr Me disdains the jalopy – its door a bloodied mouth beseeching him to enter and drive. Instead, I check the HUD map, then thumb-swagger him east towards Central. The 'Weeechung-chung! Weeeechung-chung!' of the backing track is joined by NWPhd: 'And as for thy life, consider what it is; a wind; not one constant wind neither, but every moment of an hour let out, and sucked in again. One wind – one life, one life – one wind, one wind – one life, one life – one wind . . .' The dreamy-creamy superstructure of the Coca-Cola Bottling Plant rises smoothly into my crosshairs above what should be the messy contingencies of power lines, signage and stop lights – should be, but even this far in I've spotted the patterning and concluded that this parodic LA has most probably been woven from machine code in a nerdish workroom half a world away.

Still, when a pneumatic ho pours her jugs from the backroom of a tyre shop echoing with the 'Whirrrrschunk!' of wheel nuts being drawn like monstrous teeth and coos, 'Hey, Double-U Double-U, why not step inside for a latte?' I respect the clarity of the prompt and reply with one of the 4,200 lines of scripted dialogue at my disposal, 'So long as it ain't skinny, bitch.'

'It ain't skinny at all, homie, it'll make you *froth*.'

No more stereotypical than any seductive banter – I hope you'll agree. And what of the sex act itself? From behind, natch, her cartoon face sinks into a yielding wall, her coffee haunches seesaw, the PlayStation squeaks . . . Don't get me wrong, I enjoy being manipulated as much as the next puppet, but there's work to be done: since their arrival in the late 1930s, inside the Coca-Cola plant German Expressionist émigrés have forged an indissoluble association in the collective unconscious between tooth rot and eye candy, so that no movie is complete without a waxed-paper demijohn of sugared water and caffeine pumped full of $CO_2$ . . .

'I'm gonna take these muthafuckahs down,' Mr Me says to the Jeffs, who've come up beside me. Sound Jeff pushes his cans up on his head, panda style.

'Man, WW, that's some crazy stuff,' he sighs.

'The more you know,' Mr Me says, pumping the shotgun that magically appears in my hands, 'the better. Now cover me!'

I push-button into the fray, my wild discharges set the line of innocent acacias ablaze as Mr Me sprints through the traffic across Central; pickups side-swipe saloons that front-end UPS trucks. Smoke staggers, tracers doodle, sirens yowl

and the security men take stances to unleash their impotent allusion to automatic fire: fluttery little yellow flashes, 'Da-pocketa-pocketa-pock!' Mr Me karate-chops one Hal, then the next, gains the door of the plant, forgets what he's meant to be doing . . .

And wanders away aimlessly, following his crosshairs, lost in a reverie of competence, his fingers pushing his own enigmatic buttons – the yellow, red and green, the square, circle and cross – while the HUD map oscillates wildly. The *nuages de jouer* condense into 7th Street, then the flower market, where the stalls are hung with *piñatas*. There are *piñatas* in the shape of lions, rabbits, snakes and lizards; traditional seven-pointed star *piñatas* and *piñatas* fashioned – albeit poorly – to resemble logos: a blocky 'GM', a Hummer shield, Dolce and Gabbana's copulating initials.

At the next stall to come into existence the woven-straw heads of Cheney and Rumsfeld spin slowly in the breeze on the strings that trepan their hollow heads. Ditto the Weinsteins, Karen Bass and Arnie; Nicole and Angelina kiss with a 'Tthwock!' and a riffle of their paper-streamer hair, while Thewlis and Postlethwaite duel with Cyrano noses.

When the stallholder enlarges in Mr Me's direction, I'm searching through the available lines for: *Why have these relatively minor English actors been fashioned into fiesta toys?* But he forestalls this by squawking: 'Petey Postlethwaite, man, I loved you in that Brit TV show.'

'Which one?'

'*The Sins*, man – that's why I had the *piñata* made of your head.'

I rotate the market 20 degrees. 'But why Thewlis?'

'Aw, dude.' The stallholder cups the back of the straw head. 'Ain'tcha seen *Dinotopia* – it's the greatest.'

Along the kerbs of the fashion district bolts of cloth are extruded into being, ready to be cut and sewn into the piping through which watery bodies will flow. Cars keep slewing to a standstill and offering themselves to me; light aircraft taxi up, their propellers lickety-licking like the tongues of affectionate dogs; at one point I'm even offered a jetpack. But I keep on walking, and by the time I'm following my own avatar along Broadway I've long since forgotten that it's all a game, that somewhere a *primum mobile* sits, gritty with cookie crumbs, his thumbs numb from twiddling the toggles – my disbelief is suspended, spinning in the green air that solidifies into the ornate façades of the Mayan Theater, the Belasco and the State, while the crowds of stereotypes and replicants thicken: Tyrell Corporation, heading home.

I gather the crew into a team; standing close to Gofer Jeff I can appreciate the care that's gone into plotting the downy bell curve of her standard deviation face. 'It's a wrap for you guys for the day,' I tell them, 'I won't be needing you here – sure, stuff is shot around Downtown, but it's mostly TV: suits and skirts crossing Main Street in long shot to City Hall to engage in the highest of all sciences and services, or the Walt Disney Concert Hall – architecture conceived of as a frozen moment of sandwich wrapping. Pah! I have nothing to fear from *that*!'

Camera Jeff is eyeing Mr Me quizzically, but before he can be supplied with any dialogue I turn on my zigzag legs, head on along Broadway, then swing into the foody-gloom of the Central Market. A hiatus while the interior loads, then:

comforting down lights and exposed piping spring into being, together with a sawdust-strewn floor and fruit stalls piled high with Arnie hands of bananas. Lobsters scuttle in glass tanks, noodles steam in hanks, greenbacks spit from a freestanding ATM and the replicants mill and mutter

Lawrence G. Paull had it right in his production design for *Blade Runner*: Downtown LA was *shuyu*, a borrowed urban background for a formal garden of noirish planting, equally and elegantly stunted love and hate. Mr Me and I are both transfixed by a modular plastic display stand full of sour worms, gummy sour mix, neon sour worms, sour rings and cherry sours.

And so: the game is paused while I'm left to consider this Möbius strip of celluloid: in 2008 the lobby of the Bradbury Building has been beautifully renovated, yet in the early 1980s, seriously dilapidated, it served as the apartment block of bioengineering genius J. F. Sebastian. Paull and director Ridley Scott drenched Downtown LA in a toxic rain that fell from a sky sullied with the smoke of oily flare-offs,* and made of these seventy-odd city blocks an evaginated Central Market full of jabbering Asiatic proles spearing their neon sour worms with chopsticks. Overhead a dirigible wallows in the smog; its belly nudges the top storeys of the 1920s blocks and is wrapped round with a screen-sash upon which cherry-red lips part to receive more wriggling neon sour worms.

Harrison Ford hunts replicants in 2019 (1982). The replicants track down J. F. Sebastian to the Bradbury Building (1893, but

---

* This has become known, by ecologists, as the '*Blade Runner* outcome'.

built according to principles of urban architecture advanced by Edward Bellamy in his utopian novel *Looking Backward: 2000 –1887*). To recap: in 1982 a Dutch movie star pretends to be an android in an 1893 building intended by its architect to be futuristic, but now impressed on an imagined future to leave the shape of the past . . . in the past.

Shortly before I left London I had watched a DVD* of *Blade Runner* with Sean Young, who, for the duration of the movie, played the role of my wife – or at least some of it, because I kept being interrupted by SMS text messages sent by Busner to my cell phone, a technology the ubiquity of which in 2019 wasn't anticipated in 1982. Although, to be strictly fair, we could propose an alternative timeline, BR1, in which cell phones are everywhere in 2008, then entirely gone less than two decades later, to be replaced by older devices that are prized for their ability to both mediate and disjoint communication: answer phones.

Deckard, the blade runner, has an answer phone. I didn't need to dwell on the cheesynthetic Vangelis soundtrack, or the dyed and shocked hairstyles of the women drinking blue neon cocktails in the bar where Daryl Hannah shakes her bootie, in order to find the movie dated; the answer phone's flex was already lashed round my neck and it dragged me down through successive time currents, each one full of such anachro-snags, to where I type this on my dead mother's Olivetti Lettera 22 typewriter, perfectly aware that you – perhaps in 2019 – are entirely at a loss to understand what so exercises me.

* Digital Video Disc, an optical disc storage media format developed in the early 1990s.

For as long as I'd been visiting Los Angeles the funicular alongside the Angel's Flight had been out of order. Anyway, I didn't want to take that route up Bunker Hill: boring through bank lobbies and shopping concourses, climbing flights of concrete stairs rising from parking lots to become the crenulated underside of freeways, the cobblestoned embankments of which are strewn with the discarded mattresses of the homeless. No, I had no desire to extract a core sample of this power-midden, with its bottom layer of grandiose clapboard, which, by the 1930s, had festered into the boarding houses where John Fante's young men typed and diddled; I had no wish to expose the Otis Chandler stratum, or the unholy alliance of Westside movie Democrats and Downtown propertocrats that sat on top of it.

Instead, I schlepped up 5th Street in the malodorous twilight. I had panned 360 degrees since the October evening when I mooted the death of film with the gay comedienne at the Café

Pinot, and no matter how ceaselessly the city retro-fitted itself with its own futurity, there was nothing it could do with the 35-storey-high mirrored gas tanks of the Westin Bonaventure Hotel, a structure I had last gazed upon in its guise as the Atrium in Los Santos. Having been soundly thrashed by my son, CJ, in a game of *Grand Theft Auto: San Andreas*, I lay on the sidewalk and watched him disappear into its lobby accompanied by a bevy of bitches in skin-tight micro-skirts. Still, what can you expect from an entire world a mere 13.7 miles square? One in which the omniscient deity of narrative has been abandoned, pumped full of pixels in a back alley, leaving everyone to run amok, minumental masters of their own fate?

Once I'd checked in, I stopped to chat with Felipe at the concierge desk – he was still wielding his pencil, still embroidering the gold thread of fantasy on to the uniform straitjacket of a less than congenial reality. There had, he said, been an amusing incident the week before, when one of the delegates to the Integrated Systems Convention tripped while fetching yet another muffin from the coffee stand and fell into the fountain, triggering a geyser that surged up, racing the glass elevator, until he was suspended, screaming, high above the lobby. When after twenty minutes the manager charged with choking off the jet nervily jerked the stopcock, the systems delegate was dead on arrival at Level 1, floating face down in the carbonated pool, while his moribund internal monologue fizzled out altogether.

That evening, I was the only diner in a Japanese restaurant on Level 6. I ate beef teriyaki in a woody nook, peering between paper screens at a carved and ornamented bar that gaped like a mouth full of gold crowns. I'd had indigestion before I started eating, and with each mouthful I considered: would that this – which Frederic Jameson has defined as 'the spatialization of culture under the pressure of organized capitalism' – didn't taste so fucking bad. Farting like a cannibalistic cow in a clover field, I shifted the heavy, plush-seated chair so that it pounced on my own feet with its claw ones.

All revved up, all four stomachs swollen with bio-fuels, I jetted the lift up to the twenty-third floor, then lay stranded across the bed in my room. It had been quite a day. I thought back to that moment in early afternoon, when, crossing Grand, en route from the Shrine Auditorium to the Coca-Cola Bottling Plant, I had my first clear sight of the Hollywood Hills. By rights there should have been contentment; for here was the long view that my feet, scraping away layer after layer of paving, bitumen and concrete, had exposed: the pointed breasts of the slumbering giantess, dreaming of a city of angels, radiant as Klieg lights.

Not this time. It had been the cab ride at Heathrow that had done it – a scant half-mile of rubber rolling through the tunnel to the terminal building had erased entirely what should always be written on the body: the land's enduring love for those human feet that had strived through the eons so as to be able to walk upon it. And so the Buckinghamshire lanes didn't debouch into Century Boulevard, and the Grand Union Canal didn't feed into the Los Angeles River. It bore down on me as I washed my underpants in the sink, then hung them up to dry on the shower rail, that my entire strategy had been devised not simply to repel the filmic, but to tape back together the Pangaea that had been cut up by the movies.

During the night the radio murmured: a 52-year-old woman had been found murdered in her BMW in Alhambra, a single shot to her upper torso. I tried to prop her up, to talk to her – but she wouldn't take direction and kept sliding down the gory upholstery. Now that film had died, there was no one to enforce the 30-degree rule.

# 6
## Timber Just in Lake

Not a jump cut at all – more properly understood as a graphic match, the same sight gag that Kubrick made when he cut from that first triumphantly flung war bone to the space station waltzing across the starry backcloth accompanied by the liquid strains of 'The Blue Danube'. Thus: morning discovers first the concrete logs of 4th and 5th streets felled across the trench full of the Harbor Freeway, then dissolves the heavy drapes of Room 237 to seek out my own trunk lying in a pool of sheets.

And so I awoke to the push-button phone on the malachite bedside table, the hefty hardwood armoire, the lamps swivelled in on their brass-effect wall brackets – all of it neon-furred by dream. And so I floated down the elevator shaft, through the glass roof and into the cavernous atrium, noting the jogging track that runs around the building's core. Clearly the Westin Bonaventure had been en route to Jupiter for decades now, its bulbous mirrored hulls groping through inner space while its crew remained either in suspended animation, or keep fanatically fit.

Then I was turning into Figueroa, centring my bag a little more comfortably in the small of my back while trying – despite the *nuages maritimes* that had crept back during the night – to preserve a sunny disposition. Next, I was beside the Los Angeles Central District Health Center, its dusty black cladding grafitti-smeared 'Hollywood Digz', 'Reeper' and 'Largo Rats', where I was hailed by a lithe mixed-race young man, the crotch of whose saggy-assed jeans touched the crossbar of his dinky BMX bike: 'Say, man, d'you know where the two towers are at?'

He raised himself from the saddle and hitched up his saggy-assed jeans. He couldn't possibly mean Barad-dûr and Orthanc, could he? Nor, I thought, could he be mistakenly referring to the twin towers of the World Trade Center, which had given the producers of the movie adaptation of Tolkien's novel such cause for anxiety they considered changing its name before its eventual release in 2002. Then again, recognizing the young man as an Anglo-Nigerian writer whom I had encountered a week or so before at a garden party in Notting Hill, I wondered whether or not he might – just might – be referencing Tolkien's real-life inspiration for his fantasia: Perrott's Folly and the tower of Edgbaston waterworks, both of which had been visible from the future fantasist's childhood home?

Fatal Flaw – as I thought of him – didn't appear to have recognized me, or whoever was playing me this morning. True, the last time I'd seen him his nose was dog-damp with cocaine, while he snuffled the explanation for his failure to publish anything in the past ten years: 'A fatal flaw. I mean, everyone's got one, yeah? Mine happens to be – you won't laugh, will you, promise? – OK, girls in boots with guns. Y'know, before the web it wasn't so bad – I mean, I had to work at it . . . but now, well . . .' He snotted so loudly the other guests at this tony summer party turned to look. 'Like I say, it's a fatal flaw.'

Again with the hitch and a small blue cotton cloud puffed from his waistband; invisible wires of humming tautness connected Fatal Flaw's saggy-assed jeans to those of hundreds – thousands perhaps – of other young men throughout Los Angeles, Pasadena and even into the Valley. Seeing my perplexity, he explained: 'It's the courts, man, the fuckin' courts.' Of course, the County Criminal Courts Buildings, colloquially known as the two towers, and buried in the acropolis of the nearby Civic Center.

We chatted for a while, and Fatal Flaw mugged that he didn't like the bus and so had cycled in from Melrose for his appearance that morning. His espadrilles were worn through – filthy toes fingered a bike pedal. He offered me his pouch of Bugler, but there were only a few pinches of tobacco dust. The last I saw of him was when I looked back from the junction of Figueroa and Sunset: he was deep in conversation with a bag lady pushing a shopping cart who bore a distinct resemblance to the Nobel Laureate Toni Morrison.

Years before I had queued for tickets at Cologne railway station. It was an innocently racist era in Germany, and the poster of a wanted Libyan terrorist stuck up by the Bundespolizei had been captioned below the usual Roswell photofit 'Michael Jackson phenotype'. To transmogrify from an abused child star to an abusive adult has-been – this was a far scarier metamorphosis than the jaw-stretching and fur-sprouting Jackson underwent in John Landis's fourteen-minute music video for *Thriller*.

The Jeffs were waiting on the set for this extravaganza: the Carpenter-Romantic woodhenge of Angelino Heights, a lumber yard of open-truss porches, high gabled roofs and exposed rafter ends – all of it ill with shingles. Peeking out from upper windows, banners whispered 'Support Our Troops: Bring Them Home'. Home to where Woody Woodpecker perches, 'H'h'h'h'-ha-ha! H'h'h'h'-ha-ha!', drilling his *geist* into the boards with no lubrication of beak or hole.

There it is, take it – and it goes without saying (except by a legion of postdoctoral students) that there's little more fucked up than a fairytale. Besides, between Angelino Heights and Alvarado there runs a fatal flaw in the earth's crust, one that links the Echo Park boating lake via William Mulholland's aqueduct to Benedict Canyon. Hollis Mulwray sculls along it, with his daughter's incestuously begot daughter sat prettily in the stern, while that unhappy detective Jake Giddes (when he turns up people get dead) spies on them from the parking lot. Or is that the thirteen-year-old Samantha Geimer, logy on ludes and champagne, being ferried to her rendezvous at Jack Nicholson's house near Mulholland Drive? Ah yes, a photo shoot with the diminutive director-cum-actor whose credit should read not 'Man with Knife' but 'Man Who Will Put his Dick in a Child's vagina /mouth /anus (delete where appropriate)'.

1969, Manson waits back at the ranch while Susan Atkins, Patricia Krenwinkel and Charles 'Tex' Watson head for music producer Terry Melcher's house in Benedict Canyon. 1973, the boating lake in Echo Park is a location for Polanski's *Chinatown*. 1977, the very little director does the big bad thing. The steady 4/4 rhythm of the oars, the silver nitrate surface of time flows along the fatal flaw, until, thirty-seven years later, Atkins, in the terminal stages of cancer, applies for parole. So what if she were sprung, she'd still be a lousy walking companion – what with one leg already amputated. The only people I envy in this thing are the dead.

The *nuages maritimes* had finally dispersed as I made my way along the path beside the boating lake; conservation volunteers were picking up trash, while a couple of fountains simmered

offshore. At Aimee Semple McPherson's Angelus Temple on Logan Street a gang of middle-aged bikers were doubling as extras in a TV shoot, their hogs lined up along the kerb: slices of chromed bacon. McPherson had been a devotee of *shuyu*, her Sunday sermons preached in front of a mock-up of the LA skyline, complete with two miniature aeroplanes, one piloted by Beelzebub, the other by the Good Lord.

As I scaled the hump of Montrose Street, then continued down Alvarado, the Wilshire corridor was spread out below me, frothing with greenery, wispy with smog. Shortly before I turned to the west along Beverly – in order to avoid MacArthur Park – I passed a grotty little dealership. Alvarado Auto Sales were pushing rusty pickups riddled with rust, decadent compacts and my own VW Variant Fastback, a car I'd last seen in a breaker's yard in Battersea twenty-two years previously.

The chances of this were minute – yet when I stopped to peer through the wound-down driver's window and caressed the pimply vinyl hump of the dash, there could be no mistaking it: this was the very same car, the one I'd bought from a social worker on the Broadwater Farm estate in Tottenham, shortly after the riot of October 1985 in which PC Blakelock was hacked to death by Mob with Axe.

I'd crashed the VW a year and a half later on Chelsea Bridge – and although I knew it wasn't a write-off, I'd still been in shock when the man at the breaker's menaced me with a tyre-iron and said, 'Take a tenner for it – or just fuck right off.' I found the reappearance of my old car strangely heartening: the three-car shunt that had seemingly killed it must have been a stunt, the directors of which had arranged for it to be transported here and restored. I crouched to pray, a devout machinist, and called unto the Great Car Spirit to enter me, pump the gas, slip the clutch and drive me west towards Hollywood.

When I straightened up I noticed overhead a billboard advertising *The Incredible Hulk*, the release of which was now: 11.6.08. The Chrysler Building peeked over the bugaboo boffin's green-skinned shoulder; surely, I thought, it must get tired of this shtick? Then I hitched up my short pants – which seemed ridiculously baggy – and besides, why did I find it so difficult to remember?

### *The Assassination of Robert F. Kennedy Considered as a Precursor of Express Checkout*

Somewhere between the Town House – an English manor held down in the shrubbery and force-fed pituitary gland –

and the Bullocks Wilshire, I stopped at a grocery store for an energy drink with a dumb name like Relentless. Big mistake. From its terracotta base to its oxidized copper finial, the old department store was streamlined: an autobuilding speeding from the roaring twenties to the choking noughties. In seconds I was 500 yards up the road and only six days and forty years late to meet the bullets from Sihran Sihran's .22.

Bobby Kennedy, hustled through the kitchens of the Ambassador Hotel by his security detail, had just delivered his victory speech following the 1968 Californian presidential primary. That speech! Its homage to his assassinated brother, its guileless paean to the Great Society, what . . . what were these? Ticked boxes on a card, the drinks swigged and peanuts snaffled from the minibar of democracy. Bobby is gone – unceremoniously dumped in the trunk of Monroe Stahr's 1934 Chrysler Airflow sedan, which shoots out from the porte-cochère, the chrome angel lying across its hood absorbing the up-thrust of the road through his fanned wingtips. Kathleen's in the passenger seat, her beautiful composite of a face framed by one half of the split windshield. As for Stahr, his olive complexion cannot hide the tide of death rising up from his white silk shirt collar.

As the Chrysler turns left on to Wilshire the sound of Bobby's drumming fists is clearly audible, yet neither Monroe nor Kathleen registers any emotion. Why should they give a shit about Kennedy? He's way in the future, but in their immediate past are all the greats whooping it up at the Coconut Grove – Swanson and Shearer, Valentino and Flynn, Mayer and Chaplin. They're too early, accelerating west, fuelled by the lust that will propel them all the way to Stahr's half-built house in Santa Monica, where the *nuages maritimes* will creep through the chinks in its fuselage as they fuck on his raincoat on the floor.

They are too early – and I was too late: the Ambassador had been through the crusher and all that remained were chunks of dusty-white rubble baking behind a chain-link fence. When Scorsese pitched up to shoot *The Aviator* in the Coconut Grove, he had to back it up 500 yards to the Bullocks Wilshire, and it was there that Leo DiCaprio sipped milk and schemed to swat biplanes out of the sky – an actor playing an inchoate pathology, which would one day grow into a giant corporate gorilla.

We stopped for coffee – another big mistake: there was only so much *anyone* could take in when it came to Camera Jeff's career lows. A missing poster tacked to a tree beside where we sat offered $1,000 for Scooby's safe return. I thought back to the last time I'd seen him, disappearing behind the koi sign outside Iver, and, tearing off one of the paper slips, I resolved to make the call that night, a facecloth over the receiver to disguise my voice.

When we went on, with Jeff jogging along beside me, his eye-on-a-stick staring at my shoes, something had changed. My pulse began to quicken, lump-a-lump-a-lump-a-lump-a-lump-a-lump-a-lump-a – it was paranoia on my part, certainly, but then they *were* sending them against me, these bioengineered anthropomorphic killing machines, human brains yoked to hundreds of horsepower. Waiting for the stop lights so I could cross into Hancock Park, I sympathized with those familiar features as they loomed in the screens, awfully contorted by the effort of braking. I could almost taste the sweet white flesh inside those two-millimetre-thick steel shells that had been artfully folded into Infinitis.

Lumpa-lumpa-lumpa-lumpa- I had been alone for a long time – not because I wanted to be, but because until I solved my . . . problem, there would be aspects of my personality I was unable to control. I was compelled to move from town to town, taking odd jobs where I could, staying off the books and below the radar, just an ordinary nerdy Joe with an IQ of 198 able to expand the coefficients of the binomial theorem while flossing my lacquered teeth. I might hide out here, in the eight-car garages attached to Florentine villas or Tudorbethan mansions, but sooner or later I would have to *deal with it*, did I want to fight them, or was it the dewily protuberant top lip of my only true love I saw shadowed by the sunshades?

Back on the Miracle Mile, the streamlined blocks taunt me with their *grande vitesse*, while I remain crawling along at ground level, menaced by a dump truck, lumpa-lumpa-lumpalumpluml'l' – my hands clench in front of my starting eyes, green, alien, engorged, the pastel-painted oblongs of the storefronts ripple with distortion: a fireball has been ignited behind my eyes! The orange-and-white canopy of Busby's movie theatre radiates visible spectra! A roar of rage, deep and grinding as a malfunctioning camshaft rotating all the way from Hellenistic Greece to Detroit, bursts from my barrelling chest. My T-shirt falls away in shreds, my baseball cap pops off like the plastic cap on a wine bottle. At last! Now it's clear to me why my short pants have been so saggy-assed all day! Now that I have metamorphosed they're a *perfect fit*!

I leap twenty feet in the air and come down hard on all fours, my elephantine hands and feet sending cracks fissuring through the sidewalk. I grab handfuls of hardtop and yank the roadway like a carpet runner, so that it rucks up, sending BMWs and Renegade Jeeps cannoning into one another. Oh! The heady perfume of spilt petrol, the festive tinkle of shattering glass!

I turn this way and that before the empty eyes of polystyrene heads ranged in the window of a wig store, marvelling at my own preposterous physique, abs and pecs wrapped around my ribcage like the coils of a monstrous green-skinned constrictor. Deltas of arteries radiate out from trapezius and sternocleidomastoid muscles thick as hawsers.

The thoughts of this gross a body cannot help but be visible, so, notwithstanding the drivers – who either run screaming, or grab guns from the glove compartments of their stalled and crashed cars – I pause to consider my prospects . . . my *sexual* prospects. I mean, c'mon, I'm, like, fourteen feet *high*, with a build that makes the most avid steroid-guzzler look mimsy – surely my cock 'n' balls are *to scale*? Anger and lust – never more that a synapse apart – fuse behind the baroque half-dome of my forehead with its convex mouldings and entablature of worry lines. True, these vile creatures may be my sworn enemies, but I'd still like to . . . *fuck one*.

Say . . . that one, over there, the gridlocked black Hummer, with its tinted windows wobbling a come-on, as its speakers pump out the hypnotic bass line of a rap song that's familiar despite my hydrocephalus. '*Serviat! Raptetur! Serviat! Raptetur!*' Wires and nerves threaded through my unreasonable lusts and unsociable motions pull them *tight* and I kick out, sending an auto spinning on its longitudinal axis, scattering trim, fenders, fragments of window glass, then its doors, hood, wheel trim and alloys. The anti-roll bar neatly skewers a woman drinking a frappuccino outside Starbucks to a poster advertising frappuccino – violence of such jocular savagery it can be accepted uncritically as wholesome entertainment.

As can the kicked car, which goes on spinning until all that's left is a body shell – the engine having long since plunged through the awning of the El Camino tapas bar – inside which the skull of its late driver is rattling like a pea in a whistle. Not that anyone pays any attention: the arty-slackers who were goofing beneath the awning have scattered already, whipping out their camera phones, so it's with the low definition (yet enhanced newsworthiness) afforded by the tiny screen of a Samsung SGH-G800 that we witness my next trick: a Pontiac G5 coupe grabbed *in one hand*, my huge fingers fitting so neatly into the window holes that it's impossible not to think: why hasn't anyone done this before? And an old clunker of a Dodge Intrepid grabbed in the other – then the two autos beaten like cymbals as I roar and roar and rooooooarrrr!

Suddenly squad cars are barricading off the four blocks of Wilshire between Detroit Street and Burnside Avenue, while the fat blue-and-white LAPD choppers bumble down over the rooftops, the perforated stings of .50 calibre machine-guns poking from their open hatches. Like I should care? I'm gonna hump a Hummer, so hurl the crumpled-tissue cars away, then lifting the off-road vehicle – perhaps for the first time in its life *off the road* – I tear a gash in its rear end the approximate size necessary. With disturbing tenderness I shift my grip so that I'm holding the car by its rear wheels and pull it towards my tumescent crotch.

Appalled fingers drop the SGH-G800, the view rears back and widens – but it's too late! The choreography of the scene is unmistakable: given the proportionality of my sweat-greased carcass and the dirty boulevard, this could be any poolside out in the Valley, with me an oiled stud limbering up for the money shot, but:

Uh? Uh-oh.

No one need be *that* alarmed; for one, because this is a PG or at most a PG-13. I mean, *nobody* lays out the budget for this much wantonly artful destruction without a teenage target acquired. Also, there are – as I previously remarked – aspects of my personality that are beyond my control; surely, it stands to reason that a twice-life-sized bogey boy would have an erectile dysfunction? I may pull the rear of the Hummer towards my tow-hook, my ass cheeks tensing, my rictus widening to reveal incisors the size of dentists, but even as the four Crips leap from its front doors, MAC-10s jerking their hands as if they're demented conductors, it's clear I am unable to perform.

The comity of African-American gang members and white LAPD officers is definitely the subtext to this playlet. So what? The Crips' pistols may spit fire, the cops' handguns may boom – yet only every twentieth round hits me, and then I merely yelp as if this were flung gravel. The copters' machine-guns spray this humongous gook more accurately – but I only clap a hand to my neck each time I'm bitten by a .50 calibre horsefly.

Nevertheless, like any frustrated rapist, I am doubly enraged, so snatch up more cars and hurl them at my antagonists – but when this fails to stop them I leap high in the air and come down near the summit of Desmond's department store. Grabbing the chamfered corner, I start to tear one letter after another from the neon sign, sending them skimming down into the street, where they cleaver into buses, or else up into the sky, where a boomeranging *e* deftly shreds the rotors of a police copter so that it spirals into the citrus blooms of death.

Things are going my way until the untimely arrival of a marine company armed with FIM-82 Stinger ground-to-air missiles. The first three they launch miss me and inflict devastating collateral damage on Melrose. I leap to evade the fourth and land in the La Brea Tar Pits, where I make free with the hot black gloop, disembowel model mastodons and generally amuse myself. Still, it's clear that the fight's going out of me as I wade in circles waist-high in the pit. So much so that emboldened tourists creep up behind me like kids playing grandma's footsteps, then pop their miserable flashes. The money shot – when it finally comes – is a tarry plash across their lenses.

I came to in the Farmers Market on Fairfax and 3rd, sitting at a Chinese food stall with two or three other toothless old Jews jew-jewing on noodles and kvetching our way through the hot afternoon. 'Jesus, Willy,' said one, 'you're so goddamn thin you need reverse lipo, man – some fat squirted *into* you.'

It was true: my pants were so slack they could comfortably house the Incredulous Hulk. 'Yeah,' I mumbled, 'you'd know all about getting fat squirted into you, Al, coz that's what your Dora does with her lokshen soup.'

'Heh-heh-heh,' gum-chuckled the oldsters, then went back to their jew-jewing and slurping.

I was only mildly fazed by my ability to seamlessly Matthauize with their Parkinsonian blur of liver-spotted hands; hadn't this always been the key juxtaposition of Hollywood: up on the screen the industry of souls, while in the backroom the sunshine boys black up and cry for mama? So I sat, smothered by awnings and homeyness, contemplating the Three Dogs Bakery ('Bakery for Dogs'), while from the south there emanated the wailing of sirens, the rat-a-tat-tat of automatic gunfire, and the kerboom! of ground-to-air missiles. This, the latest death rattle of the megalopolis, was something we oldsters were all familiar with, and so we went on with our ho fun, continued the green tea treatment.

I left a ten-spot for my share of the check and wobbled off into the hurdy-gurdy consumerism of the Grove Mall. All those screen gunfights, what were they, if not a brilliantly deployed strategy of Calm and Blasé against the insurgency of the Id? Of course, things could get out of hand – there was mission creep to contend with. It was only nine days since the propane cylinders on the New York set at Universal had exploded sending a King Kong cloud roaring into the sky above Hollywood. While LAFD's finest had fought the flames sporting the gold foil suits of poorly conceived aliens, 40,000 archived videotapes had burned – together with the sets of *Back to the Future*.

As I bent to pick up a strip of packing tape twined in the fence of Pan Pacific Park, Gofer Jeff came barrelling along the sidewalk on her denim kegs. 'Mr Thewlis! Mr Thewlis!' she puffed. 'We're so sorry – we kinda lost you back there.'

'Don't worry about that,' I snapped. 'So long as you keep laying down covering fire for these last three miles I'll be just fine.'

'Covering fire?' She looked at me as if I were aha-a-ha-ha-ha a cold-blooded killer.

'Sorry, I mean, so long as you keep rolling until I get to Hollywood, then . . .' I struggled to cinch my elephantine pants with the tape.

'Then what?'

I knotted the tape. 'Then it's a wrap.'


At 6922 Hollywood Boulevard there was a small terrace outside the Coffee Bean & Tea Leaf. I sat dunking two of Earl Grey's hot nuts into a styrofoam cup full of boiling water. Opposite me a bum with an uncanny resemblance to the French *romancier-maudit* Michel Houellebecq was nursing a mug rimmed with old froth. He wore a mauve shirt over a leather jacket and his sock-puppet face was scuffed and scabby. A Discman lay on the metal tabletop between his bloated fingers, the headphones of which clipped a dirty-cream panama to his ginger hair.

I had loathed him at first sight – would that I could've been planted opposite the efficient student at the next table, whose thrift-store cheongsam was split high on her chubby thigh. I eyed her well-thumbed *Pride and Prejudice* and her puppyish tummy with equal covetousness. The Houellebecqalike smelt – he muttered 'Get it together!' and other worrying exhortations.

Behind me I could hear the squeaking and baying of a rapidly gathering crowd. As I had taken my seat I'd clocked the security barriers, the bald boys in black suits and the limos pulling up outside Grauman's – there was obviously a première under way, but I wasn't going to let that interfere with my teatime, any more than P. G. Wodehouse had allowed the transportation logistics of Los Angeles to disrupt his habits, when he reported for his first day's work at MGM in Culver City, having walked the six miles from Beverly Hills.

I sipped my Earl Grey judiciously – the only movie stars left in Hollywood were the supermen's batmen, the jokers' tin men, the Elvises and the Marilyn Monroes. Still, at least the impersonators had the virtue of honest subterfuge – not so the out-of-towners treading on the stars' stars who were being drawn to the red carpet like flies to an Insect-O-Cutor. Once they got between the pavilions, under the mad eaves of the Chinese Theater, they'd get uglier: sunshine and oranges were not enough, not now they were a lowering and bitter crowd.

The traffic continued to rumble and toot, the Houellebecqalike continued to mutter and poot. The first screams were synchronized with the camera flashes reflected in the window of the Coffee Bean & Tea Leaf, but soon enough this *son et lumière* became a dinning zoetrope, then a howling stroboscope – and still I did not turn; didn't until from out of the hysteria projected a single comprehensible line of dialogue: 'That guy never gives autographs!' Then at last I swivelled in my seat to be confronted by a black face gone blubbery with joy. He held out his book so everyone on the terrace could see the page. There was the mark, the stave of the *J* serving for the *T* as well, both names lying upon a dais of a flourish and – a few feet beyond the baying hound – there was the marker.

He was wearing a shiny slate bomber jacket with its sleeves rolled up to his elbows, a $500 T-shirt, and there were sunglasses tipped forward on his charming nose. There he was, Justin Timberlake, his pale trunk tipping forward into the pool of faces, while a forest of limbs reached up to grab him. And there too, floating on the end of a blue-and-white-striped tie, was the clown-face-designed-by-committee of Mike Myers, while beside him bulged the baby puss of Jessica Alba.

'Juss-tin! Juss-tin!' the crowd chanted, while the security detail that had ushered these, the stars of the new Myers comedy vehicle, *The Love Guru*, across the road, were now frantically trying to get them back. It wasn't the cars that were the problem – their drivers sat, docilely accepting the mêlée – it was the crowd, which, having filled up the forecourt of the theater, came coursing between the stalled vehicles, a human torrent with waves of faces.

Rising unsteadily to my feet, I addressed my fellow patrons: 'C'mon, people!' I struggled to make myself heard. 'This is lunacy. Justin Timberlake! Mike Myers! Jessica-fucking-Alba? These are not big stars even by the standards of our Lilliputian era – seriously, no one's gonna riot over *them*.' I waved my arm wildly and knocked over my cup. Earl Grey leapt into the Houellebecqalike's lap. He leapt up crying, '*Roi du cons!*', grabbed me by the throat and began dragging me off the terrace.

Before I toppled into the millrace of sentiment, I was gifted with a moment of clarity: I saw that the bald boys had succeeded in corralling the money back on the far side of the boulevard, while the crowd that whirled around Grauman's had swollen mightily, its turbulence of bodies enveloping the stalled vehicles and washing up against the fronts of the buildings to twice head height. I saw that the people closest to me were highly individuated – I had only to look upon them *to know all about them.*

Valerie Schultz, a dental hygienist from Portland, Oregon, a tad overweight, a jet-bead bracelet buried in her wurst folds, a cold sore on her full lower lip, had been date-raped in 1984 and became pregnant. She gave the child up for adoption, but two years ago he tracked her down. He was angry, almost illiterate – he'd run away from foster parents in Cedar Rapids to join a biker gang. Valerie got him on a methadone programme, but he still drank – and when he drank he beat her, hence the yellowy-blue stippling of a bruise on the flap of belly exposed as, bobbing in the mob, her T-shirt rides up.

Bob, Duane and Kerry-Anne – I can smell their separate savours as they sibilate 'Juss-tin! Juss-tin!' But, just as anonymity shades in notoriety, so the further my eye roves the more stereotypical the faces of the crowd become. Then I'm being tossed and buffeted, bouncing off a belly over here, receiving a clout from a stray fist over there. As I am pitched up on to their heads and shoulders, the cacophony of moans, catcalls, shrieks, chants and applause becomes overwhelming. From up here I can make out small islets of the recognizable – a Tin Man with an oil-funnel hat, Elvis mouthing, 'Everybody let's rock!' – but these are surrounded by visages, the eyes, noses and mouths of which are no more differentiated than the funiculae, mandibles and compound eyes of a locust corvée.

To begin with I assume that it's my own proximity that can imbue these anthropoids with individuality – but I'm soon disabused, for as the agitated waves sweep me away from the terrace of the Coffee Bean & Tea Leaf, the crowd becomes more cloned. By the time I'm two blocks further and being scraped along the stone rendering of the L. Ron Hubbard Gallery, I'm surrounded by a swarm whose faces are smooth convexities of flesh, gashed with slots from which issue a monotonous drone.

My clothes are ripped to shreds, blood flows from cuts on my chest and thighs – unless I can gain a place of safety soon I'll be torn to shreds by the computer-generated mob. Think – think! The clones may be frenzied but they move only where preordained by their creators; if I can read the currents and cross-currents perhaps I can go with the flow? I note the alignment of the Orange Grove sign with a palm tree: that bearing should take me towards the Roosevelt Hotel. I twist and slip sideways into the tide coursing back towards Grauman's; then, as it draws level with the tree, I push hard at a head with both feet and reach for the trunk . . . only to be swept backwards by a rush heading the other way.

Horrified, I realize I'm in the van of a flying wedge charging straight towards a horde going in the opposite direction. Their impact flips me head over heels, and as the two columns grind against each other I'm twirled again and again, as a spar is battered by a weir. 'JussstinJussstinJussstinJussstin!' The pressure increases – if I'm sucked into an eddy I'll be trampled to death beneath the clones' feet, which, despite their binary DNA, are rigid and hard. My ribs are cracking, my shoulders and hips disjointing . . . I fight it, kicking out to keep my feet on the ground. Another moaning rush, 'JusssJusssJusss!', and I find myself in a calm spot where the pressure slackens – although now I feel a terrible stabbing pain in my lower back. It's strange, given that the forms that surround me have no more angles or projections than mass-produced souvenir Oscar statuettes . . . I can't turn but manage to twist my head: a very skinny kid wearing a Lakers cap has his sharp shoulder digging into my kidneys. Shocked by this reindividuation, I pan about and see that, yes, others of the homologues are becoming distinguishable, with here a shock of brown hair, there a scattering of freckles, over there a beaded dreadlock.

It must be that whoever animated the scene anticipated action here requiring a close-up. I crane to see under the peak of the boy's cap – he's as vague as a ghost, so, having laboriously freed my arm, I swing on him, a clumsy haymaker that comes down on top of his head and with a yelp he goes under. There's a further wild surge that washes me into another calm pool; this time I'm facing a young woman who sobs hysterically. Her cotton print dress has been ripped from the neckline to her waist – her brassière as well. Her breasts would be beautiful, were it not that one of them is missing a nipple. I push back to give her some room, but every time I move she moves with me, insinuating her leg between my thighs. I'm becoming aroused – until the girl spasms violently and her blonde bob lifts to reveal that she has no ears. 'Stop it! Fuckin' quit!' she yells – but it isn't me that's bothering her, it's the clone behind her, whose blank screen morphs into a goatish leer . . . then I see that he has his hand up her dress, while he dribbles on her bare neck.

My arm is still aloft, so I grab his ear – another action that's obviously been anticipated, for it's as well formed as an anatomical drawing. I squeeze it as hard I can and twist, but it isn't long before skin melds with cartilage and the ear disappears back into a slick egghead that's borne away from me. At least the young woman has escaped, although when I try to pick out her blonde bob in the crowd it too has been subsumed by the pixels . . . Another spasm passes through them; I find myself within an arm's length of a signpost, a second spasm and I grab it, am swung up and round into the air . . .

A final view of Hollywood Boulevard crashing with waves of sound: 'Juss-tin! Juss-tin! Juss-tin!' The pagodas of Grauman's soar thousands of feet into the sky, as do the other, less ornate buildings, all of which have been subjected to the same crude multiplier. In the deep trough between them the crowd ripples, and there's a last sensation of buoyancy as I float on this lake of doppelgängers before a providential swirl carries me into the gloomy inlet of the Roosevelt's lobby.

I stared at my idol face in the tarnished pool of an old mirror for a long time, yet there seemed no evidence of the ordeal I had just survived: my clothes were intact; my baseball cap was clamped firmly on my head. True, my expression was a little wary, but even as I looked a familiar superciliousness crept back in from the edges. I sniffed deeply, sucking up the ineradicable odour of old hotel – dust and static electricity – then padded back towards the stairs that led down to the reception desk.*

* After I had levied my Mastercard and signed the form, here, here and there, the receptionist clicked his fingers for the bellhop. I tried to say that I didn't require any assistance but the words crumbled on my tongue, and for what seemed like several hours I was suspended in a reverie during which I surveyed an entire alternative history for the North American landmass. One in which the second wave of colonization was from the west, in the tenth century CE, and by Arab traders who then converted the Native Americans to Islam, occupied the entire continent, established a caliphate, rapidly industrialized and then in the seventeenth century mounted a war of conquest against the sleepy European backwater where the Reformation – not to mention the Enlightenment – had yet to occur.

Between square pillars I could see that the tables were already laid in the restaurant, glassware and cutlery gleaming on dark wood. I checked my watch: 7.16 already – I had better get ready fast, or I'd be late for my dinner with Bret.

# 7

# My Dinner with Bret

'Is the asparagus fresh?'

   'Well, it's in a soup, so it's been, like, puréed.'

   'But was it fresh *when* it was puréed?'

   'I guess.'

   'What about the halibut?'

   'I can assure you: that's definitely fresh.'

   'Definitely?'

   'Definitely.'

Fresh the halibut may have been, although this was still the type of restaurant where dead fish were laid out for boning on squared-off mounds of clapshot or polenta. Over Bret's shoulder the dun dining room of the Roosevelt seamlessly merged with the deeper and wider murk of the Spanish Revival lobby, where an enormous crystal chandelier dripped wanly, scarcely illuminating the exposed ceiling beams, let alone the mezzanine level cornice with its pattern of desert blooms.

There had been some manoeuvring before we were installed by our own square pillar, which, like all the others in the restaurant, had been boxed off at head height by interior designer Dodd Mitchell – although probably not personally.

'I don't want to sit next to anyone in this town,' Bret had explained to the maître d' after rejecting the first two tables offered. He was wearing a cool-looking cream linen suit and a positively chilly blue silk shirt. Ray-Bans poked from his display pocket, and when he canted sideways on the banquette suede loafers poked out from beneath the table. He was being played by mid-period Orson Welles – neither the obese, sherry-swilling old roué who had taken on Busner's role, nor the young Welles who had impersonated the writer back in the mid-1980s, at the summit of his notoriety.

I didn't know who'd taken me on this evening – and Bret was giving nothing away. I thought it unlikely that Postlethwaite had been racketing around Manhattan in the nineties, which was when I'd got to know the author of *American Psycho*, but it was possible Thewlis had been there for raucous dinners at Elaine's, big drinks in the small hours at Mary Lou's in the Village, then dawn upchucking from the East River, glimpsed nauseously by vampires doing lines of cremains off somebody's butcher block in someone else's apartment.

In those days Bret had struck me as high, wide, handsome and more than a little bumptious – this was forgivable, given that he was scarcely thirty and already with the masterpiece of *Citizen Kane* to his credit. Now he seemed leaner – the Welles glimpsed only briefly on camera during the shooting of his Rockefeller-funded South American travelogue, a fiasco that had ended up way over budget. Perhaps it was this that had winnowed him out?

He finished ordering with a run through the white wines available by the glass, before settling reluctantly on a Zinfandel.

'And for you, sir?'

'Me?' I was flustered, and as my Adam's apple scraped in my dry throat I flashed back to the $1,000-per-night poolside cabana where I had checked myself out obsessively in the mirror before this rendezvous. What madness! How could I have forgotten the thinning hair, the pocked cheeks, knobbly knees and hairless ankles? I was Postlethwaite, of course, and no matter how many Kiehl's bath products I lavished on myself there was no possibility of my seducing Bret, I mean, I was hardly his *type*. 'Uh, I'll have . . . the same as him.'

It was the pathetic non-order of a subaltern of style, who knows nothing and so uses the quince spoon to ream his pipe.

Two pools of thick soup soon lay before us, inscribed in truffle oil with the worthless autograph of the sous-chef. 'A script is a commodity,' Bret was saying; 'nothing more – oftentimes a hell of a lot less. It's no longer simply a case of "to the victor the spoils"; the actual craft of screenwriting has become having the balls and the connections necessary to get your credit.'

He stopped speaking and began paddling his fibreglass face towards the soup. I already regretted having given him the whole death-of-film shtick, although at least he seemed to think it was a metaphor – and when I'd contemptuously observed Postlethwaite babbling my lines, I'd held back from admitting I was in Hollywood to find its killer or killers.

'But, Bret,' I said, 'you're a native Angeleno, your own books have been filmed – isn't *The Informers* in production right now? – you must feel an affinity for the industry?'

'Industry? It isn't an industry any more, man, it's a fucking business. I tellya, if I'd've known the whole extent of the bullshit I was going to get caught up in, I never would've come back – and now there's this other crap, the writers' strike.'

'Why did you stay?'

He sighed, an expiration that was mouldering in its dead civility: 'Phew . . . Money, dummy – I need the money.'

Welles and Ellis – they seemed like a failed anagram or a botched palindrome. Certainly, Welles had never bettered this performance, what with its re-uptake of inhibited diffidence, its Mesolithic *tedium vitae*. I recalled that shocking first sight of him as Captain Hank Quinlan in *Touch of Evil*, lunging up from his squad car, his saltpan of a face mottled and cracked. He was only forty-two when he wrote, directed and acted in the movie, yet the taint was already on him: green grave weeds, rotting at the edges. Did he see then how it would all end up, with his final role being the voiceover of Unicron, the planet-eating robot in the first *Transformers* movie?

The waiter came across and took our soup bowls. The restaurant had filled up with hay-hair honey-skin blondes in knock-off couture squired by men fully suited. Still, with no climate variation to speak of all four seasonal collections could be spanned by a few degrees: if the temperature fell to seventy, couples began promenading Sunset togged up as Nanook and Nyla of the north. The waiter returned with the halibuts and a bottle of Powerade tucked under his arm. I was about to remonstrate with him when he swerved aside and plonked it in between the tête-à-tête at the next table, so that it hovered in my own mid shot.

'Whoa,' Bret muttered, 'the hard stuff.' Then he went on about the death of film as he teased out fish bones with the tines of his fork: 'I don't think you're right, there's always dynamism in movie culture, whatever the mechanics of production. Even now with this, like, *avalanche* of product there're still innovative things getting made.'

'Like what?'

'Well, *Knocked Up* – didya see *Knocked Up?*'

I groped in the mildewed reticule of my memory and came up with, 'Um, yeah, sorta slacker comedy type thing. Not bad.'

'Not bad? It was a whole new approach to formula pictures like that. You should read the *New Yorker* review – actually, it was more like an essay—'

'By Anthony Lane, right?' I simpered disparagingly, while thinking most of what follows.[*]

### The Love Guru

Billboards advertising this movie's release dominated my circumambulation of the Los Angeles basin, and during my 120-mile, week-long walk I must have passed scores of them depicting the Canadian comedian in a fake Bhagwan beard and the orange robes of a sannyasi, sitting cross-legged, one

---

[*] The exception being the framing device – which implies retrospection – not, counter-intuitively, those events that on Thursday, 12 June 2008, still lay in the future and that I flashed forward to by using Dr Mukti's CBT techniques. The accuracy of these elements of my reverie was confirmed when they eventually came to pass.

hand grasping a yellow flower, the other held – incorrectly – in the Varada Mudra pose of Theravada Buddhism: palm out, thumb and index fingers touching. Myers was, it transpired, welcoming moviegoers into an entertainment that – even by his own unexacting standards – was a pile of shit: impotent sexual innuendoes, incontinent scatological jokes, bigoted intercultural gags – *The Love Guru* had 'em all.

I assert this, but when I eventually saw the movie in my local hot-buttered multiplex, I realized I was in no position to judge it, for so long had I been out of the celluloid loop. Sure, it was shit – but then for all I knew *all* movies were shit; either that, or, given that cinema was the world's dominant narrative medium, the silvery mirror in which Humanity viewed its own raddled features, perhaps those features were themselves *daubed* with shit.

Besides, I was not insensible to the halo effect, whereby the new work of any given filmmaker is surrounded by the penumbra of his or her earlier efforts. In Myers's case, *The Love Guru* came haloed in shit, because I'd disliked his movies from the very first time I'd seen one, on a flight back from New York in June 1992. I suppose if I had the exhaustive critical intelligence of an Anthony Lane, rather than the planet-devouring negativity of a Unicron, then I might reserve my judgement (both then and now), not having seen the original *Saturday Night Live* sketches on which *Wayne's World* was based. But I appeal to your own better judgement: would it really have made any difference?

Sixteen years ago I failed to find any charm in the two provincial bohunks and their amateurish cable TV show. My companion on the flight, Charles Hudson, was, however, happy to lose himself in the fartantics of Myers and his co-star

Dana Carvey for 94 minutes. Then we talked, drank vodka miniatures and I smoked. Strange to recall how cigarette smoke looked in plane cabins: the ghost of a smirch in the rapidly rarefying atmosphere; it's something my own children will never see, although they may well live to witness the extinction of mass air travel that my own generation saw evolve – all those dinoboeings, choked on their own tailpipes.

We drank many, many Smirnoff miniatures and decompressed from our Stateside trip in the acrid fuselage. On our first evening in Manhattan the crack vials had crunched under foot as we made our way downtown to go clubbing. Late that night I had to wake Charles up and ask him for a sedative – I knew he had some, old-school things, chalky little manhole covers inscribed with one of those Big Pharma coinages – Evaqual? Navarolt? Intephrine? – that make anxiolytic medications sound like the bastard offspring of a Turkish fisherman and a planet-eating robot.

Slowly, the Kematrol beat the cocaine hydrochloride molecules into submission. I stopped having to patrol the nylon trench in between the twin beds, ceased to be worried that the TV stand would sink further into the tufted orange hotel carpet. A couple of hours later I fiddled open the glassine envelope and tipped the last of the coke on to the toilet seat in a stall at La Guardia, then flubbered it up.

The flight to Syracuse was uneventful, if, that is, you're used to the transcendent misery of realizing you have been sent back from the future and at any minute will be killed – a murder that you yourself witnessed as a small child. I was used to this. From the airport I took a cab to the university's Health Science Center. Dr Thomas Szasz, a dapper septuagenarian in a neat blue suit, was waiting for me in a room full of ventilation ducts and polystyrene fire-retardant tiles that audibly crackled with static electricity.

I recall my conversation with Dr Szasz perfectly well (or should I say, with his impersonator, for I realized soon enough that he was being played by Donald Pleasence in his last major role), and in particular his goulash-thick Hungarian accent that added the suffix *szasz* (pronounced *zarj*) to many of his words, thus: 'Yesasz, my criticszasz are many, my enemieszasz ubiquitouszasz,' giving me the uncanny feeling that his speech was a form of prayer, consisting in the incantation of his own – possibly divine – name.

Not that there was anything self-worshipping about the veteran anti-psychiatrist (as portrayed by the valetudinarian actor). I had a journalistic assignment, but was also interested in speaking with him because he had known Zack Busner well during the early 1960s. At that time Szasz was working on what would become his signature work, *The Myth of Mental Illness*, while Busner was setting up his 'concept house' in Willesden. Both were engaged in a revolt against the dehumanizing character of institutional psychiatry, both fundamentally questioned its view of mental pathologies, but only Busner had ended up on celebrity game shows.

Peering over his bifocals, Szasz looked at me as if I were a psychic gift sent by his old comrade in arms-thrusting-from-the-walls-of-her-flat. I told him about the Riddle, and how buying up shares in the manufacturer had almost financially bankrupted Busner, just as publicizing the enquire-within tool had done for him professionally. 'I seeasz, I seeasz,' Szasz muttered as I spoke; then when I'd concluded he said: 'It isasz, I think, a caseasz of hubriszasz.'

'Hubris?'

'Exactly, hubriszasz. You seeasz, like me, Zack Busnerasz believed that schizophreniasz was not a pathology at all, only a semantic confusionasz.'

'And it isn't?'

'No, of courszasz not – researcasz in the last thirty yearszasz haszasz conclusively established the genetic basiszasz of schizophreniasz, if not its actual causzasz.'

'So, you were wrong?'

'We were wrong, which is by no meanszasz to endorszasz the way the therapeutic state treats schizophreniasz, or to admit that any other so-called mental illnessasz – such as depressionasz – are anything of the sort. But in this caszasz, we were wrong. I think perhapszasz that Busner is too proud to admit thiszasz, and so . . .'

His fingers, which had been steepled beneath his chin, now interleaved, then inverted to reveal all the pink little people straitjacketed in his institution. So, as you can see, it was an epochal encounter for me – one that had far-reaching consequences, especially when I became aware that Szasz had cofounded, with the Church of Scientology, the Citizens Commission on Human Rights.

For the rest of the interview Dr Szasz treated my questions seriouszly if peremptorily, szwiping them out of the air in such a way as to suggest he was translating from one conceptual language into another. Which made it all the more bizarre when, at the end of our hour together, he turned hospitable – *very* hospitable – and suggested that while he had no wish to detain me against my wishes, I might like – on a purely voluntary basis, of course – to be his guest in a nearby facility . . . indefinitely.

\*     \*     \*

On the same trip to the States, Charles and I went up the Twin Towers. Given subsequent events, I'd like to be able to tell you that they made a big impression on me, but that would be a lie. Indeed, I can honestly say that I never gave the vast blocks another thought from that day until 11 September 2001, whereas my revulsion from Mike Myers returned again and again over the years, rising unfunnily up my gorge whenever I caught a few seconds of a trailer for one of his movies, saw a poster, or even heard the words 'Mike' and 'Myers' in completely unrelated contexts.

The scene in *The Love Guru* that most outraged me was one involving the actor of restricted height, Verne Troyer, who Myers had imported from his earlier Austin Powers movies to play the foul-mouthed manager of the Toronto Maples ice hockey team. I suppose that given my own issues it ill behove me to be quite so censorious, but when I saw Troyer upbraiding the Guru (Myers) and his star player (Timberlake) in a scaled-down office obviously modelled on the dwarfish train carriage set in the Marx Brothers' *At the Circus*,[*] I longed for one of those vodka miniatures that I drained during the 1992 JFK to Heathrow flight to magically reappear in my hand, so that I could smash it against the wall of the cinema, then plunge it into Myers's chipmunk cheek.[†]

---

[*] Jerry Maren, who played Little Professor Atom in *At the Circus* and who was the 'prop' for the gag in which Groucho declines to take the third light from a dwarf on the basis that it's 'unlucky', has had the last laugh accorded by longevity. He's the only surviving *Wizard of Oz* Munchkin and has outlived entire legions of full-size thespians.

[†] I realize this homicidal impulse towards Myers's projected image suggests – in the jargon – inadequate reality testing on my part, but, in my defence, the indoor golfing range in Hove that I attended with my father when I was a child made a deep and lasting impression on me. He would drive a real ball towards a screen back-projected with a fairway; then it would reappear (or, rather, an actor golf ball playing it would make an entrance) bouncing towards the green.

It may be the vagaries of memory, but I think the vodka miniatures were glass. I don't believe either Charles or I behaved at all badly – we didn't even raise our voices, only unravelled the way even well-knit folk do when drinking to excess on long-haul flights. Nevertheless, about an hour before landing the stewardess approached our scaled-down barroom and told us that she refused to serve us any more liquor, and that if we didn't moderate our language she would have the pilot radio ahead and we would find the police waiting for us upon touchdown.

'He was wearing crocodile-skin shoes the last time I saw him,' Bret was saying of a former brat pack writer-buddy. 'He told me they cost $20,000.'

I pushed my spoon through the quarter-inch of *tarte au chocolat* and it clicked with china. The waiter materialized with a vodka tonic for Bret; then, as he turned away, he moved the bottle of Powerade from one point on the adjacent table to another more exactly in my own mid shot. As if this set-dressing were the cause, the voices of the other diners were now *right in my ear*.

'It'll be huge, see,' the man was saying. 'I mean, we're with this guy all the way – he doesn't know who he is any more, hell, he doesn't know who anyone else is either.'

'Uh-huh.'

I'd misread the situation: this wasn't a date; the suit was pitching to hay-hair, who had to be a studio exec.

The suit pressed on: 'Everyone he runs into is played by an actor – some well known, others not so, and people'll have a great time trying to identify who's who – that's how they identify with his, his—'

'Condition, yeah, I hear you.'

'But there's more' – he began waving his hands – 'our guy has these delusions, he sees things, he hears voices, everything is incredibly significant – everyone is in on the conspiracy –

'He's a paranoid schizophrenic, right?' She was bored. 'Lissen, Griffin, I don't want to, like, pop your bubble, but I've had people coming on to me with these psycho ideas for months now – it's all over town like a goddamn rash.'

I could understand why Bret didn't want to sit next to anyone in LA. I couldn't tell if he'd overheard the schizopitch; his face bore an expression of frightening ennui. I began babbling: 'I've been reading your *Lunar Park*, man; it's great, truly great – maybe your best yet. I love the way you play with your own identity, create a doppelgänger – but isn't that what the movies can do now, there's no disbelief so heavy that it can't be winched up with fleets of computer-generated helicopters? I mean, it's also like a *psychosis*, believing in this stuff even for a second – that's why they're putting so much into the new 3-D technology. Shazzam! And you're in the insect mines of Minroad. Shazzam! again, and you're in some poor fucker's *liver*, kayaking down his bile duct . . . and, well, this is what we *fear*, isn't it? The numbers of people with mental illnesses are increasing exponentially – bipolar, hypomania, OCD, dementia, addiction, schizo-fucking-phrenia – it's a plague, and these Hollywood movies are expressing that fear! What's so incredible about the Hulk? I'll tellya: he's got BDD, body dysmorphic disorder. He's a perfectly ordinary guy but he *thinks* he's got green skin and this, like, obscenely muscled—'

The waiter was back with a credit card receipt to sign. I scanned it and from the total realized we were going Dutch. Bret was already tucking his Mont Blanc back inside his jacket.

I had no idea if he had heard what I'd been saying – or if I'd said it at all.

'Look.' He was staring at my retreating figure in the rear-view mirror of his mind. 'All work and no play makes Jack a dull boy – this script, the rewrites, it's been grinding me down, besides I gotta drive.' Bret got up to leave, and when he turned his back I snagged the Powerade from the next table, cracked the lid and drained it in a single heady draft, then I followed his shrinking back.

While we waited under the porte-cochère for Bret's car, I tried to revive the conversation. Where was he living? Did he get out much – socialize? The more fatuous my questions, the more his face folded in on itself, an origami of mouth tucked under ear, ear poked behind eye. Eventually I resorted to blandishment: 'Ellen DeGeneres is throwing a little party for me Friday evening at the Bar Marmont.'

'For you?'

'It's a very little party – more of a gathering, really. Anyway, if you show up that would be . . . nice.'

The parking valet leapt from behind the wheel of a big black Beamerish wagon and held the door open for Bret. I was reminded of the scene in *Swann in Love*, Volker Schlöndorff's adaptation of *A la recherche du temps perdu*, in which Odette de Crécy (played by Ornella Mutti) is dressed by her maid with a sensuousness all the more compelling for being an expression of the way nineteenth-century labour relations made of one woman's body a workhorse, and another's a commodity to be sponged clean, then boxed in its clothes.

The valet clothed Bret in his black BMW, tucking him between its steely folds and binding his breasts with a nylon band. The final touch was to lift his limp legs and insert them into the leatherette hole formed by the seat and the dash before shutting the car door with the sumptuous delicacy of someone smoothing rumpled silk. The window moaned down and I was confronted by two anxious Postlethwaites leering from the lenses of Bret's Ray-Bans.

'Y'know,' he said, 'you're not fooling anyone with this, this imposture – least of all me.' He squirmed and the car juddered into drive. 'I don't know the guy well enough to know whether you're doing a good job, but let me tell you, if you're a professional actor – and come to think of it I do vaguely recognize you – if people get wind of this you'll never work in this town again.'

The car purred forward, then moved to the right. I stared at Bret's face, which remained turned towards me, as, instead of taking the exit, he came back round the circuit to where I stood. The 180-degree revolution of the writer's head was disturbing enough, but when Bret drew level he said casually, 'See you tomorrow,' then accelerated away in a cloud of nitrogen, water vapour, hydrocarbons, nitrogen oxide, particulate matter and un-burnt fuel.

Naturally, I understood what Welles had been doing: referencing the revolutionary opening shot of *Touch of Evil*, a single continuous take over three minutes long that sent the camera tracking down the main street of a dusty border town, then plunging clear through a building in order to follow the progress of a bomb planted in the trunk of a car. If Welles-as-Bret had been the camera, it must have been me who'd swallowed the dynamite.

It certainly felt that way as I ambled poolside: the halibut had reanimated and was threshing about in my belly full of stale asparagus soup. Nothing was helped by the movie star impersonators who were sitting at the circular tables in the Tropicana bar. The pool had been decorated by David Hockney, his clever embellishment consisting of the signature blue curlicues painted on the bottom, which on his own canvases gave the impression of clear water with a rippled surface, but here suggested the blue-varnished toenail clippings of giant starlets.

I assumed the impersonators were there to re-create the first Academy Awards ceremony, held at the Roosevelt in 1929, but there were far too many Charlie Chaplins, Clara Bows, Gloria Swansons and especially Errol Flynns among the guests to make the scene remotely credible. Besides, the twenties were roaring with contemporary chatter as they downed their cocktails: Atkins's parole hearing, the election campaign, the writers' strike, Bratton and Baca's set-to over racial violence, where to buy the longest-lasting garden flares . . .

I turned my back on the haunting – I couldn't stand to look them in their other people's faces. I walked along the musty dogleg of the cabana corridor and slid my key card into its slot. I hit the lights and a filament squirmed in a goldfish bowl. Christ, what a dump! Hemispherical vinyl bolsters were tacked up the wall above the bed – which was a squared-off mound of clapshot. I sat down on it and put Postlethwaite's face in my hands. The Powerade was coming up on me, the 1929 Awards were getting louder and louder – sleep would be out of the question, and worse still it was so dark I couldn't see to read.

There's a knock on the door and when I open it a solid man-shape stinking of sweat and body paint pushes straight past me.

'Hey!' I exclaim.

'Guest services – mind if I come in?' A coarse voice sounds from head height in the drear.

'You *are* in,' I snarl; 'what the fuck d'you want?'

'Man on the desk says you gotta problem with the lights, can't see to, uh, read. The dimmer switches in these cabanas are set real low, I can fix that for you.'

'Why, thank you.'

Is my tone coquettish? I hope not. There's a clanking as of a toolbox being opened and then the chink and scratch of a screwdriver applied to a switch panel. The light wells up in the cabana and I see the screwdriver twirling in midair. The voice says, 'Say, you've got quite a build on you, you work out, do weights?'

'We-ell, not exactly.' Under the warm scrutiny of this void I feel the grotesquely magnified self-consciousness of an adolescent – and with it the lust. 'But I do a lot of, um, walking.'

'Walking, huh, you mean walking like this—' The screwdriver clatters to the rug and it's upon me, invisible hands pushing up the breathable fabric of my T-shirt, invisible thumbs circling the aureoles of my nipples, invisible fingers flicking the rapidly erecting teats. I moan, and slump back against the door to the patio, my pulse begins doubling its beat as an invisible tongue snails back and forth across my belly.

It should smell of chemical sweat percolating through a dermis abraded and abraded again, by hand, with a pumice stone, in a walk-up hotel room in West Hollywood – yet doesn't. It should feel like a violation: the fat tongue shape urging into my mouth, the grappling hook caught in my hair – yet doesn't. I sense myself levitating, I mewl and struggle – not to escape but so as to arrange for my T-shirt to twirl over my head, my belt to whip away, my pants and underwear to slide along my legs, then flip over the TV set.

The vortex sets me down on top of the minibar, where I teeter on my fundament. What would the reverse shot show in this now glaring cubicle? No perfect buns, rock hard – the hollow in each gluteus maximus so pronounced that were it horizontal it could serve as a bird bath – but my own splayed thighs, my own puckered-brown anus growing pinker as it lengthens into a gaping vagina. Men as far off as Cancún or Coventry are watching this – but they can't see this piece of beefcake, its wipeable hide, its brows knit and its jaw set with the effort of whaling into me. They can see my thighs gape still further to allow an unobstructed view, but for them there's no glistening penis writhing with veins – so why should there be one for me?

I fly, legs akimbo, from the minibar to the sink in the bathroom. Kiehl's bath products rattle in the cabinet, then tumble about my shuddering shoulders. I fly from there back to the minibar, which rocks, rolls and spews its tiny Rémy Martins, gives birth to its jars of jelly babies. Then from there – at last! – to the bed. I rise up from my knees as if on an invisible horse going at a vigorous trot. I reverse this posture and joggle on. I sink down on all fours and the cabana resounds with the crack of an invisible palm that sets first one of my buttocks then the other shivering like jellies, while my face crashes into the pillows and my hand grips one of the hemispherical vinyl bolsters.

Then I'm on my back, my labia pulsing, my clitoris vibrating. I groan and squeak – as abandoned as an abandoned chest of drawers being sawn through by a rusty saw. Still, what do I expect? Pornography is the CCTV of the Id, with its fixed camera angles that capture the dullest views of suburban bedchambers and anonymous hotel rooms. But be not censorious, we actors are not malefactors – only ordinary folk going about our fucking business. It's all perfectly workaday; and since I was never going to soar over the Hollywood Hills, then down into the Valley where the flightless birds fluttered and gobbled, they'd come to me for a turkey shoot instead.

Half the adult population of the world rasps, 'I wanna come in your mouth!' and I gasp,

'Whatever.'

Their semen is as frothy as aerated cream and as toxic-tasting as typewriter correction fluid. 'Did you get that?' I ask the gauzy crew as, up on one elbow, I unceremoniously spit it into a tooth glass.

Afterwards we are surprisingly tender with each other. I lie in the crook of his arm while he tousles the mussed hair on my forehead. He sips a Rémy Martin while I reminisce:

'I used to bunk off school – y'know, play hooky – and go to the Everyman cinema up in Hampstead. I can still remember those rainy Tuesday afternoons – it's always a rainy Tuesday afternoon in the past, isn't it?'

'Sure, David,' he says, 'that's sweet.'

'I'd be alone in the fusty little cinema, watching the screen, which wavered and distorted, hot as a furnace. I'd be lying on that blistering tarmac, with the heat beating off the cowling . . .'

'So the road, that was your thing?'

'Yeah, *Electra Glide in Blue*, *Two-Lane Blacktop*, *Vanishing Point* – I loved those movies.'

'Me too.'

'But then when I was at home it was different stuff – Continental stuff the BBC would screen late at night. I'd be crouched over the black-and-white set I had on a chair in my bedroom – it used to be my father's study and the wonky shelves were still stacked with his books on planning and government. Before that it had been my elder brother's – and his double bass was propped in the corner. All the rooms I've ever had since then have been sort of sets – trying to re-create that room.'

'I understand,' he coos.

'Sitting there late at night, staring at Giulio Brogi sitting on the abandoned station platform, looking down at the weeds struggling up through the ties and realizing – you see it only in his face – that he's never going *anywhere*, that he's doomed to remain in Tara, that he is . . . he is . . .'

'His father.'

'Right.' I twist round to look at him. 'So, you know that one?'

'Sure I do – and I did the same thing. OK, it was a colour TV and I never had a hand-me-down room, but essentially it was the same in Sherman Oaks.' His voice rumbles beneath my ear, a soothing voiceover to the smell-o-rama of cigarette smoke, brandy fumes and fast-drying sweat. 'It's strange, isn't it,' he continues. 'How even as kids we sought out unerringly those movies that told us not the truth about ourselves as we were, but about what we would become.'

'Yeah,' I weep softly. 'The truth about what we've become, which is cheats.'

'Cheats?'

'Cheats, we're lousy cheats – unfaithful to film.'

\*　　\*　　\*

243

I must have slept the same dreamless sleep I endured for all the nights I was in Los Angeles. The only visions were Hal's-eye views of the beds I thrashed about in, flickering stop-action as my grub's body mutated under the sheet, until, in the grey dawn my white wings shakily unfolded and flew me to the bathroom.

At some point during those hours he had left me, and if the thousands of frames had been scrutinized there might have been five in which he tenderly disengaged my head, sat upright, then stood, the coiled diaphragm of his underwear held in a deliberating hand, the swirl of his shirt, the door half shut.

In the morning I could only deduce the memory of his presence from forensic evidence: empty Rémy Martin miniatures, the salted slug of a used condom on the wooden floor, a pummelled lube tube on top of the minibar, a screwdriver lying on the rug.

At reception I paid my bill and the clerk handed me a stiff manila envelope: 'Several gentlemen dropped this by for you earlier this morning, Mr Smith.'

'Several?'

'Well, OK, there were five of them.'

Walking a few paces away, I slit it open; inside were the forty single-spaced pages of my position paper. In the designer dimness of the Roosevelt the dense type, studded with emoticons and interwoven with diagrams bearing labels such as, '45° where the sigmoidal flexure of TC's penis is greater than 9.7', seemed to belong to an earlier era – was this the evidence of Jesus's morganatic marriage to Mary Magdalen we had all been seeking?

With the typescript there was a compliments slip printed with the legend 'From the desk of the Chairman of the Board of the Religious Technology Center', and, handwritten on this, 'Many thanks for your interesting insights and observations.' The signature was quite like Justin Timberlake's.

'Can I arrange a car for you, Mr Smith?' called over the clerk.

I laughed towards his face – and was still laughing as I strode through the dingy lobby and hit the gilded boulevard.

# 8
# The Happy Detective

A man walks these streets alone; or, more usually, he drives. He's not an especially good man – nor is he an evil one. He understands, in the immortal words of multimillionaire Harlan Potter, that 'A newspaper is a business out to make money through advertising revenue. That is predicated on its circulation and you know what the circulation depends on.' *You* – you know that a headline in the *LA Times* announcing that a US airstrike has killed eleven Pakistani infantrymen is bound to make you scrabble for change, lift the rubbery lid, smell the refried human beings.

A man walks these streets alone – why, hasn't he got a car? Has he, like the failing screenwriter played by William Holden in *Sunset Boulevard*, had it repossessed? 'You're cutting my legs off!' Yes, I remembered now: that was what Holden-as-Gillis howled despairingly as the tow truck jounced away. No, our man walks out of choice, and walks because only on foot can he engage in the sciamachy essential to his trade: fencing with the shadows of hat brims, gun muzzles and arms flung across brickwork by the beams of the Kliegs.

A man walks these streets alone: attuned to the tyre slap and engine howl, he is content in his solitude. If a Predator drone were to come dallying overhead, dipping into the canyons, then rising up to skim the apartment blocks, he would not flinch – for he is the happy detective. The happy detective knows no angst, for he has made peace with this moment and for all eternity; he remains sublimely unaffected by the thinness of his characterization while more rounded characters bemoan their stereotypy.

The happy detective accepts that when he turns up, so do the corpses: sluttish young women, their faces beaten to bloody pulp with brass statuettes; venal old men, the third eye just below their hairlines weeping blood; an Infiniti full of gang members riddled with bullet holes.* If you ask him – and believe me, I have – whether it might be better for everyone if he stayed at home, played with his kid, bickered with his wife, he'll look at you with his doggedly honest brown eyes, suck doggily on his brown moustache, hem a little, haw a tad, before replying in accents as flat as his Midwestern home state, 'No, I don't think that. I guess . . . I guess I figure it doesn't make any difference. I mean, it could be that I'm, like, the catalyst for some of these serial killings, but with an isolated homicide there's no way I could be causing them before arriving on the scene. Lissen, what I believe is that if people are gonna get killed they're gonna get killed.'

In a lesser man such an attitude would seem sociopathic; in a greater one *foudroyant*; but the happy detective is of the middling sort, the sort who come to LA either because they've made some money and want to spend it, or because they want to exhaust some spiritual capital with breatharians, sucking up *prana* or checking out *chakra*. Not that Mac Guffin is a slacker; he works full time on the *LA Times* editing the culture section, and whatever time he has left over he dedicates to his detection. He doesn't do divorce, obviously, but he'll handle missing persons, straying dogs, industrial espionage – the cases that require legwork. And if he gets tangled up in loops of wire with razor-sharp barbs, then so much the better.

* This may be the purest form of the jump cut, the eye's saccade involuntarily following the gun barrel's pan, so seeing the same wound in metal, then flesh, then metal again.

'I'm at peace with myself,' he says. 'I've found my niche. When I was a young man I wasn't exactly searching so much as yearning for something I couldn't even identify. Nowadays it's different: I'll be crunching over broken glass down a back alley out in Alhambra, I'll see the body slumped over the wheel of a BMW, and I'll breathe deeply of the cordite and the blood and the urine, and I'll think to myself—'

'It's a wonderful world?'

'Yeah, kind of.'

I hit the gilded boulevard moving purposefully. I'd arranged to have dinner with the happy detective in Culver City; it was a short drive from Venice Beach where he lived, but a ten-mile walk for me from Hollywood. I'd have to walk back to Hollywood the following day after my meet with Michael Lynton at Sony in Culver City; still, it was inevitable that on a circumambulation such as mine, which aimed to mix business, pleasure, therapy and the solution of a major cultural murder, there would be certain . . . longueurs. It helped to think of myself as a one-man Bennet sisters, clopping through a prelapsarian Hertfordshire – its elms, beeches and lime avenues superimposed on the concrete chicane of Sunset, in the same way that a 120-foot-high Jennifer Aniston was plastered across the façade of the Hyatt – and naturally, if when I arrived at Netherfield Park I had so much as a sniffle I would be compelled to put up there for weeks, wrestling with marriage proposals and the foxed endpapers of my family bible.

Along the Strip the Jeffs beamed down in front of me looking utilitarian in their baseball caps and denim shirts. Sound Jeff taped the mike to my chest while I looked away to the tattered copra that had been wind-whittled from the palms, a torn Detour candy bar wrapper, a Häagen-Dazs coffee and almond crunch box, a roasted peanut crunch wrapper and the paper napkin that had been used to wipe the eating-disordered mouth before being discarded in the gutter with all the rest. It all spoke to me – and I spoke of it – as evidence of an uncertain narrative trajectory. It was all very well suspending disbelief in the road movie of LA, but sooner or later you had to question where it might be taking you.

No one had expressed this better than L. Ron, whose Association for Better Living and Education (ABLE) I had passed shortly after leaving the Roosevelt. His sometime friend, colleague and early champion of Dianetics, A. E. Van Vogt, said of Hubbard: '(He) wrote about a million words a year . . . I have seen typists working at that speed, but never a writer.' No wonder he could maintain such resolute narrative headway, his plots moving forward like the starship *Hound of Heaven*, which, crossing the galaxy at the speed of light, exiles its crew by the passage of time, as back on earth whole generations and societies vanish for ever.

In the introduction to his final and most monumental exercise in 'pure' science fiction, *Battlefield Earth: A Saga of the Year 3000*, L. Ron reprised his own career as a genre typist, relating how he had been brought in by the publishers of John Campbell's *Astounding Stories* to inject a little humanity into these tales of futuristic hardware, because '[I] could write about real people.'

Well, I could write about real people just as well – real people like my old buddy Morgan Freeman, who, together with smouldering, stick-thin Angelina Jolie (rub up against her and you might catch fire!), was starring in *Wanted*, a thriller about a secret Illuminati of assassins, the billboard for which stood proud of the Viper Room. On our walk out to Uxbridge, Morgan had told me enough about the movie for me to feel that I'd seen it already: 'There's a neat CGI effect,' he said, 'that makes the air appear like kinda limpid water – it happens whenever we're fighting each other, and then if we fire a gun we can warp the trajectory of the bullet.'

The air that morning, 12 June 2008, seemed like limpid water, and Camera Jeff's lens a muzzle from which a bullet curled – was it the brutal, Powerade-fuelled congress in the cabana at the Roosevelt that made me feel as I had on those wet Tuesdays, when, emerging from the coruscation of the Californian highway into the familiar artificial twilight of a London night, I discovered that it wasn't familiar any more, but strangely exciting – charged?

Surely it was this feeling, rather than the movies themselves, that so entranced career film critics? Because, let's face it, there are only so many times any sane person can expose themselves to such hokum before they begin soundlessly lip-synching to the giant mouths on the screen, or running a chipped nail over the dead skin of the lips transfixed in the seat beside them. Bad rhyming quitting the Classic, leaving the Everyman, hitting the gilded boulevard, accompanied by some torpid fiddling about on the G string of a cello that suggests a troubled sexual repletion . . . The alternative – that critics retained the childlike ability to identify so closely with the sassily imperturbable Fox (Jolie) that they left their own foetuses reposing in red plush, to float up the tractor beam then dive through the screen and penetrate her drum-tight belly – was too awful for me to contemplate. It implied a relationship between critic and star analogous to that of Thetans and those genetic entities they had entered, millions of years in the past, long before they

250

crawled from the primordial slime and became critics in their own right.

Either way, they were all wankers – an English term of general disapprobation drawn from the masturbatory that, to my way of thinking, has far greater resonance than the American 'jerk-offs'. Sexual wankers, cultural wankers and – an Australian coinage this – *time* wankers, beating off their lives in the darkness while without the world goes on, a two-reeler, hand-cranked at an unrealistic speed, so that whole societies arise, then vanish forever, leaving behind only the dust of their own prematurely ejaculated *geist*. The money shot – again.

Wankers, and far more voyeuristic than honest subscribers to pornography, whose pay-perpreciation of the warped trajectory of a penis entering a vagina or an anus takes on the rarefied aestheticism of a Ruskin when set beside such gross satisfaction: piggy little eyes screwed up against the light, envaginating the madonnas on the hu-uge iconostasis over and over and over again. Is there any limit to the capacity of cineastes to be absorbed into these folds and curves of photons? They write their reviews, they expand these into essays, monographs and eventually entire books anatomizing their goddesses and gods. A chapter on their cheekbones, another on their clavicles, lengthy footnotes on the spaces in between their toes, because of the mind of the goddess – her ideas, her thoughts and feelings – there is precisely nothing to be said.

As I trudged on, my own warped trajectory brought me to the border between Hollywood and Beverly Hills. The limpid water grew thinner and bluer as the sunlight gained in intensity. The grass along the verges was dense enough for any colt to crop. At the junction with Doheny Drive I spared a thought for Bret: was he up there in his ritzy apartment hosing off the crusts of last night's fun? Was he wearily contemplating another day in the word mine, chipping away at the computer to expose veins of terse couplets?

Ray: Well, yeah, uh, I guess.

Phil: Later on, OK?

Or perhaps plotting a silken road through cyberspace to the pharmaceutical kampongs of the Far East, where brilliantly hued mounds of OxyContin, Halcion and Paxil sprawled on the ratscuttle floors, their silica slopes illuminated by the rays of light that shot through the perforations in the corrugated-iron roofs high overhead?

I well remembered the last time I had visited the pharmacy on the South Lambeth Road to fill my prescriptions for Seroxat, Dutonin and Carbamazepin, the feijoada complexion of the Portuguese assistant, in the fatty mass of which swam morsels of acne. She had looked at me – quite reasonably – as if I were mad. Busner had prescribed the Seroxat for depression and the Dutonin because of my volatile reaction to what itself was intended as a dopamine governor. Then there was the Carbamazepin, a further tranquilizer necessitated by my restless spirit. I understood why, because left to my own devices I had a way of cabbing into the West End, scoring on the street, overdosing in the alley off D'Arblay Street, then beating off the paramedics who were reviving me, only to be found hours later wandering over Vauxhall Bridge, with the crotch of my jeans torn out and my jaw half dislocated, as if in the intervening period I had been practising enthusiastic *soixante-neuf* with a werewolf. American, natch, who, after his lectures at Richmond College – where his folks have paid for a summer semester – cruises the Soho bars sporting a charmingly recherché sleeveless anorak. Or gilet.

Standing beside the rack of plug adaptors, zip-up neoprene pouches and personal grooming tools, under the watchful eyes of a plaster Alsatian on a top shelf, I could feel the sine waves plotting the metabolic half-lives of these drugs tangle in my cortex, and in that moment I decided that a life in which happiness was mixed up like a mental cocktail was no kind of life at all. So I paid the assistant, took the plastic bag of meds home, tied a knot in the handle and chucked it up on to the top shelf in my study, where it lay for years, beside the yellowing typescript of my grandfather's doctoral thesis 'The Divine Indwelling'. This was his attempt to reconcile the then (1960) modish Existentialism with Eastern religion,

Christianity and science. My father, who viewed his own failure to find a publisher for this weird synthesis as a betrayal of his patrimony, once asked me shortly before he himself died what I thought of 'The Indwelling'. I confessed that after attempting a few pages I had come to the conclusion that Grandad – a notorious autodidact who studied for seven ordinary degrees while commuting to London each day on the Brighton Belle – 'had suffered for his learning – and now it's our turn'.

'What've you done with Pete Postlethwaite?'

Camera Jeff, Sound Jeff and Gofer Jeff were standing round me in a menacing semicircle on the verge beside the Will Rogers Memorial Park. On the far side of Sunset Boulevard, the Beverly Hills Hotel was flanked by three-storey palms. In there, I imagined, execs were strong-arming deals; out here there was an intervention going on.

'What've you done with him?' reiterated Camera Jeff, the Fletcher Christian of this mutinous crew.

'We're working on this together,' I said, looking down at my Rockports nuzzling in the clover-dense grass.

'Lissen, I was prepared to shoot some footage of you when we picked you up on the Strip where we'd arranged to meet Pete, but enough's enough.'

'Enough's enough? What the fuck—'

'Yeah, enough's enough. You may think you're a player in this town, while we're nobodies, but this is . . . this is—'

'Bullshit!' Sound Jeff pushed his angry red face forward.

'Fuckin' A!' Gofer Jeff was dancing on the spot.

'OK, OK, cool it you guys.' Camera Jeff patted them down. 'Mr Thewlis, we don't want to alienate you.'

'No, right,' I laughed sarcastically. 'Because you want to get paid, don't you.'

A note of pity entered Camera Jeff's voice, 'Actually, that's not an issue here – we were paid in full in advance by Mr Postlethwaite's agent – a Mr Self?'

'The name means nothing to me,' I lied.

'Anyway, this isn't about money, it's about our professional integrity.'

'Excuse me?'

'Pete said this was going to be an experimental film – a subversive take on Hollywood consisting of a continuous take of him walking round Los Angeles for a week. From the get-go we told him it wouldn't add up to anything, but he insisted we trail him all the way from LAX Downtown, then from there to Hollywood. I didn't know what to expect from him – I mean, I'd seen some of his work, but in the flesh he was, well, skittish.'

'Skittish? You mean like "houynhmnhmnhmn"!' I bared my yellow teeth and pranced on the verge. Camera Jeff chose to ignore this.

'That's right, skittish – ordering us about, then, when we miked him up he began talking this—'

'Unbelievable bullshit!' Sound Jeff bellowed. 'I've had to listen to this crap for two days now!'

'I don't think that's exactly nuanced, Jeff,' said Camera Jeff. 'I've listened to some of the recordings and it sounded to me as if Pete is having some kind of breakdown. Then this morning you turned up instead of him but wearing the same clothes and behaving as if nothing out of the ordinary is happening – I'm gonna ask you one more time: where's Pete? Is he back at the Roosevelt? We're worried about him.'

I thought: the traffic, it's always building up, silica grains flowing into mounds dammed by stop lights. What were roads anyway? Only pipelines of exasperation pressurized by time. Crown Victoria nosed Taurus, Taurus rimmed Corolla, Corolla went down on Tahoe. Between the snout of a Fusion and the butt of an Equinox I saw long-dead dreamer Richard Brautigan sporting a headband and shades, his big pack dragging on his shoulders as he wove towards Hollywood.

'Let me get this straight.' I stepped into Camera Jeff's banally furnished personal space. 'Are we splitting up over artistic differences?'

Someone, I thought, ought to be filming this: I needed a reverse shot, so I could see my wispy moustache bristle. I needed Dolby surround sound so I could hear myself shouting: 'I don't need this shit! I hired you fuckers and I can fire you too! You're off this goddamn picture – off it, d'you hear?! Pick up your gear, bubba, and *walk!*'

But it was me who did the walking, after I'd torn off the mike, then ripped the power pack from my belt and slapped it into Sound Jeff's pudgy hand. They stood there bemused while I strode around the bougainvillea beds and away down Beverly Drive. I considered shouting back at them: 'You'll never work in this town again!', but the line can be overused, don't you think?

Carlos and Simon had made their mark on one of the birches lining Beverly Drive. Other Okies had taken time out to play noughts and crosses or score prick 'n' balls pictograms. Soon enough my angry exhilaration subsided into the tangerine dream of *première classe* suburbia, where Latinos made with the flagstones and nobody's escutcheon leant against a portico –

and the sky, the sky was no longer limpid water, only a steadily dilating Playboy bunny's hole lined with shelves upon which were stacked iPod Nanos and player-piano rolls, Box Brownies and HD video cameras, search engines and difference engines. Tipping back my head, I could see that this warm void was aching for Sergey Brin's re-entry, as he splashed back down into Marina del Rey after his midweek break at the International Space Station. What – what would he find to google at, now that whole generations and societies had passed for ever: only a savage sitting on the dock of the bay scratching a prick 'n' balls pictogram into its concrete. Under this the legend: DO NO EVIL.

I had my own small digital camera, and if I sensed the Hals clustering, or a wildcat crew creeping up on me, I could always whip it out and start filming myself, much as a boy wizard wields an invisibility cloak. The only problem I faced was the one of any ham alone in the age of technological reproducibility: who was looking at the me looking at me? Even Sergey hurtling earthwards in his steam-punk Soyuz capsule still had a back-projection of blue chiffon sky framed by the triangular porthole – this, a technique essentially unaltered since *Sunset Boulevard*, when the cops in the pursuit car stared intensely out at us, while behind them a second film of the unspooling roadway did for the *trompe l'œil*.

This then is the whole equation

projector → audience (screen) → cops driving (rear window) → Sunset Boulevard receding = reality

that, F. Scott Fitzgerald's stand-in asserted, 'Not half a dozen men have been able to keep . . . in their heads.' It was nothing to do with the residuals for *Dharma & Greg*, and, believe me, I felt brittle just containing it in my nut, and wondered as I footed down Carmelita Drive whether it might make sense to hole up in the Spadena House. No one would look for me in this symbolic assemblage of witchy elements: burnt-toast eaves, spangly windowpanes, roughed-up plaster and a toad spawn chimney stack. The little homestead of horror had originally been built as a novelty office for the Culver City Movie Company, and only latterly rolled up into Beverly Hills on a truck. I could lie low – the house would recede on a low-loader. Like Donald Crowhurst when he abandoned the 1968/9 round-the-world solo yacht race, I would fake a diary of my own circumambulation, while in a parallel notebook I frantically operated on the equation, multiplying its terms until the warped rooms were cluttered with screens and retrospectives.

There was no smoking in Beverly Hills Park. Kitted out as a bum, the Nobel Laureate Derek Walcott sat slumped in an abandoned office chair in the empty pergola – there was a beer bottle, queerly limp, drooping from his hand to his inner thigh. I crossed the road and holed up in the Coffee Café for a sandwich, observing the anthropophagi that patrolled the sidewalk in their Palomino-skin cowboy boots, the bands of jewelled denim between their hips taut as bowstrings.

For a less doughty voyager, departing the island of affluence lying between Santa Monica Boulevard, Wilshire and Rexford might have been dispiriting – yet I felt carefree, reknotting my shoelaces, reefing the strap of my backpack and stepping out with the wind behind me. It's only those who have no experience of round-the-conurbation walking who imagine suburbia as an unvarying ocean of roof peaks and garden troughs; no, here is the great individualism Americans justly pride themselves on, with each property distinguished from its neighbour: Spanish Mission instead of Neogothic, japonica in place of bougainvillea, TruGuard rather than Mercian security.

From the ridge at Pico I could see the whole dish full of smog spread out beneath me, from which popped the up-plummeting bodies of trampolining children and the inverted mop-tops of truffula trees. For a moment I hesitated – might it be an idea to set a course through the Hillcrest Country Club? I could join a lost tribe of rich Jews and wander that landscaped Sinai for . . . years. But no, I had a rendezvous with Tamisa the crossing guard, who sat in regal splendour at the junction of Beverwil and Cashio on her throne of puddled fat. 'You've gotta get offa your backside,' she told me without a smidgeon of irony. Then reassume it, I thought, part time at twelve bucks an hour.

Quite suddenly I was standing in a grocery store at Hughes Avenue buying a can of Kobe energy drink and chatting to the sales assistant, who was from Bhutan. He was unimpressed by my voyage: 'I run a trekking business in my own country,' he told me. 'Also, I am a mountaineer.'

Outside I looked up at the frozen wang of the Santa Monica Freeway and thought better of it – so poured the drink away on to the asphalt. It wouldn't do to arrive all fired up. I spat my tasteless cud of nicotine gum into my palm and was appalled to see that my jaws had expertly worried it into a perfect little voodoo doll of Orson Welles, complete with cloak and wide-brimmed hat. I shuddered, remembering the micro-manipulation of Hagop Sandaldjian, and, last fall, Sherman flung naked across the high bed – then Willy Town Mouse scuttled into the cheesy wedge of the Culver Hotel.

Which wasn't so bad – there was a high staff turnover and no one remembered me. I was given a room on the third floor with a dinky four-poster garrotted by swathes of muslin. The shower's low pressure felt historically accurate, then I sat drying off in a wing armchair looking out through breeze-buffeted net curtains at the balding Baldwin Hills, with their oil pumps rising and falling like failing hair implants. I had come almost full circle, and might reasonably have gone on to LAX and flown home to London. After all, no one else had turned up dead – yet.

Instead I phoned and in the gap between 'Hello' and 'How are you?' heard the low moan of eight lost hours and the dumb percussion of falling marbles. I wanted to ask about the crime scene tape – was it still there? But she hardly ever left the house – except by Packard; while the children – who would've known – were out at casting calls. So we said our goodbyes and hung up, and in the seconds after the marriage of the plastic I felt as if, far from having communicated, we had only defined the vast compass of the incommunicable.

Guffin was waiting for me at a table outside Ford's Filling Station, a self-styled 'American gastro-pub' on Culver Boulevard, whose 'executive chef' was none other than Ben Ford, Harrison's son from his first marriage. I nodded to Mac and for a while we sat silently in an establishing shot, absorbing the drivel on the menu: Ford's culinary philosophy was much influenced by the French slow-food movement, which favoured authentic locally sourced ingredients, simple preparation, blah-blah-bleurgh! It wasn't a philosophy that extended to the establishment's décor, with its gas station logo implying that *esturgeon confit* was another type of high-octane fuel.

The happy detective was being played by himself – he'd even grown his own trademark brown moustache for the role. It was a relief, of course, because I never knew before I actually saw someone who would be impersonating them, and even then if it was a good method actor it could still take a while to identify which one. As for me, Mac didn't seem to care who had the part, only remarking, 'You look well, man,' before moving straight to business: 'So, you've got a case for me?'

I filled him in on the conflagration at Pinewood and my escape with the quadrumanous cartoon dog. Then there was the episode on Century, and my discovery of the adulteration taking place at the Coca-Cola Bottling Plant. I alluded to the car fight at the La Brea Tar Pits, but didn't go into too much detail, then went over the horrific riot outside Grauman's so exhaustively that by the time I'd finished we were both staring down at matching *tartes tatin*. Of anything to do with Thetans I said nothing – this was a litigious town, and then there were the Scientologists.

I suppose we must have had Ipswich clam rolls and polenta cakes but saving Mr Ford's finer feelings it was all plaster casts to me – prop food that had me gulping down glass after glass of water, then calling the waiter to get more. The unemployed actor could barely conceal his annoyance, and every time he plonked down the flask he grunted like a woman tennis pro serving an ace.

Mac sucked his moustache and tousled his own hair. 'You're racking up enemies with your behaviour, man,' he said, as weary as a walrus. 'You got any protection?'

I explained about the Jeffs.

'You're screwing up big time, aren'tcha.'

'I'm sorry?'

'Well, if you're right and the movies were murdered – not just accidentally killed – then you're a real slow-moving target. Personally, I think your initial strategy was the right one – be filmed or get drilled. Now how're you gonna keep safe?'

'Tomorrow morning I'm going right into the heart of the machine.' I stabbed a finger towards the Sony lot. 'It's the last place anyone will think of shooting me.'

'And then?'

'That's where you come in. Listen.' I dropped my voice conspiratorially and, leaning towards him, took a forkful of his *tarte*.

'Hey!' Mac was outraged, and struck out at my fork with his own. We began fencing with the cutlery, until the waiter broke it up. 'You were saying?' Mac asked, picking bits of caramelized apple off the lapels of his corduroy sports jacket.

'I can't keep track of all the leads – that's the trouble with a victim that's a representational medium –'

'You say that, but everyone knows who murdered portrait painting – the camera, right?'

'Right, but portraits in oils were slow fucking food, man, one frame, hanging around on walls – they had it coming. The movies are something else – sixteen, twenty-two frames every second; for over a century they sopped up the world like a celluloid sponge, they saw everything – they depicted everyone. Sometimes they mocked up real events; other times those events were staged for them. As for the actors – they played characters based on real people; real people played themselves – or else made-up characters. That's too many linkages, Mac, too many suspects. Have you seen the titles at the end of an average Hollywood movie nowadays, there's thousands of the—'

An old homeless man, who had been standing watching us from the far side of the waist-high canvas partition penning off the patrons from the sidewalk, now approached, his hand outstretched. I looked at its dirty and cracked nails – there was an open sore on the leathery palm. 'Please,' the poor fellow croaked. 'Please, gennlemen, I only need a few cents to get a sammich. I'd be obliged.'

He bore an uncanny resemblance to the Indian-born British novelist Sir Salman Rushdie, what with his straggling grey beard and dishevelled pride, so I dropped a few coins into his hand, then said, 'But tell me one thing.'

'Yes?'

'How come you're begging – I would've thought that with your sales you'd be set up for life.'

'Oh, yeah, sales.' He shrugged philosophically. 'It's true, the books sell well enough but that's chickenfeed; the real money is in movies, and they option stuff and option it again – then they drag me out here for meetings with execs and like a sap I come. Then nuthin' happens – nuthin' at all.'

He shuffled away disconsolately, and turning back to Guffin I deftly changed the subject: 'So, Calista Flockhart, her cunt's still wedding-fresh, right?'

The happy detective spat a chunk of pastry on to the table, while all around us the baboon diners rose to their bandy legs.

'Ferchrissakes,' Mac said, recovering himself, 'd'you wanna get us lynched, or what?'

'I was only asking – I'm sure it's a question that's on everyone's lips.'

'Maybe, but they kinda slurp it back down.'

The baboons were settling back down as well, their muzzles dropped to their arugula. We sat in silence for a while.

'I dunno,' he resumed eventually. 'I'm not sure I want to take this one on – we've got troubles of our own down at the *Times*.'

'Your man Zell?'

'The word is we're looking down the barrel of a gun.'

'And people are going to get fired?'

'Absolutely – and you wanna know why? It's the same as your movie case: the readership can't suspend disbelief in newsprint any more, it's just dead meaning swatted on the page to them. They want something that lights up, scrolls down, they want inset full-motion videos and pop-up—'

'Idents.'

'Right.'

Dusk was fingering along Culver Boulevard, together with the traffic and the No. 11 Nocturne played with a jazz twist. There was a lazy intimacy to the scene – they didn't call Mac the happy detective for no reason; whatever his own problems – and he had them – he always succeeded in infusing any scene with a comfortable tannin vibe, ironic considering that when:

'You turn up people get dead – now don't they?'

He wasn't taken aback. 'So that's how it is, is it, you've got a third act problem.'

'I guess.'

'So you think: bring in Mac and the body count'll rise.'

'Something like that had occurred to me.' I took out a miniature Effie Perrine and she took out a miniature bag of Bull Durham and fiddled a cigarette into tubular existence. 'Anyway,' I resumed, 'what's your scruple? You say people're gonna get dead anyway, leastways in my scenario they get dead in the service of a decent cause – finding out who clipped the most beautifulest narrative medium the goddamn world has ever seen!'

He stood up and, pulling a rawhide wallet from his pocket, dealt a couple of twenties on to the table. 'You're fucked up, Will,' he said conversationally. 'I don't believe you give a damn who killed the movies.'

'Frankly?'

'Yeah, *frankly*. In fact, I wouldn't be surprised if it turned out you'd killed them yourself in some guarana-fuelled blackout.'

'That's harsh.'

'You think so? Well, try this on: you were a spotty brat jerking off over Ornella Mutti in the London burbs. Then you grew up and began writing your dismal fucking tales – a depressive's exercise in wish fulfilment: slash your wrists and the world slashes with you. Against all the odds you got successful enough to come out here – and whaddya find? An industry that doesn't give a damn about you, 'cause you're a cheapie, a peanut grafter, you're so goddamn small no one could even focus on you—'

'OK, OK.'

'That's not all, man, 'cause after all there's thousands like you in this town but you're different: you've got the motivation. The movies may've rejected you, but then you go and fall in love with Angel herself.'

'You believe this?'

'I've read your stuff, man, it's a fucking love letter to LA, all about how she's been betrayed by the movies, how they eyed her up, used her, then cut her up into so many pieces nobody can put her back together again – no one, that is, except you. That's what this walking tour is really about – you aren't looking for who killed the movies, you're trying to get your skinny shanks inside LA's hot haunches!'

As parting shots go it was a good one, and although he wasn't a fellow given to melodrama Mac made his exit, strolling off the Filling Station's apron and sauntering away along the boulevard.

I called after him: 'But you'll still do my legwork for me, won't you?'

He turned back. 'Oh, I dunno, man, I dunno.'

'Just check a few things out, be a friend to the cause.' He ambled back, and I whispered, 'But don't call me, it's not safe.'

'What, then?'

'Ellen DeGeneres is throwing a little party for me tomorrow evening at the Bar Marmont.'

'For you?'

'It's a very little party – more of a gathering, really. Anyway, if you show up we can talk after.'

'You better have some cash for me. Two hundred – plus whatever expenses I've incurred.'

'Naturally.'

'But don't get your hopes up, my friend, and remember: client privilege don't buy you no protection – this is a helluva tough town.'

'I know that.'

But did I, really? The elevator gate closed in a monogamous marriage of old metal, and the Culver Hotel seemed quiet enough – yet was there perhaps a trill of dwarfish laughter from the end of the corridor? What eerie visions would trouble me as I turned and turned again in my rental four-poster? Judy Garland going down on the Tin Man, her carmine lips sliding lubriciously over his steely rod, then rearing up, green oil dripping from her sharp little chin? The money shot – again.

266

When I eventually made it into my room the message light was winking: Busner had rung while I was at dinner. 'I do hope you're having a good time.' His recorded voice was far more immediate that his spoken one. 'And that you've remembered what I said . . . about avoiding the noirish.'

To my surprise I slept soundly and blankly, awakening to the Dolby hiss of another day. I ate bacon and eggs in the foyer, then, after returning to my room, expeditiously shat. I was a man with an appointment.

# 9
## The Pitch

Way back in the beeswax-scented past, Arnold Schoenberg had woken one fine morning, and, in the last heady rush of his Romanticism, decided that it would be a good idea to pen some music for exactly these sorts of comings and goings, small swoops and glissandos of strings that with uncanny prescience suggested the yaw of Escalades as they swung off the boulevard, the reeling down of tinted windows, the reeling up of tinted windows, the red-and-white-striped baton flung high to conduct them on to the Sony Pictures lot.

I dogged along behind, then picked my way between acacias and eucalyptuses towards a Palladian façade, the pediment of which was lettered IRVING THALBERG BUILDING in Art Deco bronze. There was a copper stoup bolted to the wall beside the doors. Assuming that the liquid in this must be the tears of stars delivering Oscar acceptance speeches, carefully captured in vials by their personal assistants, then deposited here at the behest of the studio, I dipped my fingers, genuflected, then went inside.

In the foyer there was a reception module womaned by central casting, and mirror-backed cabinets lined with Oscar statuettes, the tragic masks of BAFTAs, and some other awards I didn't recognize but that were symbolized by figurines of Pan sporting what looked like Stetsons.

Having been announced, I travelled along a sunlit corridor, my nape hairs erect in anticipation of the smack of a bullet. To either side open doors revealed sets of offices expertly arrayed with exactly the kind of desks, framed movie posters, filing cabinets and waggle-on-their-springs desk mascots that you would've expected. In front of the desks, tipped back in their swivel chairs, were minor players played by minor actors. Discreetly, quietly, they made marks in the margins of scripts, or else, ear-muffed by surround sound, watched product on their computer screens.

Upstairs, unity of production design, which in the movies makes of the entire world an opulent suburban home, was spectacularly in evidence. On Michael Lynton's set high, narrow windows leaked daylight between drapes of taupe crushed satin; the floor was rough-adzed boards; a Columbia icon hefted a torch on the wall; a white orchid sat on a glass table surrounded by steel-framed chairs. There were two conversation areas: one had sofas, covered in creamy fabric patterned with black coral polyps, grouped around a hardwood coffee table; the other involved mushroom leatherette club chairs menacing a discoid of white-veined marble. Somewhere in the beeswax-scented present Lynton was on a call. Nearer, in the antechamber, his secretary was finishing one. 'Love you guys,' floated through.

I sat waiting on the polyps – yet felt no discomfort. This was the Zoloft of interiors. Lynton made an entrance at the back of the open plan: he was wearing plain black shoes, grey trousers with a light check, a subdued and striped blue shirt. He had the lean, dark expressive good looks of the younger De Niro. His hand, when it shook my paw, was cool and beautifully manicured.

'So,' he said, 'you walked here, is that right?'

I admitted this was the case.

'Any particular reason?'

We sat down behind our palisades of sharp knees and the tea arrived. I gave him my spiel: how walking was the least filmic possible way of travelling, while Los Angeles was the most filmed location. I told him that I suspected that the movies were waning as the dominant cultural discourse of our era, and that this seemed the easiest way of gaining entrance to such a labyrinthine subject . . . I left out the stuff about the murder, the fugues I experienced after drinking Powerade, and the fact that he himself was in the frame. Despite these cuts Lynton still seemed engaged and when I finished – as if to season his shoulders – he shook his lightly pepper-and-salted coif and said:

'Oh, I thought you'd come to make a pitch.'

I was momentarily dumfounded, and my mind laboured through the possible permutations: I was Thewlis, I was Postlethwaite – he was De Niro, and had done the decent thing with the mole.

'No, really,' I said, recovering myself, 'I was simply interested in your take on all this; after all, here we are in the Thalberg Building, while you, I suppose, are the closest thing to a contemporary mogul.'

He smiled self-deprecatingly. 'Maybe, but in many ways I agree with you: the wow effect *has* gone from the movies – the wow effect and a certain degree of social relevance. By the way,' he said abruptly, 'I heard you were on the set at Pinewood.' I sat looking bemused, and he pressed: '*Quantum of Solace?*'

'Well, uh, yeah – I did stop by.'

*The masterful brushwork of exploding petrol, the Wagnerian curtain of roaring flame, the koi for sale from the bungalow . . . How much did he know about Scoobert?*

'A difficult shoot,' he continued conversationally. 'I heard Dan Craig sliced his fingertip off on the last day.'

*This must be some kind of code.* 'Um, yup, I heard there'd been a couple of . . . accidents.'

'Well,' De Niro said, 'this is this.' Then he continued his discursive remarks on the state of the industry, animadverting on counter-programming, *Made of Honor*, budgetary constraints, spring-versus-fall release dates, the threat of SAG industrial action – I mimed taking notes. What seemed to exercise him the most was the advent of PVRs: 'In the seventies there were maybe sixty or seventy movies released a year – now it's four hundred. If we want to get people into the multiplexes we have to focus our big TV advertising on the weekend before release, but now, well, if they skip the ads . . .'

His hand tensing, De Niro pinched the insinuation between his thumb and forefinger: this infinitesimal wilfulness had killed the movies; like participants in a perverse psychological experiment, encouraged to administer electric shocks to actors playing guinea pigs, the public had demonstrated that their empathy went no further than their own fingertips.

I must have been making the right kind of grunts – good enough for him to keep talking. Yes, he himself admired most the era of *The Deer Hunter*, *Platoon* and *The China Syndrome* – movies that minded the gap between social relevance and commercial success; but, while times may've changed, the movies still had a role. What about motion-capture and CGI? Well, the bar kept getting raised; Bob Zemeckis's *Beowulf* had showed the way: a new generation of 3-D was coming, I'd soon find out about *that*.

He stood, and I rose up into that lovely hand-job: his was firm and dry, mine limp and clammy.

'Relevance,' Lynton said, 'that's the key word.'

'Listen.' I hung on to his fingered thing long beyond the socially prescribed time. 'I do want to make a pitch: one of my therapists back in London – a guy called Shiva Mukti – he's making these films of his schizophrenic and bipolar patients during their flamboyant phases – you know the kind of thing, whirling their arms like copter blades, trying to claw the transmitters from their foreheads – then when they've calmed down he shows them what it looked like. You see, the biggest problem with these guys is that they can't accept how crazy they get if they don't take their medication – obviously the whole thing is done with their consent.' I laughed, in such a way, I hoped, as to imply that anything else would be deeply unethical – unfortunately all that emerged was a horsey lip-fart. 'But the thing is you here in Hollywood are doing the same thing on a massive scale and without anyone's consent. I mean, tell me I'm wrong, but what are these car-crushing beasts, these shape-shifting chimeras, these liquid buildings and this solid air, if not the death-ray projections of our own unfettered Ids?' Tiny beads of my spittle jewelled the luxuriant chest hair in the V of his open-necked shirt. 'Don't get me wrong,' I cantered on, 'I *approve* of this, I think humanity needs to be told to take its medication – I just think it should be done with more conviction and greater artistry. I think everyone leaving the theatre – whether in Des Moines or Dubai – should understand the magical significance of the number of footsteps it takes them to cross the foyer, should believe the voiceover telling them what to do with the knives when . . . they get home . . .'

'Great.' He released my hand. 'It's been great talking with you, and I'm glad we understand each other so well.'

I had reached the outer office when Lynton called after me: 'By the way, if you'd like to take a walk around the studio while you're here that'll be fine. I'm afraid we aren't actually shooting anything today but it's still worth a look.'

We did indeed understand each other – he had blown my cover and granted me temporary sanctuary at the same time: I would be safe at Sony. I thanked him and turned to leave.

'Bye, Pete,' Lynton called.

'Goodbye, Mr Postlethwaite,' his secretary echoed. 'And, by the way' – she made the usual moue – 'I hope you don't mind me saying it, but I loved you in *Dinotopia*.'

I walked down Main Street, passing neon signs for bowling alleys, a piano bar, the Continental Hotel. This was no torn children's book, the fragments dancing in an open fire – nor was it the Sargasso of the imagination where all the dreams ever dreamt are becalmed. No doubt somewhere in the cool, humming interiors of the sound stages, animatronic ducks were dancing in front of a blue screen, but out here there was only a carpenter lifting paint pots from a golf cart, and the open doors to a cavernous prop warehouse.

I paused, rubbing my eyes, hearing them squelch: a Spiderman caught in the web of the present. On three-storey shelves sat the *things*, the great material substratum of the enacted, its TVs and washing machines, magazine racks and rugs, bottles of Powerade and bathroom mats, telephones and coat trees, brass statuettes and Barcaloungers, pool toys and vibrators, the neurofibrillary tangles and Bronze Age funerary gifts of a culture crazed by its own capacity for replication. Even a cursory examination was enough to tell me that this hangar possessed its own stratigraphy; that the stuff of Now reposed on the highest shelves, up near the roof, while at ground level I was staring at the fox-fur stoles, Victrolas and aspidistra pots of the era when the movies had only just begun. As I looked on, a forklift truck pulled into the stores and shovelled up a henge of ancient beige plastic computing equipment. No doubt soon enough it would be shot; and then, chained to their seats in the caves of illusion, the prisoners would watch the shadows of these things cast upon the wall. So that when they arose they might go back to the plaster and plywood of their own lives, bite down on the sawdust.

Beyond the main gates Los Angeles was waiting, her hot legs spread – and I entered them, devoutly. In the Hayden Tract, a phantasmagoria of Sci-Arc buildings with broken bone girders, staircases to nowhere and oriel windows bursting like buboes, I found a café where I could sit outside. I smoked, drank tea and finished Bret's *Lunar Park*. There was room in the novel for Harrison Ford to have a walk-on part – he, who had himself once been a set carpenter, hammering away on the hulks becalmed in the Sargasso of the imagination. I left the book lying on the table – what did narrative have going for it anyway – only smelting kryptonite out of coincidence so as to trap us superheroes in the mundane.

Out here, by rights, I should have feared the zephyrs uncoiling from the brows of the Baldwin Hills – but instead I hitched up my pants and made for La Cienega; it – not they – would carry me the six miles north, back to Hollywood.

\*    \*    \*

'Surfer frat boys – that's all I can think about.'

'And you're telling me he didn't have a place to live?'

'Yeah, but he was sooo cute, but crazy – when I first started dating him he admitted it.'

'It?'

'That he'd set the fire himself – the one he received the, uh, commendation for.'

I couldn't prevent myself from eavesdropping: did she really say 'surfer frat boys'? Or from looking from the sheepskin seams of her lambbag to her charm bracelet to her anorexic bangs. Her companion was just a hair head – to me.

I'd regained consciousness in a booth in a McDonald's, and, judging by my small pot of soda and skimpy burger, I'd only popped in to use the restroom. It wasn't until I was back out in the street, striding through the tinted air, that it occurred to me to offer her this factoid: her lover was not alone. It's been estimated that 20 per cent of all fires are set by the LAFD itself – acts of daring professional closure that could only make psychiatrists gasp in admiration as they drove their patients insane with neuropharmacology.

It wasn't until I was back out on Cienega that I realized where I was: around the junction with Olympic. And this . . . this too needed to be noted: that every time Marlowe or Archer got sapped, then came to with a line of inconsequential dialogue in his ears *surfer frat boys* . . . it was a metaphor for Los Angeles's sprawl, as its long lean boulevards stretched out from the rumpled bed. Too much trouble to describe all those Hummers with their wobble-board doors bass vibrating, too much effort to block in those body shops and dental technicians, the stench of a gas station and the street persons, who, skin like bacon rind, were frying today as the smog blew away. *Keep on walking* . . . Johnnie Walker, dapper in top hat and frock coat, his boots shined, his monocle screwed into his eye, strode out towards Hollywood, yet never arrived, pinned as he was like a butterfly to the billboard.

I came to again in a bungalow at the Chateau Marmont, getting ready for the party being given in my honour. (Well, not so much a party – that implies an importance I wouldn't wish for a second to arrogate to myself; more of a gathering, really.) I was still thinking about the burning of Los Angeles and waiting for Faye to get back – it was that kind of bungalow. Naked, fresh from the shower, I wandered from the small bedroom, icy with state-of-tech TV and music system, to the kitchen, which, with its humming rhombus of an icebox, its foursquare sink – suitable for tanning hides – its chintzy muslin curtains and linoleum pong, suggested a happier era of making do belied by the dishonourable tray loaded with potato chips, cookies, cashews and liquor bottles.

I dressed and went outside to where evening had sidled between the palm leaves, and cheery lanterns lit up the mini-homesteads of this dinky banana republic. From the direction of the pool I could hear a little pre-supper goosing going on: a splash, a cry, the wet thwack of a bikini strap. Behind my bungalow Mike Myers's moon face rose up, cratered by the Mare Imbrium of his fake beard. *His karma is huge* . . .

I walked towards the thwack, let myself out through the metal gate, skirted the porte-cochère, walked down the lane, then along Sunset, and, passing between two sharp-featured young women snapped into black Lycra, entered the Bar Marmont. My key fob bulged in the pocket of my short pants as I walked up some stairs, along a narrowing corridor, through a barroom the width of a train carriage and into a second, narrow as a toilet stall, then into a third no wider than a chicken run, at the end of which I climbed through a trapdoor into a hutch cluttered with armchairs and oil paintings and people – most of whom were thrashing about in a purse seine smoking area, accessed via french windows the size of marmalade jars.

They were all there in the limelight: the Jeffs and Bret, Michael Lynton and Ellen DeGeneres, James Crespinel and Judy Brown, Michael Laughlin* – who was explaining

---

\* It was anomalous that no one seemed to be played by anyone else at this gathering, although when I came to reflect on it later there was one exception – Ellen DeGeneres as Stevie Rosenbloom. I cannot account for the veridical nature of the events recounted below, except to suggest that I was thrown by the contrast with the last Hollywood party I'd been to, almost a decade before, at Carrie Fisher's house. That was a true 'night of a thousand stars' – or at least, I think it was. At one point I found myself in the line-up for the chicken gumbo with Rod Stewart, Geena Davis and the entire featured cast of Blake Edwards's *The Party* (excluding, of course, Peter Sellers); then later on I asked the crown of Jack Nicholson's head if: 'You get out much?'

Being in one space – albeit the sort of hypertrophied living room-cum-terrace mandatory for second-generation movie royalty – with that much notoriety could've been the beginning of the Syndrome, because, while these faces were as familiar to me as my own (and, in many cases, having examined the play of their features for many hours, far more so), I had the disagreeable sensation that they were not who the world claimed them to be, but rather a bunch of saddo impersonators, scooped up off the sidewalk outside Grauman's and taken on by Fisher as a job lot to amuse persons unknown who were sitting hidden behind two-way mirrors, snorting cocaine and laughing hysterically.

the genesis of his self-designed sneakers to a young woman whose name I never did learn – and Mac Guffin, who immediately drew me to one side: 'Jesus, man,' he said. 'I picked up five fucking tickets minding your back all the way up Cienega.'

'No one asked you to do that,' I hissed. 'And if you had to, why didn't you ditch the wheels?'

'Aw, c'mon fellah, don't be like that – I'm just trying to look out for you; they're on your tail – y'know that, don'tcha? They're sharpening their knives, putting on their leather faces, cranking up their chainsaws, I mean, it's *because* you're paranoid that they're now coming to get you—' He broke off to take a highball glass full of fruit from a waitress struggling through the throng.

'Yeah, thanks for nothing, Mac,' I snarled; 'why not just piss all over my party.'

'Party?' He shook his Labrador head, then began slobbering on a pineapple chunk. 'Isn't that a little grandiose – it looks more like a—'

'Nice gathering,' Bret said, cutting in appositely. 'This is Brad.' A tall, good-looking young man in blue jeans and a silky-black hoodie, the pink drapes of whose top lip parted to reveal expertly bleached teeth.

'Hi,' said Brad chirpily.

'Brad is directing a movie called *The Shrink*.'

'Really?' I said with maximum disdain. 'And what of it?'

'He wondered if you might like to drop by the set – they're shooting on location down at Venice; wouldn't that be on your way back to LAX?'

'Uh, yeah, I guess,' I said, trying to sound unconcerned, although I was whining inside: *Is he trying to get rid of me?*

'Bret says you're walking clear round LA,' said Brad.

'That's the aim.'

'Any special reason?'

'I'm location spotting for a movie about a guy who circumambulates Los Angeles,' I told him. 'I originated the script, did the development myself, put together a lot of the finance, then took it to Sony.' I jabbed a finger towards Lynton. 'They've green-lit the project and I'll be directing as well.'

'And starring?'

I really didn't like this Brad – he was snider than an ill-gotten Madison hidden in a coffee can.

'Well, no, since you ask – obviously not. I may have some profile as an actor but I'm not *that* bankable. Leo DiCaprio will be playing me – although he's gonna need a body double for the walking scenes.'

Brad was smirking and I foresaw that our next exchange would cross the border at Tijuana into outright savagery. Luckily DeGeneres took my elbow and guided me away, throwing over her shoulder, 'Don't mind us, guys, there're some people I'd like David to meet.'

There was Dervla, who as she spoke took strand after strand of her own chestnut hair in her scissoring fingers – as a hairdresser might – and who wondered if I would be interested in her idea: 'Based on an original phobia of my own – fear of candlesticks.' And there was Ogden, who had bitten his nails so badly he had to wear ten finger puppets. 'What's the pitch?' He threw his chucklesqueak into the felt mouth of the Mickey Mouse one. 'I'll tellya, it's about a guy who's nervous, nervous, noy-vuss – set in Manhattan, natch – or at least, on a set of Manhattan crowded with scrumptious twenty-somethings deafened by canned laughter.' And then there was Artie, who had spent the last thirty years in a remote cabin in Montana obsessively writing and rewriting a movie script about a reclusive anarcho-Luddite who launches a bombing campaign aimed at derailing the relentless reproducibility of technology: 'I worked on birch bark,' Artie confided, 'using a bone stylus and pigments I had extracted from wildflowers. Then, when I finally returned to civilization, I found out about the Unabomber – man, was I pissed – my whole fuckin' idea stolen for real.'

They were all interesting pitches, yet I found it difficult to concentrate and kept grabbing Coke after Coke from the trays swirling through the smallish crowd. So there was my mounting and gaseous turbulence – and also the disconcerting presence of Susan Atkins's amputated leg (which, so far as I knew, no one had invited), which kept kicking the guests' butts, a grim travesty of the murders it would undoubtedly have tried to perform if it could've got their necks behind its knee.

'What's with the severed leg?' I asked Ellen. 'I mean, is it some kind of ironic comment on my walk?'

'Lighten up, David,' she said. 'Think of Atkins's leg as just another Mac Guffin – like the hands of Orlac.'

'You're not gonna graft that thing on to me, lady. I mean, I've got enough homicidal tendencies of my own.'

She looked at me with an odd expression, but only said: 'Shall we go on and have some dinner at the hotel? The others are already there.'

It was then that I noticed that the once-threshing crowd had been landed – the purse seine was empty except for me, Ellen, the leg and the legman. 'Will you join us?' I asked Mac, but he only handed me a manila envelope.

'It's all in there,' he said. 'Everything I could find out; read it later and then call me.' He snagged Atkins's leg, which was hopping past, and tucked it under his arm like an umbrella. 'The sick shit that goes down in this town,' he muttered as he duck walked in front of us along the chicken run, but I knew his comments weren't addressed to anyone in particular, just as I also knew that he was as happy as a pig in it.

The evening began to end in the hotel restaurant. We were eating paella made with giant insects, and although the antennae caught in my teeth they didn't taste too bad. I was sandwiched between a movie lawyer and the teenage wife of a mogul who was fully gravid – it seemed she might give birth at any moment, a baby doll torn bloody from beneath the hem of her baby doll dress. The lawyer was telling me he represented Rutger Hauer – although what that had to do with anything (even Hauer himself) was entirely obscure. Then he said, 'I live out at the Palisades in a one-storey house. Y'know people aren't killed by earthquakes at all – they're killed by houses.'

The evening was killed off by my bungalow. Coming along the path from the pool, I saw that the moon had risen above the billboard advertising *The Love Guru*, and I cursed myself for my earlier trope: the Mare Ibrium was nothing like a fake beard – Myers's or anyone else's.

I sat smoking a Joya de Nicaragua and got out Mac's report – which turned out to be a photocopy of my own. I leafed through the forty-odd pages, smiling grimly at the smiley faces and scattering cigar ash on the elaborate diagrams. Mac had scrawled a few words across the final page: 'Copies of this are being widely circulated – if you can't join 'em, beat 'em.'

## 10

# The Virgil of Laurel Canyon

It must have been a hell of night, because when I awoke – tucked as savagely into my bed as I had been by the disapproving nurse at Heath Hospital thirty years before – I found I'd had breast implants done. And not just any breast implants – Laura Harring's. At least, I fantasized that they might be Laura Harring's breast implants, because when I examined them in the full-length mirror on the bathroom door they had a combination of inelasticity and prominence that reminded me of the improbability of her chest – relative to the slimness of her back – when Harring and Naomi Watts took off their tops to fake love in David Lynch's *Mulholland Drive*\* (2001).

I wondered whether implying that anyone might have had breast implants was libellous – but the alternative – that these were Laura Harring's *actual breasts* – was too awful to contemplate. I mean, there was I, idly caressing them, while Harring might well be lying somewhere dreadfully hacked about. In an interview I had read with the actress she said: 'Life is a beautiful journey. Every episode of my life is like a dream and I am at peace and happy with what life has given me.' But there was no way she could factor a sadistic double-mastectomy into such a beneficent dream – this was a thieving nightmare. Or had Harring been murdered, her beautiful face beaten to a pulp with a brass statuette of a monkey? If so I was off the hook for libel – but without an alibi for the caesura of the past twelve hours.

---

\* A scene that was shot – or so she assured me – in Stevie's old apartment building; or possibly Ellen DeGeneres's (which, might be more apt); anyway, one or the other.

Clearly, it was time to force the pace of events: if they were messing with me to this extent I'd better take the fight to them. I leafed through the *Yellow Pages*, found the number, called it and discovered there was a meeting in Hollywood that very morning. Good, I'd have some breakfast, then stroll over.

Slumping in the kitchenette, teapot on the table, and beside it the newly polished brass statuette of a monkey, I poked one long lean thigh languorously out from the folds of the hotel bathrobe. Ignoring the multiple sections of the *LA Times* strewn all around, I felt as iconic as a Terry O'Neill photo – which was just as well, because even in a town renowned for sick shit it was going to take some guts to hit the streets with my purloined tits.

I needn't have worried, by the time I'd shaved and dressed, the breasts – or implants – had begun to subside, becoming first perfectly normal middle-aged bubs and then the budding nubbins of a teenage girl. Locking the door to the bungalow, I slid a hand up under my T-shirt and was relieved to discover coarse hair. The whole tit-thing must have been the after-effect of a particularly polymorphous erotic dream, and although I felt a little cheated it had to be better than murder.

I found the meeting up on Hawthorn in some kind of community centre. There was a Formica table covered with leaflets and a forty-year-old woman with braces *and* a tongue stud serving coffee through a hatch. Savouring the ghostly aroma of last week's cheap meals, I took one, figuring it was only Nescafé, and thinking also of how it was I walked among them, these seraphic folk, able to suspend disbelief in

films, in TV adverts, in pop songs, in microwaved food – and even in age itself. Maybe – just maybe – this could work for me too.

All the rest of the cast was assembled – exactly the players you'd expect for a self-help production almost anywhere in the maldeveloped world: following men and trailing ladies, character-defect actors, bit failures and spare extras. I slotted right into this stereotypy and no one paid me the least attention as I threw myself down on a canvas bottomed chair, muttering and slurping and giving off that supersonic whine that's unfailingly associated with mental distress.

I watched and listened as the children of Xenu were called onstage to testify to their treatment at the hands of the cult. This frail girl, all elbows and ears, the ends of her hair as fractured as her psyche, explained how she had been recruited into the Sea

Org* at the age of twelve and spent eight years being bullied and abused – four of them as a suppressive person, forced to wear an orange jumpsuit and wield a mop for fourteen hours a day. She wept.

As did a burly man, who said that while he had managed to make the break, his parents – despite everything that had happened to him – continued to believe that they were Thetans who had been exiled to earth 75 million years ago, and that after arriving at an implant station housed in an extinct volcano, they had clung to genetic entity after genetic entity, piggybacking their way through evolution, until they ended up passing out leaflets on Hollywood Boulevard. He himself had had a breakdown after leaving, and when his parents – 'They still love me . . .' – had the temerity to meet with him, they too had been labelled 'suppressive persons'.

'You guys know what that's like,' he sobbed. 'Nobody can talk to them, sit with them, hand them a friggin' cup of coffee – and you know the awfulest thing, I kinda feel that way too. I feel like I'm a suppressive person even out here in the real world – I just can't connect.'

The testimonies were getting to me. I'd known in general terms the secret arcana that Scientologists became privy to only when they attained the grade of Level 3 Operating Thetans, but still: to hear how this hokum had corrupted minds and distorted

---

* The Sea Org was formed by Hubbard as his Praetorian Guard in the 1970s, when, facing what he viewed as persecution (or taxation, as it's commonly known), the core group of Scientologists took to the waves in a couple of clunky old merchant vessels. Mostly comprised of pubescent girls clad in itty-bitty miniskirts and sailor tops, the Org members, while not actually physically abused by Hubbard, were manipulated by him into the most fanatical loyalists.

lives was . . . salutary. I looked at the slack skin on the backs of my hands. True, it would've been a reassurance to be admitted to the religion – neither of the actors playing me was getting any younger, and while I was confident they'd still be having offers for years to come, what kind of parts would they be? I didn't want to end up in soaps – or sitcoms. Whereas if I were a Thetan, I'd effectively become an actor with a billion-year contract and there'd be no resting at all: as soon as one part (or 'life') ended, another would begin—

'Are you going to join us on the demo?'

'I'm sorry?'

'Are you coming with – on the demo?'

I had been romping in my reverie of full and eternal employment, with its personations flowing seamlessly, each into the next, never the dull requirement to *just be myself*, when suddenly there were the braces and the tongue stud and the petty earnestness of it all.

'Well, uh, where?'

'We're going to picket the centre up on Hollywood – you don't have to if you don't feel comfortable, I mean, we'd understand.'

'Sure we would,' said the burly man, coming up behind her with an ursine undulation of his sloping shoulders. 'I mean, you could be recognized by someone – and that can cause problems in this town, you could end up as *fair game.*'

I knew what he was talking about: to be branded 'fair game' was the Scientological equivalent of being forced to wear a yellow star in Germany after the promulgation of the Nuremberg Laws. Persons designated 'fair game' could be 'deprived of property or injured by any means by any Scientologist', and this included being 'tricked, sued, or lied to or destroyed'.

'I gotta tellya,' said the burly son of Xenu, leaning down to me conspiratorially, 'I had no idea you had any involvement with the Church.'

'Um, well, not *formally*,' I stressed, 'but I did go to Saint Hill a few times – y'know, in England.'

'Sure, sure, I understand – loved you in *Dinotopia* by the way. Lissen.' He held up a swatch of black cloth and a white mask.* 'You could always wear these if you don't want to be recognized, and we'd be grateful, we could use the numbers.'

I stood up and took the robe and mask from him. 'Sure,' I said, 'I'll come along – I could use a walk.'

They couldn't – the children of Xenu piled into a minibus and several cars, leaving me to plod the couple of miles to where the demo was assembling at Hollywood and Vine. They said they'd try to wait – but, as Busner often used to say, 'Trying is lying.' I'd been thinking of him on the walk over, and what he'd make of these odd polarities – here was I, joining the anti-Scientology march, while over there, on Sunset, was the office of the Citizens Commission on Human Rights, the anti-psychiatric pressure group szupported by Szasz and the Scientologists.

From the corner I could see the Scientology kids wending their way through the crowds along the boulevard, all of them in their V masks, and carrying placards with slogans such

* Interestingly enough the Guy Fawkes kind – saturnine features accentuated by slashes of 'tache and goatee beard – sported by the anarchist revolutionary V in Alan Moore's *V for Vendetta* graphic novel. Moore himself had violently objected to the Wachowski Brothers movie adaptation of his book, stating: 'It's been turned into a Bush-era parable by people too timid to set a political satire in their own country.' The question was – and is – which V were the children of Xenu hiding behind?

as 'They Want Your Money and Your Sanity', 'Scientology Disconnects Families' and 'Tax-Exempt Pyramid Scheme'. This last seemed the most problematic – after all, just about all of late capitalism was founded on a tax-exempt pyramid scheme; or so it seemed to me, on Saturday, 14 June 2008.

I shrugged on my own black robe, donned my V mask, then hustled through the tourists and the cruisers and the movie star impersonators – but the demo kept on marching, while I was only floundering: walking to Hollywood was one thing; running quite another. In a way, it was relief when a van slewed into the kerb beside me, its side door slammed open, and two Mormonesque heavies leapt out, grabbed me and hustled me inside. 'C'mon,' said one of them. 'You've done enough walking for a lifetime – why not take a ride.'

The last thing I saw before the door was slammed shut was Margaret Atwood slumped by a storefront, a pathetic styrofoam begging cup on the sidewalk in front of her. I'd had no idea dystopic novels were selling that badly. Then, as the van pulled away, through the tinted rear windows, I spotted Kazuo Ishiguro, the British novelist – another writer who'd had many of his works adapted for screen; but, while to be down and out in Hollywood was one thing, why was he wearing that curious robe, which looked like a couple of camping mats and an election placard strapped round his torso? And what was he wearing on his head? Was it a hat – or a house? And if it was a house – which one? Darlington Hall, as featured in *The Remains of the Day*, or Netherfield Park?

But I had no time to reflect any further on these mysteries, for the van's driver – who was hidden from me in a sealed compartment – must have seen a break in the traffic and accelerated, and I was thrust backwards on to the point of a hypo. I felt the drug ooze into me – then my consciousness, tissue-thin to begin with, was balled up, wadded and thrown away.

I get it back standing stark naked in what appears initially to be a featureless room: plain white walls, a high ceiling with recessed lighting diodes. Then I see, lying on the smooth white floor, the silky pool of a Spandex bodysuit. Next, I notice a single prop: a stop light, such as you might see at any LA intersection. It's working, and as I look it changes from the red DON'T WALK to the green stick-figure with its legs parted. There's no smell at all, except the stray whiffs of my own sweaty armpits – yet I sense altitude and aridity, and wonder if the room might be in a desert, say, the Mojave.

'Put on the bodysuit,' a voice crackles through a hidden speaker. I'm a little miffed – at forty-six I'm proud of my toned appearance, and, despite the kidnapping and the drugging, the idea of displaying myself naked to unseen voyeurs is the most arousing experience I've had since the girl in the CGI riot involuntarily came on to me.

The speaker crackles again, 'Put on the bodysuit – or we will send someone in to put it on you.' This time I reluctantly obey. It fits me like bespoke and, as delighted by my new clothing as I'd been with my nakedness, I swing my arms this way and that, then flex my legs. 'Be still!' the disembodied voice orders me. A door whines open and a huddle of white lab coats come bustling in, one of them pushing a shopping cart full of small balls covered in Velcro. They're all wearing V masks and as they cluster round me I ask – I think entirely reasonably – 'What's going on, guys, is this part of the demo?'

But if they're the children of Xenu they aren't letting on; without speaking they begin sticking the Velcro balls on to my bodysuit, one each at all of my joints: ankle, knee, hip and so on. It's done in a matter of seconds, then they retreat back through the moaning portal. I'm equally pleased with my new bobble suit, which resembles one of Leigh Bowery's rather more restrained costumes. I start doing knee bends and humming Divine's 'You Think You're a Man' until meany-voice rasps: 'Stop that!', then begins ordering me about:

'Now, do exactly what I tell you: walk towards the stop light, then wait for the green man. No! That's too fast, begin again . . . Better. Now wait . . . OK, cross.'

I don't snap back, 'Cross what, exactly?' I understand what's wanted of me – you don't get anywhere in life without being able to take direction. Besides, I enjoy strutting about in my bobble suit, while crossing intersections is something I've been doing for days now – it may be typecasting, but at least it's *my* casting.

After we've done crossing for a while, the voice commands me to amble around the periphery of the room, then to assume various conversational postures, then pretend to take notes, then photographs. Next the V masks reappear, pushing before them a platform on wheels and a swivel chair, while two more bring up the rear carrying a table. With these new props the voice's directions become more complex: it wants me to pretend to sit at the table and eat, to write, and then to make a phone call. After which I'm urged to lie down on the platform and feign sleep – in a foetal position, and also thrashing about in the flicker of REM. Next I'm to roll over and fake masturbation, before rising, sitting backwards on the swivel chair and straining my way through a realistically effortful shit.

All in all, over the course of an hour or so, a Marcel Marceau on crystal meth, I recapitulate the entire gamut of physical actions I might expect to perform in the average day. It's an exhilarating workout, but, even as I prance and dance and stop and swing, something's nagging at me – eventually I ignore the next direction and instead stand with my face petulantly downcast.

'Bend over,' orders the voice. 'I said bend over,' it reiterates. 'Bend over or we will MAKE YOU bend over!' it barks.

'I truly want to do my best for you guys,' I pout, 'but what I want to know is what's my motivation here?'

'OK, OK,' the voice fizzes, 'you gotta point. Just bend over for us this last time and then we'll get to your motivation, OK?'

I bend over.

The Vs come bustling back in; some spirit away the platform and the table, others remove the Velcro balls from my suit and depart with them. 'Sit on the chair,' orders the voice. A pair of Vs return with a basket of tiny plastic balls and begin expertly attaching these all over my face using some kind of clear adhesive. They stick balls to my lips, top and bottom, to my frown lines and to still more of my frown lines, all along my brows and on my eyelids, they near beard my chin with these nurdles. When they're done there must be over a hundred of the things hanging off me, while presumably I look like a sufferer from some hideous alien skin condition.

'Face the wall,' the voice spits, then it coos, 'Ree-lax.'

If the body workout was exhausting, the psychic one is both more demanding and more satisfying. The voice begins simply enough, getting me to frown, smile, scowl, laugh, mime soliloquizing, dialoguing, arguing and shouting. Soon enough, however, the directions become more complex: I'm to adopt an expression of weary pity, existential angst, frozen pride, justified hauteur. Then I'm asked by the voice to appear as if I'm listening intently to the recursive eddies of flute and woodwind that flow into the oceanic melodies of the Andante to Mahler's Sixth—

'Whoa,' I cry, 'that's a hell of a subtle mien!'

'You can do it,' the voice urges – and so I unstitch my brows, flutter my eyelids and suck in my already hollow cheeks, because I'm beginning to warm to the voice – love it a little even. I can imagine that if we were penned up together for long enough in this rehearsal room we might have an affair – hadn't I already pretended to masturbate for it?

'Great!' the voice cries. 'I *believed* that one. 'Next try conveying the countenance a character in a narrative might adopt, were he to realize not only that he *was* a character, but that the narrative itself was—'

'What? Unstable – deconstructed altogether?'

'Let's just say . . . decentred.'


'Interesting,' the voice sighs. 'Although perhaps just a tad forced.'

'All right, d'you want me to go again at that one?'

'No, let's move on, we don't have all day – how about this: a kind of "whither the Left" wistfulness, incorporating an acknowledgement of the bitter-sweetness of the fall of the Berlin Wall, and a harder-edged perception of the fissiparous effects of post-9/11 conflict?'

'That? – *That*!' I guffaw. 'C'mon, that's first-grade stuff: watch me.'

When I'm done, the voice seems gratifyingly transported. 'Beautiful,' it groans, 'just too, too beautiful, darling . . .' Then it pulls itself together and crackles. 'A still easier one: give me man-having-tiny-plastic-balls-torn-from-his-face, followed by a mickey finn.'

And that one is easy, because the V masks come barrelling back in and I have someone to do the scene with. I'm still frantically mugging when the pearlescent drop appears at the bevelled end of the hypodermic and the house lights go down, and the spot focuses in tighter . . . tighter on my face . . . and . . . blanks . . . out.

I came to being thrown from the back of a Lincoln Town Car that was taking the bend in Mulholland Drive immediately to the north of Runyon Canyon Park at twice the limit – or so I estimated as I windmilled into a ditch right at the feet of a family of joggers in full nylon kit.

'Oh my God!' the mommy ejaculated.

'Oh my god,' the daddy rather more agnostically echoed her.

'OMG,' their tweenage daughter cried.

'Oh!' said a toddler in an all-terrain buggy.

'Wuff!' said their Airedale, nuzzling between my thighs with his square-haired head.

'Frodo!' the mommy called it, reeling the poor unfortunate in by its extendable lead. Once the dog was landed the daddy approached:

'Are you, like, OK?'

'Kind sir,' I said, clambering to my feet and straightening my torn clothes, 'there is no question of similitude at all; thanks to Laura Harring's breasts I have been spared any serious injury.'

He didn't recoil, nor did the rest of the FoJ – once they'd floated off on their air soles, paws and tyres I realized why: it may've *felt* as if shells full of silicone gel had broken my fall, but for the second time that day my fingers crept up my T-shirt and discovered only the same old skimpy pectorals. Ho-hum, I sighed, picking bitumen from my knees, snuffling up the bouquet garni of the mesquite and looking out over the Los Angeles Basin. I may've lost the breasts, but I stood at last on those exposed ribs and gullies of the Sierra, stacked with hundreds of thousands of dollars of firewood and the palm froth of kindling. In the distance the skyscrapers of Downtown rose up straight as ruled lines, the Y-axis for Huxley's graph of civilization's boom and bust.

From the angle of the sun I estimated it was a couple of hours until dusk. A more timorous hiker would've probably given up at this point, slumped back down the hillside to his bungalow at the Marmont, eaten far too many cashews and nutted-out in front of the TV, but I was made of more suicidal stuff: I would follow the great silicone migration along the escarpment. True, my circumambulation had been ruptured by the van and the car rides, and I had also been kidnapped, possibly even abused, although this was debatable: was an actor like a child, passively acquiescing to perverted direction because she knew no other authority?

And now that I came to think back over the episode, as at first I made my way along the verge of Mulholland, then dived down a winding side road into the dark heart of affluent suburbia, it dawned on me that not once during that strange interlude had the voice referred to me by name. Who was playing me, then? As I walked I ran my hands over my face repeatedly – but one angular middle-aged male face feels pretty much the same as the next, and it wasn't until I crept under a carport and crouched to frame my features in the wing mirror of an Infiniti that my hunch was confirmed: this was not homely Pete Postlethwaite's face, or Thewlis's haughty mien. But as to whose lumpy nose, rag-rolled cheeks and equine teeth were described on this face mask – well, I was at a loss, so I squeezed a blackhead.

And soon lost interest, plodding on along the road towards Mount Olympus. Somewhere up here Huxley's house had burnt down, a domesticated fireball of mystic books – what was it his friend Gerald Heard had said? 'Man is the general name applied to successions of inconsistent conduct having their source within a two-legged and featherless body.' Poor Aldous, his visual field so savagely foreshortened by myopia and his attention span – sooo long, a stretch limmo of awareness, capacious enough to seat the entire casts of all the movies ever shot in Hollywood, in Culver City, in Burbank, in the Valley. Will Hay and the Fat Boy sat up with the driver, and in the back compartment Manuel P. Zlotnik carousing with Miss Pearlstein, Carol Goodenough . . . and all the rest.

That was Aldous's misfortune: spaced out in Schwab's, he had seen Los Angeles's hair was burning, that her hills were filled with fire, and with that he broke through from the monochrome world of the 1950s to the other Technicolor side. Poor Aldous: if all the movies ever made had been spliced together, wound on to a reel the size of a Ferris wheel and projected on to a screen two inches in front of him, it still wouldn't have been long enough to divert him, it still would've *seemed* over in a blink of his mescaline eyes. For he had seen the future: the after-image of the movies, flickering on the inside of his lids.

\*     \*     \*

I had noted the flyers for Location Services stuck in the mailboxes along Willow Drive, and now I reached Laurel Canyon Boulevard only to discover that in my flat-footed abstraction I had lost the straight way and that the sun had dipped behind the shoulder of the mountain. The canyon was a deep place and with Saturday fast fading the snorting beasts were rampaging back from the beaches, their headlights piercing the gathering shadows. The hardtop snaked between steep bluffs terraced with real estate and there was no sidewalk. I got out the map crumpled into my pocket, but once I'd unfolded it saw that the available routes back to Sunset were all equally wiggling – they wormed across the rumpled paper, the apotheosis of the grid, as if the plotting pens of an EEG had simultaneously registered the nightmares of the city's entire populace.

I tried walking on the left-hand side of the road, but each time I rounded a bend I was horribly aware I was invisible to the beasts that came at forty, fifty, sixty miles an hour, panting hydrocarbons, their fenders-for-jaws snagging the pandanus along the verge. I sprinted across to the right – but here my terror was still greater, for each time a beast came charging up the hill, its headlights ignited visions in my eyes – while they, I knew mos' def', could see nothing at all.

I tried switching from one side of the boulevard to the other as it wound down through the canyon, so as to provide the beasts coming from either direction with the greatest possible visibility – but this was no good, for darkness was upon us all now, and as I pelted like a picaro (or do I mean a picador?) beneath the points of their chrome horns I couldn't prevent myself from witnessing the abominations inside these Escalades and Infinitis and Tahoes. I may have been a cryogenically preserved Disney head bowled chuckling down this lane of death, I may have been a silica grain impelled by time, but at least I wasn't like these . . . these . . . *sinners.*

No wonder they couldn't slow down, when this lustful man's penis was so engorged, so turgid, that I could see it thrusting up towards the windshield. No wonder they couldn't see me, when this gluttonous family's minivan was so stuffed with their own fat and discarded food that even as they screamed by I noted the high tide of gnawed drumsticks, frayed corncobs and crescent burgers pressed by paps and thighs against the greasy windows. No wonder they had no care for the future, when, like this derivatives trader, they urged their Crown Victorias forward, while their heads were *reversed.*

This last beast, sightless, sunless, ravenous, clipped my shoulder and sent me flailing into a drive. I wasn't injured – at least the skin wasn't broken, and only swirled into an oily multicoloured whorl when I pressed it with my thumb – but I was finished. I slumped down on the concrete, my throat combusting with nitrogen, nitrogen oxides, water vapour, particulate matter and, of course, hydrocarbons. It was the nadir – and then he came, and I was lifted up.

He came, tripping down the side of the boulevard, his silky three-quarter-length pants shimmying as his highly toned calves took the stresses of descent in their stride. He came, strips shaven into his scalp beneath the arms of his shades, a tattoo of a torpedo on his stringy neck, a tuft of hair on his decisive chin. He came – and when he saw me there, washed up on the shore by the metallic storm, he stepped aside and pulled away the headphones that cosseted his noble ears.

Despite the whoosh of the boulevard, I registered familiar close harmonies, staccato yet melodious cheeping from the tinny-tiny speakers: 'Whatsoever thou dost affect, whatsoever thou dost project, so do, so do . . . (Aff-ect! Pro-ject!) And so project all, as one who, for aught thou knowest, may at this very present depart out of this life . . . out of it, out of it . . . (Pro-ject! Dee-part!) And as for death, if there be any gods, it is no grievous thing to leave the so-ci-ety of men—'

'Hey,' I said, 'what happened to the Latin?'

'Excuse me?' He hadn't noticed me before I spoke.

'That's NWPhd, isn't it? I saw those guys rehearsing down at USC a couple of days ago.'

'Aw,' he said, shaking his head dismissively, 'I don't know nothin' 'bout that, this is my roommate's MP3. I just grabbed it as I took off – this ain't my kind of shit at all.'

'You don't dig Aurelius?'

'Or who?'

'Marcus Aurelius, Roman emperor and stoic philosopher – it's his *Meditations* those guys are rapping, I just wondered what'd happened to the Latin, they usually do the Latin as well as the English.'

'Oh, OK, I getcha – my roomie, he did say this was some kinduva remix, so maybe they, like, dropped the Latin to make it more commercial, or some kinda shit like that.'

It had been a long and substantive speech – which I was grateful for, but I needed more; he, however, seemed intent on leaving, pulling the headphones back on and turning to resume his goatish descent. 'Hey, wait!' I cried.

'Say what?' He turned back.

'You aren't going to walk all the way down Laurel Canyon, are you?'

'Fool, I live up there a-ways, so I do the walk down to Sunset twice daily – I've a little problem with my licence, you dig. The only time I *don't* walk down is when I skateboard.'

'Skateboard?'

'You heard it. I got me one of those big three-foot boards with the meaty wheels. I start back up a-ways by the park. Man, I tellya that thing *goes* – I guess I must be hitting thirty by the time I get to here, and when I drop back an' brake, the sparks *fly*.'

'But what about the sinners?'

'Excuse me?'

'I mean the traffic – the cars.'

'Ain't no traffic late at night to speak of, and when I'm walking I go right directly t'wards 'em. Then they see you – so long as they see you they won't hit you. And if they do hit you, well.' He started to rap: 'It-is-no-grievous-thing to-leave-the-so-ci-ety of men.'

I was impressed by his nerve – and told him so, then asked, 'Would you mind if I followed along behind you? The traffic terrifies me.'

He grinned. 'Sure, man, whatever you need.'


It took us around half an hour to cover the two miles back down to Sunset. He loped on ahead, his life story trailing over his shoulder like the silk scarf of a valiant fighter pilot. Which in a way he was now – strafing the enemy with his gaze as they came swooping up towards us.

'You know that TV show, man, *Intervention*?'

'Can't say I do.'

'My folks, they set me up for that. One day I was sitting in my condo in West Hollywood doin' meth, the next I was in the

Betty Ford Clinic in Palm Beach, Florida. Craziest thing ever happened to me. I'm only telling this you this' – he glanced back at me earnestly – "cause I'm pretty much recognized wherever I go. See this: I'm only going down to Radio Shack to get them to look at this busted cell phone I got, but I'll be hollered at least three times. Three times!'

I was grateful to him – but put him down as another fantasist. The town was full up with them, after all, and if the senescent could masquerade as the juvenescent, and starlets could go supernova – why couldn't a deluded drug addict be the star of a reality show? But then we hit Sunset and right away a car slowed down and the driver leant out the window: 'Good to see ya, Virgil!' he roared. 'You stay away from that shit now, y'hear.'

'I hear you, man,' Virgil called back, but his face – a perfect vacuum of nature-abhorring need – belied his words.

I thanked Virgil for guiding me, and was on the verge of asking him back to the hotel for a drink when some cloudy premonition got in the way. The last I saw of him was his jaunty pair of pants fluorescing in the headlights as it floated across an intersection towards the discount electrical goods store.

Back at the Chateau Marmont the desk clerk wouldn't let go when I grabbed the key fob. We tugged it this way and that for a while; she was trying to get through to me that: 'There's a gentleman to see you Mister Self, he's waiting in the bar.' But it had been so long since anyone had called me that I thought she must be addressing the man waiting behind me, scuffing his shoe irritably on the carpet. Eventually she gave up, released the key and passed across a stack of phone message slips, all of which bore the same name: Dr Zack Busner, together with a series of times – 8.30 a.m., 9.30 a.m., 10.00 a.m. – that grew progressively closer to one another, until, as the present drew nigh, he had been calling repeatedly: 6.58 p.m., 6.59 p.m., 6.66 p.m.

He was indeed waiting for me in the bar with his red froggy face, and his pale yellow young Orson Welles face, and his dead-black Sandeman Port face. His six eyes were weeping ('It's the smog,' he explained), and his six wings were beating ('I just flew in'), and there were so many ice buckets ranged round him on stands that it looked as if this great monster were waist deep in the crystalline chips and cubes.

'Ah,' he said, 'there you are! Don't you ever answer your phone? I've been leaving messages on it all day – calling here as well. I mean, the last thing I wanted to do was *surprise* you.' He passed a clawed hand over his face and I felt it.

I sat down opposite him, not speaking, just getting the measure of the situation and the degree of danger I was in. A waitress brought a menu and I ordered a bottle of Powerade®. It was quiet in the bar, that blissful early-evening calm when the barman is dusting all the bottles on the shelves so that they shine, and the atmosphere is quivery with the anticipation of what that night's patrons will do to each other once their blood begins to boil.

When the waitress returned with my energy drink and poured it into a highball glass, I added a couple of ice cubes from one of the buckets and took a long draught. Setting the glass back down, I looked from one pair of eyes to the next, then said levelly, 'There's something you really ought to know.'

'Oh?'

'I never did see *Citizen Kane*.'

# II

# A Touch of Evil

Going home always feels like the real getaway to me. To depart on a journey is to simplify your identity: you must present a serviceable persona to strangers shorn of ambiguities – be just *x*, or *y*, or possibly *j*. But when you scoop the strange coins from the unfamiliar bedside table and funnel them into your pocket, when you flex your passport and put it away in the zip-lock bag inside the zippered compartment, when you look at your face in the mirror above the sink – and queasily catch sight of the back of your spacey head in the mirror on the bathroom door – you begin to feel the first stirrings of adventurousness: who will I be when I get back? Will I have changed? Will *they* have changed? The world is all used up – only tourists or salesmen set off on journeys; the real explorers strike out for the known.

These were some of my more spacious thoughts as I got ready to quit my bungalow at the Chateau Marmont on the morning of 15 June 2008. Making some coffee in the kitchenette, packing my small bag, drinking the coffee and eating a cinnamon donut while I scanned the map – these were actions: easy enough to suspend disbelief in, having as they did the robotic character of the pre-credits sequence for a movie that's gone straight to video before it's even in the can.

Touch, taste – smell! Don't make me laugh – all these are barnyard senses, grossly overrated, only pigs would want points. That my thoughts had a quality of being somehow *pre-cogitated* – at once a little glib and overworked – I didn't let bother me.

Nor did I make too much of the way that I was conscious of these thoughts not merely as subjective intimations but as actual declamations that resounded in space. It was inevitable that I'd be feeling a little spaced out – it had been quite a trip, although I couldn't remember much about it. Still, I had a long day's walk ahead of me if I wanted to make my flight, so: 'I'd better not linger.'

At 8.12 a.m. I was standing at the junction of Sunset and La Cienega, looking down the long gentle slope into the *nuages automoteurs* that blanketed the Los Angeles Basin, out of which came the occasional set of headlights, dragging behind them a car. A billboard rose above the intersection, on it the sad black face of a giant captioned in the art director's conception of the giant's own handwriting 'I lost me too meth.' 'Me too, brother,' I muttered as I loped past. 'Me too.' Then I was working my way down, block by block, to Santa Monica Boulevard, egged on by Johnnie Walker, who seemed to be striding out from every billboard that didn't feature a gargantuan speed freak. 'Keep Walking!' Johnnie's copywriter exhorted – although he himself remained pinioned. 'Keep Walking!' I admonished myself, then noticed a strange phenomenon: my own shadow, legs parted, cast on to the smogbank by the rays of the rising sun.

Keep walking – early morning on Sundays is the time allotted for pedestrianism in LA. For an hour or so those of us on foot had the city to ourselves. There was a mackerel sky over the Santa Monica Freeway and a steady stream of joggers coming between the mirrored donjons of Century City. Then there were the street persons, old hags bent double under sacks who turned their backs on the haunting flares of sunlight. 'You have really pretty eyes,' said a scuffed-up ladyboy who pulled me up outside a deli somewhere around Glen Boulevard. 'Can I have a light?' I took in the shaving rash, the baseball cap, the hip-hugging cut-offs and the just-picked-up butt of filter tip stuck in a face that was dustily lacking in registration.

I gave him one, although he too had a disconcerting air of being pre-known, as did the petals lying around a storm drain and the WARNING. THIS AREA CONTAINS CHEMICALS KNOWN TO THE STATE OF CALIFORNIA TO CAUSE CANCER, BIRTH DEFECTS AND OTHER REPRODUCTIVE HARM, as did the Elysian Fields of the Los Angeles Country Club.

A linguini of LAFD hoses had been vomited across the sidewalk from the engines parked by the kerb, and there, sitting at the metal tables in front of a Coffee Bean & Tea Leaf, were the fire starters themselves, companionably planning their day's arson. I stopped for a smoke and a coffee – decaf, of course. But, even so, this was a big mistake, because as I kept walking my bladder swelled and mutated until I was but a hollow man who could barely put one leg full of urine in front of the other.

What to do? Gas station after gas station taunted me with its signs: RESTROOM FOR CUSTOMER USE ONLY. Until I got it into my thick head and became a customer myself – but what to buy, not a candy bar, or a spare cap for my gas tank. No need for a newspaper or a rubber mat either . . . Aha! Quick Energy Drink® – small, portable, inoffensive. I paid and knocked it back. Then the Cha'an meditation illness began, in front of the urinal, it was of course state law that employees wash their hands, but as for the rest of us we were free to walk the streets with our hands dripping blood and excreta. The incontinent recall of Buddhist texts, which is the symptom of this overstraining of the pupil's psyche, can be rectified only by the master hitting him hard on the head with a stick. Otherwise the texts range themselves, left to right, across the pupil's visual field, not interrupting his view of a homeless man foetal on the sidewalk – but augmenting it. More disturbingly, the texts are no mere phenomenological wallpaper – the meaning of every word is instantly grasped by the pupil, even as he stares through them at the sign for historic Route 66.

And still the texts proliferate – at first only ones the pupil is familiar with, but soon enough these are joined by others he has only heard of. Yet these too are comprehended in their entirety, at once, even though he can see straight through them to a plate-glass window, and beyond that a store full of running machines. The pupil's mind becomes bloated with a consciousness that inexorably ramifies, his ego, free-will, intentionality – whatever – it is trapped like a swarming water drop pinioned in a microscope slide. There is worse to come, as flying from all angles wing still more texts that the pupil is compelled to include in his screaming wits – these are texts he has never heard of at all, texts he didn't know could exist, texts written by alien civilizations, texts doodled on the Etch A Sketch of God by archangels peaking on acid –

The Quick Energy Drink® had to have been a mistake, because this was the mosh-pit of soma I was chucked into as I continued west to Santa Monica – with one key distinction: I saw not texts but video clips. Clips of me walking out from the arrivals terminal at LAX and on to Century Boulevard, clips of me freaking out in a gas station, clips of me checking in to the Uqbar Inn, clips of me passing by donutmorphic drive-ins, clips of me surging through *nuages maritimes* in the Baldwin

Hills, clips of me beating on *piñatas* east of Broadway – in short, video clips of me at every stage of my circumambulation, and not just the ones I knew had been taken by the perfidious Jeffs, but all the clips from the security cameras I'd long stopped trying to avoid.

I was pondering this – in as much as anyone could ponder such an extravagant onslaught of visual imagery, tens – hundreds even – of thousands of full-motion shots of himself walking, streamed straight to his visual cortex – when I realized that one of the clips was in real time and that it coincided, more or less, with my own POV. I was passing by the John Wayne Cancer Institute; it was a pretty big cancer institute – but then he had been a pretty big guy. I had reached Santa Monica and regained some sort of equilibrium, standing on the sidewalk like any other rube and reading the following text:

'Here are described the humble beginnings of the once swamp dweller whose fortune was lost many generations before his own birth due to the unfortunate and unexplainable misplacement of his great, great, great, great, great grandfather's will and the deed to 21,138 acres of land which once encompassed the greater part of what is now San Francisco. Legend also tells that the soul of SCUSSUXYKOR III, an ancient Egyptian pharoah murdered by his very own soothsayer priest, sometimes dwells within his flesh. The astrological sign of the squid from the zodiac of the planet Jamzübati-Remoti on the outer Stewart Skippy Socrates solar system centered on the SUZ11R23 galaxy exemplifies the Amazing Chain Man.'

Which was written in marker pen on a piece of cardboard stuck on top of shopping cart, beside which sat a street person I thought I recognized. He was rattling hanks of chain between his hands. His bald head was surmounted by a twist of bandana, and above his beard was the benign expression of someone who believes that the everyday slights of this world can be fully explained by pan-galactic conspiracy theories.

'Hey, Chain Man,' I said.

'Hey,' he replied.

'That's a fine piece of writing.'

'Thanks.'

'Not to be picky, but it's p-h-a-r-a-o-h.'

'A-o-h what?'

'Pharaoh – you've reversed the *o* and *a*.'

'Right, whatever, dude.' He let the chain hank fall to his lap. 'But I'm a writer – not a fuckin' speller.'

I make no excuses, I was weary and anyway facetiousness comes naturally to me: 'Oh, OK,' I chuckled, 'so what do you write?'

The Amazing Chain Man got out a bit of a Marlboro and lit it before continuing, 'Before the strike I had a pretty good gig churning out scripts for *Stargate SG-1*, did some stuff for *Atlantis* and *Universe* too – that was my eating money anyways.'

'Oh – you mean you're a *real* writer.'

'Like, d'oh, we're *all* real writers.' He waved the tip of his cigarette to encompass the tramps, winos and bums who had congregated on these benches at the intersection of 7th and Santa Monica. 'Whaddya think, that the WGA had a generous strike fund? There was too much fuckin' product anyway, now they've gone head to head over the new media residuals for *Dharma & Greg*, well, most of us will never work again. Some of these guys, though, they're, like, idealists.'

'Like idealists – you mean they're transcendental idealists?'

'No, dummy, they're novelists, short story writers – even biographers. They've come from all over to back the strike. They can read the writing on the wall: if it that's all she wrote, that's all they'll be wroting too.'

I let this solecism slide and confined myself to the matter near to hand:

'So this' – I pointed at the cardboard – 'is what exactly?'

'That's my shill, man, people see that they get to talking, maybe they ask me to write something for them – tell 'em a story perhaps, y'know oral literature may be the way the whole thing is going, kinda back to the future trip.'

It was lost on me – the shill, the riff – I was already heading on towards the beach. Thomas Mann was calling to me from his exile in the sewer pipe – the Santa Monica Pier was calling to me too. Not all writers were down and out. I ignored the

Amazing Chain Man's cry, which followed me down the block: 'I do kids parties too!'

There were no surfer frat boys for me down at the beach, no muscle Manns either, only tourists de-evolving into Segways, and kites tethered to the sand, and craft stalls selling serapes made from tin foil, and glass-bead purses, and figures carved out of pine with quartzite pebble eyes and detachable penises. And there was the Freak Show and the boardwalk cafés, and a wino who looked like Ernest Hemingway with a sign that read 'Why lie, I need a beer', and quaint little bungalows festooned with flags, and jogging families, and fat teens hunting for weed, and all the carnival of a Sunday afternoon that I had been exiled from by a circumambulation I now realized had been completely traduced, for I was but one of a legion of writers tramping round LA, we were all the same: poorly registered, our very images thieved from us – just another chapter in the tale of our immiseration. And in final confirmation of this Kazuo Ishiguro danced past, Netherfield Park tied to his head: he'd made it to Venice before me, together with the Bennet sisters.

I left the beach and floundered inland to where, at the intersection of Windward and Pacific avenues, a section of the old arcade was still standing, with its Corinthian columns striding along the sidewalk. I was so disoriented – so dispirited. If I'd had anything to write on I would've made a shill of my own, but instead the very ordinary chained man leant against a pillar and felt the whole city – from LAX to South Central, from South Central to Downtown, from Downtown to Hollywood, and from Hollywood to here – revolve about his head, a whirlpool of 'burbs and malls and office blocks and country clubs, through which cars drove and Metro trains clattered with absolute disregard.

\*     \*     \*

Some scenes from Brad's movie *The Shrink* were being shot on location nearby, so I headed on over to Dell Avenue with a view to hanging out for a while – the circumambulation might have failed, but not to visit a murder scene when I was in LA to find a killer seemed like a dereliction. This neighbourhood boasted the last-remaining canals, long troughs of stagnant water reflecting the façades of the self-conscious buildings. The vibe was arty, not artful – men who moisturized sat outside upmarket patisseries in the hot June sunlight, sipping cappuccinos with cashmere pullovers tied round their necks.

I spotted where the filming was going on from a long way off: there were maybe twenty or thirty trucks and SUVs parked along the kerb, and around a hundred techies wearing carpenter jeans and T-shirts merchandising Pacific Northwest grunge bands were milling about performing essential tasks. They were all elbows and earrings and had mouthfuls of crocodile clips but no time for me because time was at a $50-per-hour premium. So I pushed on through and discovered maybe fifty or so boys and girls armed with clipboards, and one of them fetched Brad, who swished his lips open in what I supposed was a welcoming smile – either that, or he might've been trying to dazzle me with his teeth.

'There's not a lot happening,' he said, 'but feel free to wander around – we'll be doing a couple of takes . . . soonish.'

The house was a 1980s riff on the modernist Case Study aesthetic, all sliding glass doors, wide windows and external conversation pits. A portable generator burbled power on the ground floor, and this was piped up the steep concrete stairs to where cameras, lights and monitors were clustered about the small zone that was to be immortalized. It took over an hour for the eight producers, four directors, seven lighting cameramen, fifteen sound recordists and thirty-eight lighting technicians to be happy with the set-up. I found the process utterly absorbing, all the more so because in order to get the lighting and the camera angle exactly right I was asked to sit on one of the banquettes as a stand-in for Pete Postlethwaite, who was late on set.

When he eventually arrived he came skipping up the stairs looking tanned, relaxed, fit and debonair, with two or three achingly beautiful personal assistants tripping along behind. He barely glanced at me as Brad made a fragment of an introduction – 'Pete, this is—' – and skipped on to a zone of mirrors and clothes racks where twenty or thirty makeup artists and wardrobe assistants began prepping him.

I might have been offended, were it not that Postlethwaite's arrival was immediately succeeded by a still greater commotion – a running back and forth of production crew, the collective making of manifold phone calls, the passing of orders up and down the chain of command, the mournful note of a bosun's whistle. I hunkered down in a corner and made myself as small as possible; when I looked up again a mass of denim legs was shuffling along the corridor. I stood and peered over their shoulders.

The cynosure of all this activity was looking grimly at a tray being held in front of his overly familiar face, a tray containing a selection of watches – the straps gold, chrome, leather; the faces jewelled, plain or black. It was Kevin Spacey – I recognized him instantly, because in common with all movie stars he had that quality of being pre-known, his face not so much a visage as an *a priori* category waiting to be filled with a serviceable identity. In this case the limp pennant of a mohair tie, the clever prostheses that filled out his cheeks and neck, the still more skilled weeding out of his hair and the inspired tarnishing of his teeth confirmed that he was portraying Dr Zack Busner.

As Spacey's hand ranged over the watches, picking one up and then dropping it with a 'chink' clearly audible because of the hushed reverence of the 250-strong crew, I was visited with an overpowering intimation of death: Death pressed me back against the rough concrete wall, Death rubbed my belly, Death circled my wrist with his bony finger and bony thumb and all the rottenness of this world oozed from the holes in his skull.

'OK, rolling.' Brad's instruction was incredibly downbeat – no bullhorn, no gofers yelling, 'Quiet on the set please!' We couldn't see the players from where we stood, only a monitor upon which the fuzzy black-and-white figures of Spacey and Postlethwaite confronted each other, seated either side of a concrete coffee table. A clapperboard was waved in front of the camera scrawled with: '107 #1. INT. DAY. Busner's consulting room, Venice Beach'. Then:

BUSNER: How's it going with Shiva Mukti?
CLIENT: OK, I guess.
BUSNER [*provocatively*]: He's a neat guy, Shiva, but kinda dull.
CLIENT: He shot movies of me when I was, like, freaking – then played them back to me.
BUSNER: Did it help?
CLIENT [*giggling*]: Help . . . well, I guess with the movies – and a little bit with reality—

'OK, that's cool,' Brad called, and the whole schmozzle ground to a halt. Spacey stood up and began rolling his shoulders, presumably to ease the tension of performance.

'Where's Philbin?' Brad asked a nearby AD, 'I need Philbin here right now – and tell him to bring the sides.'

'Philbin!' 'Philbin!' 'Philbin!' The name echoed away through the house and in a short while a fussed-looking writerly type – small, glasses, needlessly sensitive face – came hustling up clutching a handful of A5-sized yellow pages.

'OK, Philbin.' Brad took the sides from him and shuffled through them rapidly to find the right scene. Maybe seven or fifteen men and women in business suits materialized out of nowhere, and the entire group adjourned sideways through sliding doors on to a roof terrace, where they formed a promenade of couples, passing the yellow pages back and forth between them.

Eventually some sort of consensus was reached, because Brad and the blackleg writer came back with the relevant side and they bent over it together. Brad said, 'Uh, yuh, uh, so . . . here, and here – I don't like that – that doesn't seem to me the kinda way he'd say that at all.'

'It's too, uh, teen?' Philbin ventured tentatively.

'Yeah!' Brad was delighted. 'You got it, Philbin, it's too goddamn *teen*, now put some words in his mouth that have got more . . . more . . .'

'Gravitas?'

'I'll grab your fuckin' ass if you don't hustle, Philbin,' Brad laughed, and the writer withdrew to a corner with the script editor and the script editor's four assistants. Spacey was now doing neck rolls.

After a few minutes Philbin was back with the new sides and Brad okayed them and Spacey and Postlethwaite scanned them fast like the pros they were, and the makeup and wardrobe people stampeded out of shot and the clapperboard was waved in front of the camera again: '107 #2. INT. DAY. Busner's consulting room, Venice Beach'. Then:

BUSNER: How's it going with Shiva Mukti?
CLIENT: OK, I guess.
BUSNER [*provocatively*]: He's a cool guy, Shiva, but sorta dull.
CLIENT: He shot movies of me when I was, like, freaking – then played them back to me.
BUSNER: Did it help?
CLIENT [*giggling*]: Help . . . well, I guess with the movies – and a little bit with reality

There was no denying: it was an improvement – far more plausible. But I knew there'd be at least twenty or fifty more takes before they nailed the scene down and I had six or seven miles still to go. I didn't want to disturb Brad while he was shooting, so I asked one of the gofers to tell him goodbye from me. She said she'd make sure Brad's PA got the message: 'He should know you've gone by early next week – midweek at the latest.'

I set off along Dell pursued by the sinister intimations I'd had when Spacey was sorting through the watches. Watches! Such a cliché – whether on wrists, mantelpieces, or melting in the corner of Dalí canvasses, timepieces were always just that. Still, what did I have to fear? I'd survived it all, and here were the cheery apartment blocks surrounding Marina del Rey, their balconies like the open draws of filing cabinets, their sunbathing tenants brown-papery in the afternoon sun.

I'd survived it all, and here were out-of-work hoofers break-dancing with placards advertising real estate brokers at the intersection of Washington and Lincoln boulevards – tossing them up in the air, then catching them behind their backs. There was a metaphor there, but I was too weary and footsore to reach for it; I only wanted to keep on going across the Ballona wetlands, where Leonardo DiCaprio had flown his Spruce Goose, and the Native American juju had repelled the developers and the toxic effluent from Hughes Aircraft had been pumped away and the egrets and the herons waded . . . I only wanted to keep going, but there was this awful tinnitus plaguing me – bass notes and bum notes, a sax riff that pierced me from ear to ear.

The sidewalk gave out and I went on, the fenders of SUVs shaving my cheek. I wanted to keep going – but out here in the middle of the marsh, where freshwater floods met saltwater tides and the wrack was Infinitis and Escalades and trucks and town cars, all mired in solid oil, I spied a figure tailing me from the front. How long had he been there? Had he been keeping tabs on me all the way from the Chateau Marmont, or from still further back along my circuit? He was in shirtsleeves, a jacket slung over his shoulder, and although I thought I recognized the set of his shoulders and the shuffle of his gait, every time I tried to catch up (the bass doubling time, the sax beginning to rock), he accelerated as well. I slowed down and he slowed down, I hopped and he hopped, I skipped and he skipped.

Tiring of this, I stopped – and he stopped. The tinnitus faded to a distant plink-honk. We stood twenty yards apart for a minute or so. I turned back to face Marina del Rey, then whipped back round – I'd caught him out: it was Mac Guffin. 'So it's you,' I called. 'Should I be afraid? I mean, when you turn up people generally get dead – even your clients.'

'Especially my clients,' he called back. 'My clients have a near 100 per cent fatality rate.'

'But you don't let it get to you, do you, Mac?'

'I try to maintain a regular disposition.' He held his hands palm up, the laughter lines creased around his trustworthy brown eyes.

'What're you trying to tell me, Mac – that the worst has already happened?'

'I figure someone had to, Will: you're a dead man walking. You've been dead since Laurel Canyon.'

'Was it the implants?' I asked, kneading my breasts through the damp fabric of my T-shirt. 'I mean, I know suicide rates are way higher for the women – the people who've had them.'

'No.' He shook his head pityingly. 'It wasn't the implants; it was that dumb-ass report you wrote. You didn't think you could get away with saying those things about the sigmoidal flexure of TC's penis without getting clipped, didya?'

'Well, I dunno . . .' I hung my head in the sweet breeze coming in off the wetlands.

'Y'know what it was, Will, it was attention-seeking.' Mac shook his head; he didn't seem so happy today.

'I . . . I just wanted to belong.'

'Well, now you do belong: to the departed. And, while we're at it, it's 10.2 and 67 degrees.'

'I had no idea it was that . . . big.'

'No' – again the weary shake – 'you had no idea.' And he turned his back on me and trudged on along the scrappy verge. Having no alternative, I followed my Charon, the swish-swash of the traffic fading imperceptibly into the moody horns and sucrose strings of a pickup orchestra fucking over *The Isle of the Dead* in Westwood.

Which faded out on the rise, where Mac halted and I turned back, hoping for a sweeping panorama of the coastline, but saw only a sign for La Vista Motel and the highway in its mid-ground of embankment and plantation, up above the blue screen and a few dabbles of cirrus. 'Well,' he said, 'I've gotta leave you here, man; there's a hiking trail along the bluff to the playa – kinda neat walk.'

'Neat walk!' I spat. 'What is this crap?'

'Y'know,' Mac said, observing me with impatience and pity, 'some people walk for fun, Will, for leisure – to have a good time.'

'I . . . I don't know what to say . . .'

'You mean there's no illusion of a core self that's giving you direction?'

'Ye-es, I s'pose so.'

'Well, what can I tell you,' he said, sucking his moustache; 'this is an amazingly complex piece of software – there're bound to be some glitches. I mean to say, this has to be the first time anyone's tried it.'

'Tried what exactly?'

'Kidnapping someone, forcing them to undergo systematic motion-capture filming and standard-deviation face tracking, then replacing them with a 3-D image of themselves.'

'So that's what was going on – I wondered. Boy' – I shook my empty head – 'they must have been laughing when I asked what my motivation was.'

'Yeah, kinda ironic: they knew all about your motivation – and I have'ta give it to you, Will, you were on to something, you got close, but there was no way they were going let you find out who killed the movies—'

'So they killed me and replaced the actors playing me with an animation.'

'You got it.'

That's why I'd been feeling so exiguous, so thinly drawn – and that's why my thoughts came to me unbidden, and I had no sense of smell, taste or . . . touch. I wondered how far back it all went – to the CGI riot in Hollywood or even before that? But there was no point in speculating, not when I'd paid someone to discover the truth for me. 'Tell me, Mac.' As I spoke, I expertly rolled a cigarette with one hand, struck a non-safety match on my thumbnail and lit it – now that I was a simulacrum of myself cliché came unbidden, and smoking was a stylish breeze. 'If I'm a 3-D image of myself, then what exactly am I being projected on to? I mean, what's all this stuff, is it LA or just a blue screen?'

Pity gave way to impatience as Mac rolled down his sleeves and fastened his cuffs. The dirty work had been done. 'I'm a detective,' he snapped; 'not a fucking metaphysician. You want answers to that kinda appearance/reality stuff, go ask the Wachowskis.'

That was it: no farewell, no bear hug; he just turned and strolled away from me, the happy detective out for a Sunday afternoon promenade. While somewhere out in the Valley, in a darkened home studio, an overweight claustrophobic, headphones clamped on his head, crunching Cheerios and messing about with a synthesizer, turned the volume back up on the Rachmaninschmaltz.

Having nothing else to do, I went on. Isn't this what we do: go on, no matter how depersonalized and useless we feel, no matter how lost in our own lives and confused about our role in the universal – if any? I went on past the Westchester golf course and saw the first sharks' fins cutting through the wavy air on the far side of the savage fences. I went on to the junction with Sepulveda and made a right, and then a right again for the terminal. I went on through the curtains of light falling from between the decks of the overpasses, and I went on past the birches in their triangular concrete pots and the benches shaped like aerofoils – fly away, you writing bums! I went on until my rubber soles married with the treads of the escalator and carried me up to departures, and I went on through security and groped my way towards the Air France lounge.

Sitting in there, I looked about me at the other whey-faced travellers contemplating the imminent hurl skywards. They did their best, rattling the sections of that Sunday's *LA Times*, making last-minute phone calls, fiddling in their laptops – but it was hard. The light in the lounge was yellowing, like a fish tank that hasn't been cleaned, and the sounds were all muted except for Lionel Ritchie singing 'All Night Long' – which was far too loud. And I thought, well, I may be dead, but who's to say everyone else isn't as well?

So I did my best to conform and called Stevie Rosenbloom to say goodbye – and got Ellen DeGeneres: 'That's you gone, is it?' she said, and I could only mewl:

'You knew, didn't you?'

'I kinda did,' she admitted, 'although I wasn't in on the whole thing, I mean it was like the tag line for the movie, "The Strangest Vengeance Ever Planned".'

'What movie?'

'*Touch of Evil.*'


I broke the connection without saying goodbye. Of course! And that's why when I reached the colonnade in Venice I had felt so peculiar. I had never circumambulated Los Angeles at all, only remained standing exactly where Welles had executed his famously circuitous tracking shot while the entire city walked around me.

The Heathrow flight was called and I staggered towards it. Then we were taxiing and then we were taking off, accelerating along the timeline of the Sierra as it described civilization's boom and bust, and then the plane lifted off from the runway of LAX and began almost immediately to bank round over the ocean, bumpily gaining altitude. I looked back and below to see enormous cracks snaking across the Los Angeles Basin, some following the boulevards, others cutting through the freeways. I watched, bored, as the Baldwin Hills slid into Crenshaw and Hollywood tumbled down into the Wilshire corridor. The Downtown towers bowed, then curtseyed, then disappeared in boiling clouds of dust, the Sierra itself humped up into a vast breaker of earth, lava and fire that came surging down, annihilating all of Pasadena and East LA in a matter of seconds.

The final thing I saw before the first clouds began flickering by was the dome of the Shrine Auditorium standing proud of the maelstrom, the crescent atop its elegant spire glinting in the rays of twilight's last gleaming.

# Will Hay and the Fat Boy

'And that's what happens to you when you don't take your medication,' Shiva Mukti said in the matter-of-fact way psychiatrists affect in order to cope with the extremities of mental delusion.

We sat and stared for a while, first at the pots and packets of my medications, which he had lined up on the desk – the Seroxat, Dutonin and Carbamazepin – then at the near-obsolete VDU monitor with its mushroom plastic casing that sat whirring at a queer angle on the fake wood veneer of a refectory table.

'Humph.' I was not to be persuaded so easily. 'You say that, but perhaps that's what happens to entire civilizations when they don't take *their* medication.'

'Listen,' Mukti said, solicitous, 'I understand that you may feel a little . . . put out.'

'Put out! Of course I'm put out – wouldn't you be if you discovered it had all been a videotape that your psychiatrist had made of you? And such lousy production values as well.' I drummed the table with my quick-bitten fingertips and longed for a cigarette.

'You have to appreciate, don't you, that these symptoms are potentially very dangerous: the paranoia, the visual and auditory hallucinations—'

'Next you'll be telling me that everyone I meet isn't played by a well-known screen actor!'

He took a ballpoint pen from his jacket pocket and began to draw a series of boxes on the sheet of paper next to my medication. What was this, the beginnings of a storyboard?

'No, that's right – they aren't actors, any more than you are. Capgras and Fregoli's delusions, these are well described in the literature: the impersonation of people known to the, ah, patient – either by the famous, or by doubles. I admit, you seem to be experiencing a rather unusual combination of both, but, as Dr Busner has remarked, yours is an especially ebullient and productive schizothymia.'

'You don't understand, do you?' I countered. 'I *like* my delusions. They're a form of entertainment for me – what the hell else is there to amuse me any more, now that film is dead?'

This seemed to stymie Mukti and he left off his doodling to examine me more intently through his antiquated pince-nez. Really, it was a ludicrous bit of miscasting: the white skin, the fluting voice, the thinning hair and the hoary old comic delivery – still, I was happy with it if it kept the credits sequence short. What I was less happy with was my trousers, which were painfully tight. Holding Mukti's gaze, I surreptitiously loosened my belt – it wouldn't be good if he realized that I had realized that he was being played by Will Hay.

# Spurn Head

And past the poppies bluish neutral distance
Ends the land suddenly beyond a beach
Of shapes and shingle. Here is unfenced existence:
Facing the sun, untalkative, out of reach.

– Philip Larkin, 'Here'

# I

# Daycare

It was not long after I returned from Los Angeles, in the middle of June 2008, that I began to suspect there was something wrong – with the wider world, certainly, but perhaps also with me. At first I linked the fuzziness and forgetfulness that increasingly plagued me with the bizarre experience of walking to Hollywood; it seemed only just that the extraordinarily rich ebullition gifted me – particularly on the morning when I walked from the Chateau Marmont to Venice along Santa Monica Boulevard – should be compensated for by mental impoverishment.

The body, always a sturdier vessel, had righted itself soon enough: the superpowers I had possessed in LA – enabling me to leap tall buildings, stop buses with the palm of my hand and warp the trajectory of bullets – faded as soon as I reached home. When I tried to show my smaller sons what a hero I'd become by leaping over the wire-mesh fence of the all-weather football pitch in the local park, I threw myself straight into it. The five-a-side players left their ball pattering and came over to mock me where I lay.

But, while physically I simply returned to normal – the dull accommodation of my body, its strip-lit limbs and identical en suite organs – my mental faculties continued to deteriorate. When I came to consider the matter, the fact was that my memory had been eroding for some time: the grey waters of Lethe undercutting its soft cliffs, so that individual recollections – which, no matter how tasteless and bogus, nonetheless had the virtue of being owned outright, not mortgaged – tumbled on to the beach below. I could only posit forgetfulness-within-amnesia to explain how I had confused this with the standard-issue agnosia of middle age: names and faces shuffled together, so that I often spent a half-hour or more at a party talking to someone I knew perfectly well, yet whose identity remained obstinately hidden.

Stupidly, I had indulged in special pleading on my own behalf – and for several years this did act as a groyne with which to impede the longshore drift. There was my notoriety, which served to make me more memorable to those I had met than I would've been otherwise, and so encouraged them to come forward: 'You don't remember me, do you, but . . .' Then there was also the nature of my work, which meant that either I was in solitary reclusion, or else revolving around the country promoting my novels at bookshops and literary festivals. Thrust, blinking, on to podium after stage, I suspected that, while I might be providing sharply etched vignettes for audiences, to me the experience was but part of an on-blurring.

It was true that in the decade since I had stopped drinking and taking drugs my short-term memory seemed to have improved; at any rate, I no longer needed the elaborate system of Post-it notes stuck to the walls of my writing room that had for years served me as a kind of random access. If I maintained this, it was more as an art installation, or magic ritual, designed both to represent the combinatorial powers of the imagination – and to stimulate them to order, then reorder, the tropes, gags, metaphors and observations with which I built my papery habitations. Recency may have been a slippery proposition, happy sociable families a demanding game, but I cleaved to the notion that my textual memory was better than ever. Sadly, this was a delusion; rather, it was my skill alone that had improved: I now wrote books with the workmanlike despatch of a carpenter turning out tables, this busy practice obscuring the loss of much I had once known.

In London, walking from the tube station, before I reached the grey whales' backs of Frederick Button's 1952 ferroconcrete bus garage, I passed a row of lime trees planted in circular beds raised above the pavement. Around the low brick walls the tarmac writhed with the slow subterranean flexing of the limes' roots; while at the base of their trunks was all manner of rubbish: cigarette packets, aluminium cans, beer bottles and sweet wrappers were impaled on spiky shoots. It made an arresting image – this coppicing of trash – and ever since the winter, when I'd first noticed it, I'd reminded myself almost daily to go and photograph the waste-withies. Now it was summer and a thick canopy of leaves hid the mundane fruit.

Now it was foetid summer – the atmosphere super-saturated with sweat-metal – and I realized, belatedly, that I had taken the limes for granted.

It was the same with the trees in the local park. As evening shadows flowed between the tower blocks, young men would bring their Staffordshire bull terriers out to be exercised. They tacked back and forth along the spore-smelling streets, human leaning away from canine as if hauling on a rope attached to a wayward boom. Then, in the park, the boys would complacently observe the dogs as they shat, before urging them on to attack the trees. The dogs broke the boughs' necks, they gored the wrinkled hides – when they were done the oaks, rowans and birches looked as if a shell had exploded nearby, stripping long, white-green slats from their trunks. Eventually, these fell away, leaving only a necklace of dead bark immediately beneath the crown of the tree – and it was this that I forgot to record.

I couldn't remember names, faces, places I had been and books I had read – but there was also a sinister awareness of estrangement from my immediate vicinity. London, the city of my birth – which I knew, not exhaustively, but well enough to set out from home and find my way almost anywhere intuitively – was becoming alien to me. Weaving among the lunchtime joggers along Rotten Row, then rounding Wellington's old gaff at Number One, London, I would find myself in uncharted waters, with the effortlessly oriented gulls wheeling insultingly overhead: 'Heeeere! Heeeere! Heeeere!' That middle-aged Italian couple – he with puff of smoky beard, she with too youthful T-shirt and bum-bag – would it be too perverse to enquire if I might consult the map they held stretched between them? For I no longer recognized this city, this *Londra*.

At home, every day I expected to be exposed: my wife or children to arrest me on the stairs and cry, 'I do not know you!' Or, worse still, 'You do not know me, do you?' Basic mnemonics, long used by me to recall PIN numbers, or the name of the man in the bike shop, now had to be contrived for my nearest and dearest: she is not fat; fat people are D-shaped side on – therefore, her name begins with a D.

I linked the amnesia and the facial agnosia with my growing myopia. Print wasn't attending to personal grooming: the index of the *A–Z* began to grow stubble; next it was the turn of the thesaurus. There seemed some logic to this: first I became disoriented – then I was unable to check my orientation; first I failed to recognize my interlocutors – then I was unable to search for synonyms, and so all shades of meaning were balled into monism. 'This,' as De Niro's character in *The Deer Hunter* philosophized upon a bullet, 'is this.' But what did 'this' mean? I'd forgotten and could no longer consult the dictionary without glasses.

Still, I kept writing. I was correcting the proofs for a story-cycle that was to be published that autumn. For all that I professed – to friends, colleagues, whoever would listen – that I was no longer focused on producing books (like tables, or bullets), but rather thought of the work as my fundamental praxis, my way of mixing my mind with the world and so extending my being – bits of text still had titles, the author's name and my mugshot on the jacket.

The only memory I could summon with complete clarity was of a series of events that hadn't happened to me at all, scenes from a documentary about a woman suffering from early-onset Alzheimer's that had been made – simply and affectingly – by

her daughter. The woman was still feisty at the beginning of the film; thrice-married, but now on her own, she was only in her late fifties. She had her house, her garden, a job as a librarian in the university town where she lived. After her diagnosis, with sickening rapidity, she tipped backward into the coalhole of amnesia.

To begin with she was giddy with the fall – amused by her own forgetfulness. Like me, she devised mnemonics and stuck up Post-it notes; she kept a laboriously calibrated chart attached to the fridge, so she could discover what she should be – or actually was – doing. At first she checked this from day to day, then hour to hour, and eventually moment to moment. Soon enough she became depressed – and this coincided with her trips to a daycare centre, her raven hair nestling on the minibus beside all those snowy cowls.

Depressed and distressed. She sought alleviation, and throughout her miserable deterioration kept asking her daughter to take her to Southwold on the Suffolk coast, a picturesque resort where they had often holidayed and she had loved to sea bathe. But her daughter – in frank asides to the camera – explained that this was a wish she felt unable to accede to, for fear that her beloved mother would simply swim out to sea and submerge her own incomprehension in the liquid unknown.

Mercifully, the woman's memory quickly became so circumscribed that she was encased in a mere droplet of self-awareness, a permanent Now, the silvery surface tension of which gifted her once more with girlish high spirits. Purged of foresight and all but a few dregs of sensual recollection, she was free to simply Be; and it was then, finally, that her daughter – no longer fearful that she would commit suicide, for she lacked the capacity to formulate a plan – granted her boon.

The last we, the viewers, saw of the woman was her entering the glaucous waters, looking baby-like in her one-piece black bathing costume, and striking out for the horizon through the gentle swell. The entire film was unutterably poignant, but what struck me most forcibly was that she swam with the same idiosyncratic stroke as my father used to; a sort of sideways doggy paddle, hands pawing at the water, feet ambling through it. And like my long-dead father, the senile woman had an expression that was at once effortful and seraphic.

This image, the woman's joyful face as her mind swam in the Now, and her body in the enduring sea, as I say, returned to me again and again, breaking the silvery surface of the bathroom mirror on the mornings when I remembered to shave; and, had I known of the malaise termed 'paramnesia', I would've understood that these things – the checklist on the fridge, the trips to the Cambridge daycare centre, the awkward hobble down over the Southwold shingle, my adipose body, seal-black and seal-slick in its nylon skin – hadn't happened to me at all.

Someone had sent me – in the way that kindly people do – a book on coping with Alzheimer's. I read it and wondered if my wife had read it as well. Either she had, or she understood intuitively that the way to deal with people who are confused and upset is to provide them with simple cues from their concretized past that match currently baffling situations.

*Who is that child?*

*Why, it's your friend Julian. You love playing with your friend Julian, don't you? Riding your bikes through Sandy Wood, climbing trees and making secret dens.*

She stopped asking me questions and only provided answers: *You'd like to go upstairs now and do some typing.*

She grasped that properly managed I could spend all day existing solely in the manifold of those things that I had once enjoyed: typing in my secret den, while prattling to childhood companions who were, in fact, my own children.

Nevertheless, as the surface tension of June bulged seamlessly into July, I made the decision to undertake another walking tour; one that would, I hoped, either heal, or at least legitimize, what was happening to me.

Of course, all of my little walking tours were methods of legitimizing. Towards the end of my drug addiction it had occurred to me that the manias of cocaine, the torpors of heroin and the psychoses of the hallucinogens – all these were pre-existing states of mental anguish that only appeared to be self-induced, and so, perhaps, controllable, because of the drugs. So it was with the walking, which was a busman's holiday; for, while I trudged along, through fields, over hills, beside bypasses, I remained sunk deep in my own solipsism – then I returned to the chronic, elective loneliness of the writing life. The only real difference I could see between walking and writing was that engaged in the former my digestion achieved a certain ... regularity, while when I wrote I became terribly constipated: a stylite typing atop a column of his own shit.

Walking my six-year-old son to his school, I held his hand fiercely. I ran my fingers over his knuckles, acutely sensitized to skin, bone, muscle and tendons; hugely aware of scale, the way his hand was a smaller version of my own. Yet, while he sought my big hand out – a gentle fluttering – it was I who needed his small one to make love intelligible.

He asked me to resume the story I had been telling him the previous morning, 'George and the Dragon'. With their fierily seductive breath, dragons had burnt up his previous passion, puppies; but, of course, I couldn't remember to what point the free-forming narrative had progressed. 'The cardboard dragon,' he prompted me – and then I got it: George had flown to the top of the mountain. The little dragons had wings, but George, being a human boy alone in Dragonia, had been given a balloon made from sloughed-off dragon skin. Little George had a special mouthpiece, which meant he could breath fire and so fill the balloon with hot air.

At the summit they discovered a whitewashed cottage with a neat garden. The little dragons flew back down – the mountaintop was taboo – but Little George landed his balloon and encountered old Sir George, the knight, who had come to Dragonia many years before in pursuit of dragons and ended up exiled here. However, he told Little George that his reclusion hadn't been too awful, for every day the dragons brought him a packed lunch consisting of a cheese sandwich, a Nutri-Grain bar, a shiny red apple and a carton of mango juice. Sir George had saved all the empty cartons, and over the years used them to build a spectacularly realistic, near-life-sized model of a dragon.

As usual, after filling in the back-story, then adding a few trivial embellishments, we had reached the school. I handed my son his packed lunch and book bag, then he scampered through the gates into the playground.

The dog was straining at the leash, and I had already turned towards the little park near the school when I spotted something lying in the gutter. I stooped to pick it up. It was a scrap of a black-and-white photograph – the top-right-hand corner, implying that the whole had been torn in half and then half again. I looked at it wonderingly. There was the anachronism of a print in this digital age, and there was the still more old-fashioned *feel* of the monochrome image.

I seized upon it – as if it might be a clue of a special kind. Not that it portrayed anything remarkable: only most of the head of a fleshy-faced white man in his mid-thirties; a man who sported a scraggy beard that kept to the bottom of his chin, and whose scalp was outflanking – on both sides – an attempt at a quiff. He looked amiable enough – or, harmless until proved psychopathic by the legwork the clue seemed to demand. He wore a watch with a steel strap; the ragged tear at the bottom and side of the scrap framed the shoulder and cuff of a chequered shirt; behind him were lager bottles, the handles of beer taps and, dimly, what must be shelves of glasses. Above his head a row of optics gleamed.

I found the scrap of photograph unsettling – wrong, even. Once I'd taken it home and clipped it to the shade of an Anglepoise lamp in my writing room, far from receding into the rest of the tat, the man in it forced himself into my consciousness, his eyes frequently catching mine. The mirror behind the bar he sat at, unseen in the photograph, but perceptible as a luminescence countering the camera flash on the beer taps; the utter anonymity of the man, the image created by impulse, in two rips – all this made of it a contemporary version of those painted Russian icons where perspective is deformed in the service of worship. This outsized and hieratic figure was, I concluded, a saint, to be viewed through a hagioscope from the side aisle where I sat, worshipfully typing.

I corrected the proofs for the new collection, and, although long accustomed to the excruciation of my own prose, there was a fresh focus for this. Previously, it had been the bloody style coagulating on the page – that, and the very grating mechanism of metaphor itself: such and such was like such and such; this was like that . . . arrant nonsense! Ask De Niro as Vronsky: this is always this; things are nothing more – or less – than themselves. Now individual words began to get to me. Badly. In this particular text it was 'even', as in the sentence, 'At night, even in the nick, he rubbed whitening powder into his tan cheeks.' Irrespective of context, changing 'even' to 'especially' would hardly change the sense – at least, not so as anyone would give a shit. The evens – which were everywhere I looked – were trumpeting to me, if to nobody else, the increasingly parenthetic (and thus provisional) nature of my own work. I even hated the look of the word, a failed palindrome. I stared at it malevolently, willing it to transform into 'never'.

The very evenness of even disgusted me; a spondee, its syllables equally stressed, I found it doubly stress*ful*. It also reminded me of my father, of whom it was often remarked that he had 'a remarkably even temper'. Even to think of his phlegm was enough to rouse my choler. In the years since his death I had resolved my issues with him, operating like a family therapist who views dysfunction comfortably from behind the mirrored glass of mortality, yet I knew that he'd think the books I was writing exhibited both a profound negativity as well as a satirical miniaturism that he was fairly (fairly!) critical of when alive. True, his mildness meant he was ill cast as a punitive superego, and when I compared his gentle critiques with the execrations that issued forth from the death masks of friends' parents, it occurred to me that, although I was losing my memory and my sight, I remained preternaturally sensitive.

So, there were these: the amnesia and agnosia, the myopia and logophobia. I was as disengaged from the zeitgeist as my father – who had been a conscientious objector during the Second War – for, while much of the commonality were passionately engaged with their support for – or alienation from – campaigns against nouns (the 'War on Drugs' and that on 'Terror' being the most salient), I was trying to defeat *an adverb*. In sum: it was all these yappy feelings that herded sheepy me towards another walking tour, whilst the very erosion of my memory drew me, seemingly ineluctably, towards the Holderness coast of East Yorkshire, the 35-mile stretch of crumbling glacial till between the chalk cliffs of Flamborough Head and the shingle spit of Spurn Head.

Carried along in the mudslide of my amnesia were pathetic fragments of childhood recall. One was of Michael Barratt, the presenter of the long-lived BBC1 current affairs programme *Nationwide*, interviewing a man in a house that was tumbling down a clayey cliff. The homeowner was saying, in broad Yorkshire accents, as he stood in one half of a conservatory – the other half was nowt but a jumble of broken spars and cracked panes – 'I can't oonderstand it, I only poot those UPVC windows in two year ago – and now loook at the place!'

Even at the time – and I cannot have been more than eleven or twelve – I remember thinking that this fellow must have been formidably stupid to have invested in a property on the brink of a sea cliff; for had Barratt not just told the viewers that this was the fastest-eroding coast in Europe? That its biscuity loess was being dunked, then chomped, by the North Sea at the prodigious rate of two whole yards every year, as fast, in geological terms, as a speeding bullet?

Then again, I may be giving too much credence to a capacity for retention that I've already conceded is ruptured, because, now I come to think of it, Barratt seldom ventured beyond the Lime Grove studios from where *Nationwide* was put out live. These local interviews were conducted by regional reporters and screened via a feed. Barratt, with his distinctively 1970s hairdo – a splodge of ice cream rippling over his forehead – was a rock of a presenter, who, even when the mass medium was only twenty-odd years old, still managed to fuse dash and paternalism in a uniquely televisual way.

A snappy clarion of horns, a rappel of strings: 'Dada-daaa! Dada-daaa!' 'The Good Word' by Johnny Scott leapt down the scale accompanying the beguiling title sequence. Archetypes of modern Britain appeared in quick succession: a car accelerating up on to the Severn Bridge; a man with a child in his arms; the Tyne at Newcastle; a man speaking on a car phone the size of a small car; electricity pylons stalking across countryside; the ectomorphic cooling towers of a power station with sheep grazing in the foreground; a train disgorging commuters.

These vignettes took up alternate spaces with the *Nationwide* logo in a 3 x 3 grid, the logo being simply the letters 'NW', with the arm of the *W* and the leg of *N* curled so as to cuddle the couple. In retrospect this logo was strongly evocative of the Nazi swastika, while the sequence evoked our own naive faith in technological advance. The very rapidity of these images of motion, then the way the 'NW' logo multiplied, streaming in threads across the screen to form four revolving cogs, while 'The Good Word' went on 'Dada-daaa! Dada-daaa!'ing – all this I am able to summon up despite *Nationwide* being closer to the Normandy landings than I am now to it. I wonder, has each generation's perception of time – its decadences, its stratigraphy – always been like this? Or is our current sense of time piling up into a necessarily terminal moraine of events simply a function of the digitization of knowledge, which makes it inevitable that the entire networked society will end up, like poor Funes in Borges's tale 'Funes the Memorious', unable to delete a single paltry occurrence or cultural factoid?

And so, there will be Holocaust Remembrance Day, and Holocaust Remembrance Day Remembrance Day, and Holocaust Remembrance Day Remembrance Day Remembrance Day, and Holocaust Remembrance Day Remembrance Day Remembrance Day Remembrance Day – until the significance of the Holocaust itself – which no one any longer living has had direct experience of – is quite forgotten.

I repeat, a culture that is afflicted with such a hyperthymestic syndrome will never recoup itself, never experience the necessary downtime for renaissance to occur. 'It was very difficult for him to sleep. To sleep is to be abstracted from the world; Funes, on his back in his cot, in the shadows, imagined every crevice and every moulding of the various houses which surrounded him. (I repeat, the least important of his recollections was more minutely precise and more lively than our perception of a physical pleasure or a physical torment.)'

There was a raw constructivism to the *Nationwide* title sequence – and a peculiar masculinity also. There were no women nationwide – at least, not in this erect procession of images, whose subtext was a series of phallicisms: Progress, the well-lubricated interpenetration of Town and Country, Benign Paternalism. I loved *Nationwide*; my brother and

I would watch it whenever we could – which wasn't often, because our insufferably *bien-pensant* parents had, in their infinite snobbery, got rid of our television. Usually, the current affairs the show reported were emphatically soft and mushy: items about skateboarding ducks, or a monastic order that manufactured toothbrushes; hard news resounded elsewhere. It was presumably in this spirit of quirky human interest that the man at Skipsea Sands on the Holderness coast had been interviewed.

Middle age – the fulcrum around which the mind-world turns. In youth the future is murky, while the past has a seeming clarity – but now it's the future that becomes crystal clear: blackberries shining in a hawthorn hedge after sudden autumnal rain. Decline – then death. Meanwhile the past recedes, lapping back from a muddied shore across which it's unsafe to wade – who knows what might have happened there?

At New Year there had been a photograph in the newspaper headed 'Hazardous New Year' and captioned 'Houses close to a cliff in Skipsea, Yorkshire, have been gradually falling over the edge and it is thought unlikely that they will survive the year.' They? Survive? Echoes surely of the personification of property that had dominated Britain in the early years of the century, but, setting this to one side, there remained the uncanny feeling that while the householders had been watching for years as the void encroached on their loved ones – undercutting the gardens, munching on the rockeries, crunching up the cucumber frames, then picking its teeth with raspberry canes – I had been watching them watch.

*       *       *

I conceived of taking a walk from Flamborough Head, north of Bridlington, where the chalk synclines of the Yorkshire Wolds are sheered off by the brown sea, to Spurn Head, that peculiar three-mile shingle bracket that hooks round into the wide mouth of the River Humber. It occurred to me that were I to keep for the entire distance within six feet of either cliff edge or shoreline, I would, very likely, have completed a journey it would be impossible for anyone to ever make again. By the time another year had passed the solid ground that had risen up to meet my feet would have disappeared forever.

This would be a unique walk of erasure – a forty-mile extended metaphor for my own embattled persona, as its foundations were washed away by what I suspected was early-onset Alzheimer's. Perhaps it was also sympathetic magic: the walk devised as a ritualized erection of groynes, which might impede the longshore drift of my psyche.

To counter this – frankly morbid – self-absorption, I scanned the data on long-, short- and medium-term cliff erosion rates. I checked out coastal evolution and beach plan shape modelling. I examined the evidence of site inspections, and the various proposals – including the Mappleton coastal defences – that had been advanced against the ceding of solid to liquid. I read the reports of expert witnesses, and looked at the aerial photographs they had posted on the web, marked up so as to make explicit the underlying dynamics.

The names of the towns and villages that had been inundated since the medieval era were legion: Wilsthorpe, Hartburn, Hyde, Withow and Cleton; Hornsea Burton, Hornsea Beck and Southorpe; Great Golden, Golden Parva and Old Aldborough – and so on; like mortality itself, the sea had ground into utter oblivion, these, the habitations of already faceless villeins. Near to Spurn Head itself had stood the substantial town of Ravenser, a sturdy plantation of spires and spars where Henry Bolingbroke landed in 1399, and which, until the rise of Hull, was the principal port of Yorkshire. Since the Roman occupation more than fifty square miles of land had gone from Holderness, and still it disintegrated, clods and stones plash-plopping into the shallow sea.

As I undertook these researches the conviction grew in me that far from the erosion of two yards of land every year being a tragedy, it should be regarded as uplifting – for here was a landscape that was more transient than an individual human. The bungalows would be rebuilt inland, the UPVC windows reinstalled, the caravans would head north to Filey – only the earth was drowning.

I had never visited the Holderness coast, although, on a couple of occasions, I'd gone up to Hull to do book readings. The first time I went the crowd at the bar where I read seemed convivial, and afterwards I fell into conversation with a local man, talk that – I now realize – had itself been rendered parenthetical by the great bracketing of nearby Spurn Head. (He was a tall British-Asian with angular, faceted looks that mirrored my own – including the sunken cheeks, pockmarked with old acne scars.)

The man explained how he and his son liked to drive out on a Sunday, through the lush reclaimed lowland of Sunk Island to the peninsula, and how the sense of abandonment and loss they both felt – the family was broken, they were deracinated – was almost pleasurably compounded by Spurn Head itself, where on the eastern flank of the peninsula a Victorian lighthouse stood, surrounded at high tide by the waters of the estuary, for the shingle and sand spit where it had once rested had wavered away to the west.

On their walks along the beaches, the man and his son happened upon slimed reefs of discarded chattels – fridges, televisions, washing machines, the dinosaur bones of antediluvian agricultural equipment – all of it caught in serried piles, which in previous centuries had been driven into this skittish land in a forlorn attempt to *pin it down*. And as I listened to the man talk – he was not articulate, but expressive, what with his shrugs and hand-chops and hesitations – I was thrust back to the Paragon Station at which I had arrived a couple of hours previously.

It was a proper terminus – emphatically at the end of the line. As I had lurched stiffly from the train, I was struck by how lofty the vaulted roof seemed; tiny humans beetled along the grey platforms beside the worms' casts of the rolling stock, while from up on high cold loads of light were let down through translucent perspex. By the time I had reached the booking hall the fugue had intensified: the old oaken island of a branch of W. H. Smith's and the blind arches along the walls faced with caramel-brown tiling shored up the mounting sensation that I had arrived too late; that this was the voided – although not yet decaying – outpost of an empire that, rather than being overthrown, had been undermined by creeping indifference.

That was the first visit. The second time I went to Hull I was early for my event and so walked through the shopping zone to visit the museum down by the old dock area, passing a pub that advertised Lindisfarne Fruit Wines and mixed drinks with names such as 'Dr Pepper's Depth Charge' and 'Shit-on-the-Grass'. In the cobbled streets of the eighteenth-century town the silence was louder than bombs.

It was a quiet weekday afternoon in summer, and almost museum closing time. Once I'd passed the somnolent staff in the shop full of moulded plastic and printed cotton, I found myself alone in a series of comfortingly predictable spaces. Polystyrene rocks housed dioramas of the Holderness coast of 120,000 years previously, when elephants wandered the jungly cliff that ran miles to the west of the present-day coastline. Then came a dummy of a Holocene mammoth, standing foursquare on the linoleum tiles; then there were Neolithic artefacts and a life-sized, mop-topped human dummy that had been buried in a fibreglass sarcophagus.

Passing between the glass cases full of earthenware and bronze anklets, I became aware of an eerie hissing sound and a woman muttering in a half-foreign tongue. Exactly at the moment I realized this must be a recording, I saw the lit-up glass case containing the late Bronze Age wooden figurines known – after the Holderness drainage ditch where they were discovered in 1836 – as the Roos Carr Figures.

As I read the information cards, and stared at the curious spindly men, carved from pine over 2,000 years previously, I found that my mind was racing – forward in time, back in time, circling my own lifetime, then plotting its curve on to the widening gyre of history itself – while my body was paralysed, drenched in sweat.

The pebble eyes inserted in the pinheads of the four figures that had been placed upright in the carved boat held me captive for long minutes, then released me to stagger into the mock-up of an Iron Age village. The muttering was, as I suspected, a curator's notion of proto-English, placed in the mouth of a manikin at a treadle. I stood gathering my wits for a while, under the cutaway thatch of a newly ancient hovel, until the staff member assigned to check the galleries were empty came past me. 'Oh! You frightened me,' she said, and then: 'I suppose I should be used to it by now.' It being, I supposed, the presence of live humans in among the instructional dummies.

Later on, I was approached after the reading by a man who told me that his wife had very much wanted to attend but was unable to do so because she was trapped in their house by a swarm of bees. It was a warm evening and it took us about ten minutes to walk there. The bees were densely clustered on the front door of the two-up, two-down, their translucent wings, gingery bodies and black extremities conveying an impression that this living micro-mosaic was but a detail of a far larger picture.

We went round to the back door and found his wife drinking gin with a friend in the kitchen, while clearly relishing her

predicament. 'I called the police hours ago,' she said. 'But they've not sent anyone yet.'

I pictured the beekeepers who must be on stand-by during the swarming season; half dreading, half hoping that they would be called upon to go and twirl the living candyfloss on to a stick, put it in a box, put the box in the back of a small van. *The bespoke suit of tiny bodies agitating your skin . . . the galvanic stress of knowing they are about to poison you from every angle.*

That night I ate in an empty Bengali restaurant. There were overhead strip-lights, and neon tubes rimmed the plate-glass windows. The tablecloth fluoresced beneath my sad hands as I ate far more chana masala than I'd intended. Later, my belly slopped in my dinkily awful room at the Royal, which was one of those hotels built into the wall of a station like the Grosvenor at London's Victoria Station, or the Great Eastern at Liverpool Street. As a child the Grosvenor had entranced me; its fusty reception rooms and wide staircases seemed doubly interior – rooms inside a big building that was itself inside a bigger building. Yet Victoria, like the Paragon Station in Hull, was open to the elements, swirling with soot and pigeons, and so the hotels were perhaps only gatehouses between one world and the next.

In the predawn I awoke to crouch grimly for a rope-burn of an evacuation, then slept again, uneasily, and dreamt I was standing in the booking hall of the station, staring up through the oculus. I was aware of the tremendous emptiness of sky over sea, and, on stepping out through the main doors, I discovered not the expected thuggery of the shopping centre opposite, but the peninsula of Spurn Head tapering into the distance, its shingle, furze and sand a collage that had no relief or hue but lay flat on the still flatter sea. Just visible, at the very end of the spit, was a vapour trail such as you sometimes see streaming from the tip of an aircraft wing, or a Himalayan peak.

# 2

# Static Homes

I left home at 7.00 a.m. on the Thursday, 24 July 2008. It had been a damp summer and, perversely, I was hoping for poor weather – a Hollywood rain of milky droplets to veil my departure, through which I could scuttle along shining pavements before burrowing into the tube. Down there, in the hypocaust of the city, warmed by the commuters' foodybreath – well, it would be like relapsing into sleep once more; then, I'd reawaken to the sooty chill of King's Cross, a space that no amount of renovation could ever rejuvenate.

Instead there was bright sunlight and butterflies clipped the flowering buddleia by the front gate with their blade-thin wings. At the end of our block there was a pavement shrine: a score of cellophane-wrapped bouquets leant against the iron railings, the spikes of which were festooned with T-shirts, wristbands and laminated cards covered in rap poetry. Spreading out almost to the kerb were tea lights arranged to form the slogan I LOVE FREDDY. There were two or three brightly coloured plastic water guns propped among the shrivelled floral tributes, and as I passed by one of a pair of youths who were contemplating the shrine bent to touch a play weapon, while remarking to his companion, ''E turned 'is back an' ven vay plunged 'im.'

I had with me a notebook and considered stopping to note this down – but then forgot all about it within yards. In the past, at the start of a journey, its pages would be blankly awaiting the obsessively tight stitching of my handwriting as I tried to sew observation to thought. But now it was already quite full of train times, the places I intended visiting and those where I was booked to stay; a detailed itinerary that was necessary, lest, from one hour to the next, I forgot why it was I had gone to East Yorkshire, where I hailed from – and so was lost entirely.

If I were to be found wandering, mute and disoriented, I wondered what my rescuer might make of those pages where, in anticipation of being unable to recall the right words or phrases, I had pre-emptively set out a multiple-choice list of alternative descriptions, thus:

Flamborough Head is: (a) impressive (b) windy and desolate (c) desolate and oppressive (d) a jolly place, what with the wheeling gulls and the trippers taking tea beneath a candy-striped lighthouse (e) with its humped back and baleen cliffs, suggestive of a beached leviathan.

There were also examples of credible self-knowledge that I could select from upon waking, either from sleep or an amnesiac spell, such as: (a) I dreamt of the lost children again – is there something I am repressing? (b) I have my father's powerful self-absorption together with my mother's fearful neurosis. (c) The anger I felt when the woman in the newsagent's sniggered at me was qualitatively *exactly* the same as that I experienced aged eleven when teased because of my haircut. (d) Impotence can be a refuge. (e) There is no time left now – yet self-obsession is a dimension of its own.

All I had to do – or so I had convinced myself – was circle the appropriate letter and I would add another niblet of commentary to the great multi-and-no-faith Talmud. Yet, by the time I was sprawled on the chequerboard of sweaty plush, the scheme seemed at best unworkable – at worst futile. As the train pulled away from Victoria a recorded announcement intoned: 'The next stop is Victoria, change here for District,

Circle and Piccadilly lines and mainline rail services.' At the time I thought it was a mistake.

The east coast line franchise had been won that summer by a company called Grand Central. The ends of the carriages bore blown-up photographs of Marilyn Monroe and James Dean; passengers – had there been any besides me – might have meditated on the desirability of self-murder and good looks, or else played upon the *Monopoly* and chess boards incorporated into the tables. As I say, the train was nearly empty, yet still it strained to achieve escape velocity, struggling through Camden Town and past Alexandra Palace before leaving the planetoid of London brick behind around Watford.

At Hitchin a Montessori school and a pole-dancing club shared the same single-storey premises. I wondered idly which institution the sign on the flat roof – 'Wonderland' – referred to. Ash trees did a dusty hula-hula along the field margins, gloss-black cattle stood in the deep shadow beneath the massy crowns of oaks. I went to the buffet car in my socks. The steward placed a lidded styrofoam cup in a small paper carrier bag, together with a tea bag in a sachet, a tube of UHT milk and another sachet – this one of sugar. I explained to him – as I withdrew the cup, ripped open the sachet and dunked the tea bag – that tea was an infusion, which meant that it was *vital* for the water to be actually boiling when it came into contact with the leaves. He looked at me furiously – his appeal to health and safety was the hiss of a cornered snake. My probing head felt small, hard, shiny and wedged into the top corner of the carriage like a security camera. I knew – without being able to recall a single instance – that I had behaved like this many times before: taking Canute's stance in the path of the great surge of ill-brewed tepid tea that was inundating England. The steward's glare cut me into diamond shapes that sparkled in the sunlight, then condensed into droplets whipped away from the carriage window – a vaporous trail.

I grabbed a complimentary copy of *The Times* from the counter and beat a retreat to my seat.

The fight went out of the train and it sidled to a halt beside an irrigation system that was jetting liquid assets over a field full of subsidies. I rattled the paper open on this headline: 'Scepticism Mounts over Installation of Holderness Wind Turbines'. There was an aerial photograph showing the thirty-mile outer curve being described by the giant turbines as they were implanted in the seabed between Flamborough Head and Spurn Head.

How could I have forgotten *this*? The largest public works project in living memory, one that had been compared in its scale and dynamism to the Tennessee Valley Authority – or, more tendentiously, the Mittelbau-Dora labour camps that served the V-2 rocket factories. The government's commitment to generate 10 per cent of the nation's electricity using renewable technologies had been the centrepiece of its regeneration programme and seldom out of the news. The long-term unemployed of Tyneside and South Shields had been dragooned back into work, and by some accounts were being treated by the contractors – a German company – with a toughness bordering on brutality. Others said that this was nonsense, that the 30,000-strong workforce was being either newly inducted or retrained in an exemplary fashion and to the highest standards. Once the turbines had been built and installed, these men and women would form the core of a fully revitalized heavy-industry sector in the Northeast: a new generation of welders, fabricators and turners who would rival

– then exceed – the output of those who had built the great warships and artillery pieces of the Imperial era.

When they came on-line, each one of the massive, three-bladed turbines would generate five megawatts of clean power – and there were to be a hundred of them strung along the Holderness coast alone. Naturally there was opposition; an uneasy alliance had sprung up between the power station workers – who saw their jobs blowing away in the wind – and the more extreme environmentalists, who, while they may have campaigned aggressively for renewable energy, never envisaged it being generated on quite this scale, nor predicated upon a gargantuan reindustrialization. And then there were the inhabitants – the operators of shrinking caravan parks and the farmers of diminishing acreages, aghast that so much tax payers' money should be poured into the German Ocean, while their own sea defences – with the exception of those at Hornsea and Withernsea – had been abandoned on the grounds that they weren't cost-effective. In the pubs and golf club bars from Bridlington to Easington it was reported that dark mutterings could be heard, of sabotage – and worse.

I looked up from the article to discover that the train had slow-danced into the flatlands of the Humber estuary. The green corduroy of the fields smoothed away on either side; to the east there squatted the fat-bellied cooling towers of the Drax power station at Selby, belching smoke; while to the west an obese grey-white cloud waddled up into the blue sky, its source the Ferrybridge power station at Knottingley. Was it possible, I mused, to judge by eye alone which of these genies was bigger, or to distinguish limbs from heads? Or was this anthropomorphizing itself evidence of my part in a futile collective denial? For they were nothing, really, these clouds

– only a portion of the thirty million tons of carbon the pair vomited out every year.

Not just the Drax and the Ferrybridge – hereabouts the coal-fired power stations were as windmills in a Dutch landscape; there was the Eggborough at Goole and the Salt End in Hull itself. All those trillions of carbon particles roiling up, then caught by the wind shear and so driven offshore into the turbine blades; dirty power twined by clean into a vaporous trail that wavered over the waves. In the synoptic eye of my fervid mind the turbines became the propellers of a monstrous airship – or landship, for the craft was the seabed and the Holderness coast; straining, the turbines wrenched the crumbling cliffs, the caravans' hard standings, even entire flint-knapped churches away from the East Riding, away from the desert island of Britain.

Under the elegant glass and cast-iron roof of York Station I bought a medium latte with a triple shot of espresso. The caffeine was a bad idea – my bowels liquefied, but the platforms were thronged and there was no time to queue for the toilets, so I pressed in among day trippers who were crowding against the doors of the small, five-coach Scarborough train. Then I struggled past bare arms as pendulous as fat bellies to achieve a single seat. I opened *The Times* again, and as the train chuckled away from York read that the film adaptation of Bret Easton Ellis's *American Psycho* would be screened on a cable channel that evening. 'It's a fascinating insight into an inhuman mind,' the previewer wittered, 'with a late twist revealing the sheer insanity at the core of Bateman's character.'

Bateman? Ellis? The names had a certain familiarity, as did the vignette-sized photograph of a chubby-cheeked man not unlike the young Orson Welles – yet I couldn't pin down the facts: did I know either of them, or had I only seen the movie?

On family car journeys we played the memory game. Each member, in turn, recited the formula 'On my holiday I took with me . . .', then added their own item, whether bucket, spade or pink sun dress. The next player had to remember all the previous things and then add another. Could this be a useful strategy for me, one to add to the mnemonics, the lists of routine activities, and the technique – which I had easily mastered – of not asking myself any questions, or contradicting myself, only supplying a steady flow of reassuring answers?

The passengers sat surrounding me, jammed into the smoothly adzed wooden vessel; their torsos were rigid, their arm-length detachable penises lay by their feet. Their quartzite eyes flickered as cuttings, embankments, trees and barns hurried past the little train, which was mounting now, up into the Yorkshire Wolds. Had they all faked their own deaths, I wondered. If so, where were those things they had taken on their holiday, the floating buckets, the sinking spades, the billowing sun dresses – if not scattered on the cold green waves?

Besides, if I listed *everything* – a 1.5 litre bottle of Coke, a tracksuit top with *trompe l'œil* chainmail sleeves, a child's rubber figurine wearing a Churchillian siren suit but with the head of a pig – wasn't there my paramnesia to contend with? Might I incorporate things that didn't belong to me – and had never even been in my visual field? And so I dredged up an unimpeachable memory: the British Ghanaian writer who had accosted me at a West London summer party, where the guests sheltered from the rain in a palatial playhouse, and, his jaw prognathous with cocaine gurning, clutched my arm as he explained his failure to publish was a result of 'My fatal flaw, see, it's girls in boots with guns. Before the internet it wasn't a problem – I mean, I could control it – access was difficult; but now . . . *Man!* There's too much – a superabundance!'

So I took his flaw with me on my holiday, together with the five empty Ribena cartons that clustered in the rain hood of a Maclaren buggy. Further along the carriage one of the wooden idols cracked its mouth and said, 'I'm a systems analyst.' While I thought, aren't we all?

At Seamer I left the train, laced my boots, then went away through a metal gate to piss among nettles and brambles, their stems and thorns trussed with flung silage. Not good, this modern Millais, the white rim of a discarded paper cup beaded with urine taking the place of Ophelia's wrist, breaking the surface of the pool. The next train was full of commuters heading south to Hull – they took me with them on their business trips, together with the boots, the guns, the girls and the child's rubber figurine wearing a Churchillian siren suit but with the head of a pig.

I detrained at Bempton. The landscape rolled modestly through the final waves of syncline and anticline before the chalk cliffs of Flamborough Head. I had envisioned the train chugging around the crescent bay of Filey, holidaymakers saluting it with uplifted spades, a portly McGill man in a one-piece striped bathing costume leaping, crab nipping his big toe. Instead, there was only this: thick white cumuli tumbling down on the spectral willows, a monotonous breeze, and pebble-dashed bungalows, each neat front garden equipped with a paddling pool and a trampoline. I edged past, stopping every hundred yards or so to see if, by some minor adjustment, I could make my boots more comfortable.

Most of the trampolines had security netting both at the sides and overhead. I was still perplexed; surely the parents were being irresponsible, there had been over 4,000 disappearances this year already. One moment the child happily bouncing, the next raised up not in Rapture but abject terror. Up and up they flew, human balloons trailing thin screams. They never came down again. Inevitably there were many occasions when a sibling or playmate grabbed hold of those about to be disappeared by their trainers, only to let go when too far up. One little girl who had survived the fall was in the hospital at York. Interviewed by detectives, she said she saw nothing, knew nothing and felt nothing but pain. Still the children went on trampolining.

The straight way between two nondescript Yorkshire villages, drivers' mouths wobbling as they swerved to avoid me; a group of sinisterly black toadstools in the grooves of a felled ash; the elongated barrow of an overgrown old railway embankment; the beige earth littered with plough-share-halved flints; Seaways Farm, Home of Agricycle, WARNING: GUARD DOGS, WARNING C.C.T.V. installed on these premises. Then Flamborough village clustered around two fish and chip shops, its peripheral brick semis tucked like *Monopoly* properties in the corner of raggedy fields. The old octagonal lighthouse tipped above the horizon, quaint as a doge's hat; next golfers grazing on their fairways, after that the new lighthouse and after this the cold and salty shock of the white-flecked waves retreating towards a hazy horizon guarded by – Oh! How could I have forgotten *them*?

On my holiday I took with me the fatal flaw of girls in boots with guns, quartzite eyes, a detachable wooden penis, a child's rubber figurine wearing a Churchillian siren suit but with the head of a pig – and these: beyond the whitewashed Coastguard station, and the steely latticing of a pair of radio masts, came marching the tripods with their three-bladed heads. I was shocked by their size – at least 500 feet high, the ones closest to Flamborough Head stood wave-waisted, entire, while those further out each had a bobbing flotilla of barges and service vessels. Further still, where the vast parenthesis tended to the south, the turbines were still being erected; the floating cranes' platforms were measurable by acreage, their davits implausible – their being of human manufacture, that is.

Cheery walkers – 'Hello, matey' – passed me by as I scooted over the headland, my eyes not on grassy quiff but the great bracket of the turbines wavering away in the sea haze. At the cliff edge, I stopped, got out my stove and made tea. Sipping and smoking, I checked the three, shiny-new maps I'd brought, counting the kilometre squares to Bridlington, then Bramston, then on to Skipsea, where I planned staying the night. While I stared into the map's pale clarity of line and colour factoring all dimensions into two, everything appeared intelligible; yet if I peered over my paper lap, down to the shattered chalk at the cliff base, it looked uncannily like broken-up blocks of old metal type. This place, far from legitimizing my amnesia, might prove a fatal shore for my comprehension. I packed up and pressed on, leaving the maps lying on the fan of grass where I'd been sitting.

On my holiday I took with me the fatal flaw – not girls in boots with guns, but Socrates' cashiered madman, who had to be yanked along behind me, drool on his chin, roused only by the surreal lubrications I whispered in his ugly ear. Then there was the rubber figurine – at most two or three inches high – sporting a navy blue siren suit buttoned tightly to the neck and with the head of a pig. However, I forgot the maps and by the time I noticed I'd walked on a couple of miles along the declining cliffs – drawing level with Sewerby Hall, a stately enough pile, although now surrounded by the pavilions and pennants of a caravanning jamboree – and it was pointless going back. My way was physically straightforward and temporally warped; no mapping could explain the grinding away to silt and sand of all those generations who had toiled in the lost fields and beaten back the vanished hedgerows.

My breath in my ears, the rhythm of the waves, the steady tramp of my molars on latex impregnated with nicotine. I still smoked, a bit, but this gum was the scrag-end of my addiction. I had sucked in clouds of self-absorption for decades, shaped then moulded them with tooth, tongue and lip, until finally they were compacted into this dense yet mutable wad.

The cliff face grew fuller and was grassed over. I was in a municipal park where serious pilots had ambitions completely out of scale with their model planes; would-be paragliders hopped about, adipose as bumblebees, their black nylon suits striped with logos, their empty wing cases sagging on their backs. One had managed to get his glider aloft, and it filled out, then curled into a 25-foot parenthesis; he tugged on the guidelines and made local leaps, but I doubted he'd ever get aloft – his chute bracketed him with the land.

The path became lined with benches towards which I felt great compassion. I knew the Yorkshire folk took their passing over seriously and carted their senescent ones here, to the east, where they drowsed out the balance of their lives; becoming stiffer, squatter, more wooden in the sun porches of residential care homes, days and nights speeding across their faces, until, at the moment of expiration, they metamorphosed into these noble sit-upons, at the ends of which their descendants could prop floral offerings.

I'd assumed from the gull cries of the children skating across the slick beach that the town was crowded – then suddenly I was in among the smoked-glass barns full of slot machines and the bits of Victorian terrace, and there was hardly anyone about. Along the front there was a handful of family groups, most consisting of elderly parents eating donuts and a grown-up Down's child with a toffee apple. Lumpy teens jostled in the finely drawn shadows, their cheeks livid with candyfloss. The atmosphere was so sugary the air was granulated, then, at the funfair, the Jungle Ride's dugout canoes were all screamingly empty as they were winched on their cataract over the beach.

I sat down by the old harbour, savouring the fishy smell. A few remaining inshore boats were jostled by a clinking mass of sailing dinghies with aluminium masts, which in turn had been pushed to the barnacled seawall by two giant, crudely formed steel feet. Rising, I went down to the quayside so that the feet towered four storeys above me, rust-streaked rivets running around the insteps and up the shins. To seaward the swell of the calves almost blocked the harbour entrance, but I could make out the thickening thighs, the oil rig of the hips and pelvis, and beyond this the tanker-sized chest stranded on the sands.

It was less the anthropoid form of the turbine that bothered me than the fact of it being there at all. Even if the structure was hollow the highest of tides still wouldn't float it. How had it come to be beached here in Bridlington, rather than implanted with its robotic fellows, the long line of which I could see stitching the horizon with their slow-revolving blades? I wanted to ask someone what *the hell* was going on. How long had the turbine been run aground here? Was it under repair? I couldn't understand why there wasn't a crowd of gawpers – at the very least a fisherman coiling a rope or chipping paint, but there was no one, and when I reached the top of the harbour wall the entire disconcerting length of the turbine was revealed: it was decapitated, bladeless – or armless – and with its slightly bandy legs and deep chest appeared out of kilter. The enormous turbine reminded me of someone, but who? I resolved to find out when I reached Skipsea.

The last Michelin people rolled past me along the low concrete walls bounding some defunct fast-food joints, the beach blew out before me, a quarter- then a half-mile wide. Families were silhouetted behind the bellying canvas of their windbreaks, while lone men flew their outsized kites, each another ellipsis added to the gulls' wings quoting the sky. The lone men staggered, skidded, the kites sliced down on to the sand. The lone men went to curl up behind them.

Inching towards me at my own dogged pace came some stuff washed up along the tide line. Was it frills of seaweed or more durable wrack, detergent bottles and car tyres? The dogs had dragged their walkers off, the kite flyers had skittered away, the wind was rising, and there were no particulars anymore with which to judge the scale of things, only the universals of sea, sand and sky. I started when the first pillbox popped up at my feet, tilted, its single oblong eye black and weeping. Beyond this sentinel there were more and still more hammered down into the wet sand, limpid pools at their gnarled feet. Were they mourning their failure – not to defend the country, for no invasion had ever been mounted – but the land itself, land that, in the seventy years since they had been built, had been driven back a hundred yards to where it now cowered, its raised hackles a field of barley?

I went up there and laid some apostrophic turds among the crop. There was no one around; besides, I doubted that I could really be leaving any spoor. I sensed already that the walk was doing its own mysterious business, so that with each step I took, far from creating a footprint, I rubbed away whatever marks had been left on my memory, leaving it as smooth as the sable plain ahead.

Local Indians stood by their quad-bike steeds, their squaws danced to a boom box; an arrow of WWII fighters flew overhead. This was all: the hours filed by me, the beach narrowed, its innumerable grains flowing through the glassy pinch-point of my contemplation. The shoreline humped up into a muddy cliff of domestic proportions – maybe only sixty feet high. On my holiday I took with me the madman on his chain, the rubber figurine, these clayey flotches and bulbous little stalagmites, in among them the slow surge of the long-since broken waves. I took entire sections of brick wall, washed round and smooth as cushions, tight ribbons of mortar cutting into them.

The muddy cliff morphed into thousands of dragons' teeth, then concrete-filled oil cans; a slipway staggered past, atop it a compound of caravans reached by a rusty iron flight. The cliff slid on, and now up above me lanced the spars and beams of structures recently undermined. Drainpipes thrust up from the mud, together with coils of wire, dead-birds'-wings of polythene, three courses of a garden wall complete with curlicues of cast-iron decoration spanned a gulch in the mudface, above this the nibbled end of a road to nowhere. To the west, unseen, the sun was setting into this clag, the sky silvered, then greiged.

Surely by now I must be near to Tipsea? Dipsea? Skipsea? whatever the place was called. Even if I wasn't, I'd have to head inland, for darkness was coming and the tide had risen to within twenty yards of the cliff, while up above hung the outlines of half-shacks, quarter-bungalows and the oblongs of hard standings recently abandoned by static homes. The one-sided alleyway of dereliction was stark against the evening sky. I had been walking for over seven hours since I stepped down from the train; landward there was nothing I could recall, while to the east, I knew, lay Wilsthorpe and

Auburn, Hartburn, Hyde and Withow, their salted fields and silted cottages, their shingle-filled belfries and long-rotted inhabitants, whose grinning skulls were stuffed with seaweed and crabs.

I worked my way up the cleft of a drainage ditch and so came to the cliff top. The bisected alley was still gloomier up close: the abandoned chicken coops, their tarpaper roofs lifting away like scabs; the epidermal layers of linoleum left exposed in the corpse of a bungalow. I thought I heard footsteps in this half a home, a muttered curse, a shoulder roughing up a wall. I felt no inclination to investigate – in the declining light the turbines stood along the horizon like gibbets, or crucifixes. All but one had been anchored for the night, and as I turned inland its blades waved goodbye.

At the Board Inn the liqueur coffees were £3.10 and the girl in the big white blouse said, 'Ahl av a loook faw ya,' and went off to see if the lamb balti was on. I sat, staring blankly at the raffia placemats and the bentwood chairs gathered around them. I was the sole customer for the mini savouries combi platter, the only person who could be urged, 'Treat Yourself to Spanish "Rioja"'. As someone schooled in the Oxford Analytic tradition, I feared that punctuation might well be logic, and so these quotation marks implied a certain dubiety, that the wine was indeed Rioja was only hearsay.

The girl returned with an affirmative and took my order, then a while later she came back again with a little karahi on a plate, a stack of tiny rotis beside it and a small mound of white rice. I decanted the meaty sludge and began eating with the laboured precision that is the very hallmark of solitude. This *stuff* – the lamp contrived from four bunches of metal grapes, a fish tank in a gilt frame, photographs of the Inn in the 1960s showing Morris Travellers plumping up soft verges – all of it swirled briny before my tired eyes.

And then, a few tables away, there was a quartet of large German engineers in tartan shirts, upsetting stonewashed jeans and high-topped lace-up rubber boots. They were getting physical with pints of lager and a bottle of 'Rioja'. One second – as I chased rice grain with tine around the stadium of my plate – they weren't there, the next they were, decompressing from the day's exertion, their mud-smeared fingers definite, feeling. They hadn't simply materialized, for there was their Toyota pickup, outside the window, the treads of its outsized tyres knobbly like tripe.

The place name 'Bridlington' projected from the erosive wash of their German, and so I went over and, excusing myself, asked if, by any chance, they were working on the wind farm project? Absolutely! They invited me to join them – what was I drinking, would I take some wine? (Although, confidentially, they very much doubted it was Rioja.) I retrieved my tonic water from my own table, leery of too great an intimacy. I might be asked questions about myself that I could only answer by consulting my notebook.

The big feet stamping in Bridlington harbour, had they been a summer madness of mine? No, they reassured me, this turbine was indeed human-shaped. 'To be precise,' the most academic-looking of the engineers said, 'it is the body form of a famous British artist.' He mentioned a name, but it meant nothing to me. 'He is doing this kind of thing all over the places, I think – all these big statues, scaled up from a cast of his own body. It is very interesting I think that he is also, how you say . . . *ein Zwerg?*'

'A dwarf, I think.' One of his colleagues offered.

'A dwarf, exactly so.'

The German had bifocals, an upswept wispy moustache. He spoke with no malice, and I noticed then that his companions' faces were in fact equally refined, altogether at variance with their rough hands and workmen's clothing.

He continued, explaining that the famous artist was very driven, and that his specifications for the anthropoid turbine had to be met with great precision. 'The oxidization, you are knowing this has to be all over the same, so . . .' This was why it had to be beached at Bridlington: it was waiting to be rusty. '*Unt* then, the fixing of the blades, two only, so they will . . . how you say? *Anheln*, yes, resemble, so they will resemble arms, this is so very difficult, while the costing, this is "phut!"' He held up his hands, grabbing at bunches of cash. 'I do not know why your government is paying for this – not now.'

I had left my rucksack at the bed and breakfast opposite the pub. When I'd arrived, Pauline, who was whippet-thin, had asked me a trifle shamefacedly to go round to the back of the substantial brick farmhouse, and I obliged, musing on how like genteel pimping keeping a B&B was: you give me £30, I let you sleep with my sheets.

The room was in an annexe. It was a new conversion, spic and span with recessed spotlights and varnished blond wood. A basket of potpourri sat on the lid of the cistern in the wet room. There could be no question of spending any time there other than to sleep, so after leaving the Board Inn I resisted the ebb back to the sea and dragged myself further inland, through the village, then across the fields to Skipsea Brough, a substantial Norman mott-and-bailey that stood, overgrown with gorse and brambles, in misty cow pasture. The light, which down on the beach had been fast fading, endured here, and I sat on top of the old cone for a while, puffing away, and hanging on for grim death while a glossy crew of rooks made misery in the trees.

Yet still the light quivered, and eventually I could no longer resist it and set off back to the cliff. By the time I got there night had fallen and I could hear the relentless pulsion of the longshore drift, the grumbling into nothing of the friable land. Out of the darkness an image came to me of the cascade arcade game I'd played as a child on Brighton's West Pier, the heavy old pennies, with their tarnished heads of Georges, Edwards and even Victoria, all of them clunking down from one moving platform to the next.

My boots were pinching and I could feel blisters forming on my insteps – yet still I went on, intent on that shattered alley where I had heard something moving in the bisected bungalow. There it was, dirty poplin curtains whiting the sad little eyes of the windows in its porch. I forced the rotten front door and spilled into a mildewed parlour. The lino was scattered with fallen plaster and an open doorway opposite framed a dead mackerel sky above leaden waters; dominating this queer pictorial space – as if the subject of cosmic portraiture – loomed the head of a turbine.

I froze listening to my own wheezing, then heard the snaps and crackles of someone else's bronchial misery. I moved forward and discovered him on the far side of the doorway, his back against the externalized wallpaper, his feet dangling in the void. Without looking at me he said abruptly, 'Have you any water?'

I gave him my naive bottle and he took a slug, then, wiping his mouth, he said in a voice flattened by fear, 'What does it mean? What do these things mean?'

Keeping my back against the wall I hunkered down, earthy granules rattling away over the flopping old lino. I knew the drop was only sixty feet or so, and that the soft mud slumped, rather than fell sheer, to the shingle – but no one wants to fall from half a house. Sensing me beside him, the man extended a nocturnal hand, which crawled on to my sleeve.

'Why are these things permitted?' he continued. 'What've we done wrong? It was only a little place, somewhere to relax and do some painting. I come back from a walk this afternoon and it'd collapsed! Like I were being punished – all my work, down there' – the hand leapt into the air – 'trashed! What are these bloody *things*!' The hand grabbed at the turbine head on the horizon.

'What're we?' I answered, clearing my throat. I had an acute sense of this fellow, the water colourist, as pale, freckled, soft-featured, thirtyish, liberal and impotent. He put his arms around the dark hillock of his legs and pulled them close. I felt his pale eyes on me.

'I went in t'village to have a pint,' he said.

'What, to the Board Inn?' I replied, eager to show I had local knowledge, and so gain mastery.

'No' – he gestured – 'along t'top to Skipsea Sands, there's a leisure centre there that's got a licence. There's a bunch of us that drink there – we've all been under threat. I must've 'ad a few – too many.' Suddenly, he spasmed, then spat, 'Fuck the fucking Micronesians! Fuck 'em!' Then he shook his head and went on levelly, 'I went out walking along t'roads – to clear me head, like; then, when I got back here it were like a fucking earthquake, everything trashed! The little studio we built only three year ago, we put in UPVC windows and all sorts. Gone! Swept out of existence, and all because of those little brown buggers!'

I felt the floor move beneath my backside, a slight undulation suggesting a reposing giant about to turn in its sleep. Yet I felt no especial fear – possibly I was partaking of the water colourist's despair, and for him the worst had already happened, everything – teacups, forks, paints, brushes, unused prophylactics, towels, rubber bones – had slid away.

'Surely,' I said, adopting a conciliatory tone for a harsh message, 'you can't blame the turbines for this; this coastline has been eroding for centuries – millennia; you must've known this when you came here?'

''Course,' he spat again, a feeble little flob. 'But the erosion was steady enough, a few feet every year, it were predictable, like – we knew 'ow long we'd got. When they rebuilt the coastal defences up at Scarborough it got a bit worse – pushed the longshore drift down here, see – but when they began sinking the piles for those bloody monsters. I dunno, it must be 'cause they sorta funnel the current or summat. This stuff, it's nowt but muck, really. It's like playing a bloody hose on a bloody sandcastle. I'm a foolish fucking man!' he cried. 'Built my house upon the sand, and the rain descended, and the floods came, and the winds blew and beat upon that house; and it fell, and great was the falling of it!'

I'd got his number by this time. For him the domestic tragedy of the earth's overcooked fate was as nothing – it was only this: his own stupidly spilt milk that had driven him to the brink of his reason.

'How long will it take me to walk along the beach to Hornsea?' I asked matter-of-factly.

'Beach!' he guffawed bitterly. 'There's no beach at this time – can't you hear the sea, man?'

Strange to relate, I hadn't heard it – I'd entirely forgotten the rising tide that had hustled me up only a couple of hours earlier. Now canting forward, I could make out beyond the lip of lino the gargling of foam, and my ears filled with the rhythmic chuntering.

'Things have changed,' I said to the water colourist, while slowly easing myself back along the wall to the doorway. 'You must get a grip on yourself.' I gripped the exposed brickwork of the lintel, vibrantly aware that if it were to fall nothing could be more ridiculous than my holding on to it.

'These things are everywhere,' he wailed. 'There's hundreds of 'em up on the North York moors already – and for why? What do I care about the fucking Bangladeshis? I just wanted somewhere quiet to paint! I tellya, man, this is the beginning of the end – it's not just Skipsea that's gonna be washed away, they'll put these things right along the east coast, then you fancy pants down in London'll know all about it, you'll wake up drowned in your fucking beds!'

I'd made it through the doorway and was levering myself backwards across the parlour. I stood and dusted the plaster and earth from my trousers. 'Be a man,' I said caustically. 'You quote the Bible, eh? Well, what good is religion if it falls apart in a calamity? Think of what earthquakes and floods, wars and volcanoes, have done before to people. Did you think God was going to factor Skipsea out of the equation – he's not a fucking actuary, or a loss adjuster for that matter!'

Maybe I was a little harsh, but I wanted to jerk him out of his self-pity. I meant it as a parting shot, yet lingered expecting an angry retort. He only sat for a while in blank silence, then asked, 'What's that flicker in the sky?' Moving back to the doorway at first I saw nothing, then around the head of the turbine straight ahead of us there gathered a ghostly luminescence, arteries of galvanic lightning that intensified, white-bright as a military flare, and sent beams skipping across the wave peaks towards us.

I drew back, half blinded, then the water colourist cried out again and I returned: the entire file of turbines, as far in either direction as I could see, was being lit up. A pulse of brilliance streaked from one to the next along the Holderness coastline. 'We're in the midst of it,' I muttered to myself. 'Quiet as it is, this is the gathering storm.' And I turned on my hurting heels, exited the sagging bungalow and made my way back along the alley to the single-track road. If I turned left I would reach the village in half an hour; if I turned right I would come soon enough to the bitten-off edge of tarmac, and beyond that a traveller needs must skip from wave crest to crest, if he wanted to reach the place where Withow once was.

On my holiday I took with me the fatal flaw of not altogether caring; a rubber figurine only two or three inches high and clad in a Churchillian siren suit but with the head of a pig. I had a 1.5 litre bottle that I filled from a tap whenever I had the opportunity, and three water colours – sea scenes, amateurish to begin with and now badly muddied, of no real merit, certainly, but a convenient size to tuck under one arm.

As I gained the road I thought I heard a low rumble, a fusilade of falling pebbles and a high, wild cry. These sounds were open to more than one interpretation – I chose the most obvious, and so pressed on, intent on the late television news, a mug of tea and a packet of shortbread.

# 3

# The Seal Pup

Fruit pudding, white pudding, black pudding, bacon, sausage, two fried eggs, three rounds of toast, a grilled tomato, mushrooms and beans – all of it washed down with orange juice and a cafetière of coffee. During the night I had forgotten about all this chomping, had dreamt of butterfly girls sipping viridian nectar, and android men who only needed the monthly replacement of one rusty fuel cell with another shiny one. I had forgotten also Pauline, who stood over me freshly scrubbed, slim and shiny as a PVC drainpipe in her tightly tied plastic apron, urging me to eat more while she told me about her childhood in Driffield, and how having grown up on the coast she never found its steady disappearance that peculiar.

'Fair enough,' she said, placing her fists where her hips ought to have been. 'When they put the Millennium Stone in at Barmston, and I saw a couple of year later how much closer the cliff had got, well . . . made me think a little.'

So I left her in her well-equipped kitchen, in its gravelled courtyard, which lay within the larger enclosure of Skipsea itself, with its painted paling fences, pink hollyhocks and silver-metallic Nissan hatchbacks circled in the cul-de-sacs. The means of mobility employed as a defence – could there be any better bulwark against what was going under a mile to the east?

I hurriedly bought an apple and some cheese at the village store and set off, desperate to return to the coast. I had not time for rape fields or poplar rows – besides, field margins were overgrown, convolvulus snaked across the lanes, a sewer stank, and pigeons gorged themselves on ripening wheat. The countryside seemed proud purely on the basis that it was, rather than was not, and taking a path running alongside a grassy knoll I looked at the caravans thereon, each complacently yoked to the national grid. Yet what were they, that they should only be tacked on behind, the appendices of hearth and home?

The farmer's wife had been up at six to stuff me; now I paid her back with my most liquid currency: amnesia. Why was I, I mused, so flatulent? Why was my belly so uncomfortably swollen? I fixated on the exposed coils of an electricity substation humming in nettles, and so was quite unprepared for the moto enclosure that lay beyond this.

The big old boar lay half inside a corrugated-iron humpy; the sow wallowed in a muddy slough. She was suckling a pair of mopeds, who, rears wriggling, gored her with their greed.

'Oo goin' thee-thyd?' she lisped as I strode past, and, pausing long enough to confront her bristly baby face, I replied, 'Yes, I mean to get as far as . . .', then faltered, because of course I couldn't remember where it was I was going, so had to get my notebook out and check, all the while cursing myself for the ridiculousness of engaging in conversation with a creature that couldn't possibly understand.

'Yes.' I found the entry. 'I'm going as far as Hollym today.'

The sow raised herself up on her elbow, fluttering her thick eyelashes, a coquettishness at odds with the pleated gash of her exposed genitals. 'Thee-thyd,' she mused. 'Oo goin' thee-thyd.'

The mopeds grunted and squealed.

'Well,' I snapped, 'that's quite enough of that!'

I put the notebook away and headed on, although as I continued along the path, kicking out distractedly at molehills, I could still hear her maddening singsong, 'Thee-thyd, thee-thyd, thee-thyd . . .' and the gobbling of her young.

At the seaside the mist was plumped up, a sweaty pillow on the wrinkled sheet of the waves. North along the bluff I could make out the leftovers of a hamlet; on the landward side of an alley there were wooden shacks and tiny bungalows, while to seaward only broken walls, a few fence posts, a hopeless 'For Sale' sign, and detritus strewn over the edge of the cliff. The tide was in, undercutting the bellying mudface that in other places had splurged down in a slow-motion convulsion. Observing the saturated postage stamps of useless water colours floating on the swell, the phrase 'rotational slumping' slid into my mind, and so I turned south under a Teflon sky.

I had cosseted the Granny Smith apple in my palm since Skipsea, and now bit into it, releasing a sour concomitant: a bad news thread that spooled in front of my eyes, *Deposits of amyloid visible as apple-green yellow birefringence under polarized light. The amyloid forms plaques and neurofibrillary tangles that progress through the centres of the brain.* Bite of apple, wet and sharp – bite of boots, the stupid costly bespoke things. Somewhere in the Midlands there was a last, a scale wooden model of my foot growing dusty on a shelf. I'd stretched plaster across the hard ridges of the metatarsals that morning. It didn't matter – I knew the skin would break before the end of the walking tour and I, an immigrant merman who'd never seen my submarine homeland, would be condemned to walk on knives.

A golf course arrived, heralded by CCTV cameras and signs WARNING of crumpling cliff edges and flying golf balls. Next came a caravan park, with long lanes between the vans that followed the contour lines of the increasingly high and sheer cliff. It was past eight, and I greeted the dog walkers who were about, but they were having none of it. They stuck close to their metal hutches, while I was beyond the chain-link fence, hard by the cliff edge, a creature of sea and sky.

Then another park, the inhabitants of which were more rooted still, their static homes girded round with mini-picket fences, behind which sprouted potted gardens – wincey shrubberies and shocks of pampas grass. Aspen, Vogue, Celebration and Windsor all went by. Windsor had a nautical air, and the standard of St George stiffly riffled beside its jutting prow. A man stood watch outside its picture window, his feet spread on hardwood decking, his elbows propped on a taffrail. He looked like the bulldog on his tea mug, the same barrel chest, slope shoulders and bowlegs. His muzzle – red as the Holderness loess – was amiable enough, and so I hailed him, 'Don't you ever get worried?'

He raised a monobrow.

'About the cliff?'

Was this perhaps a ridiculous solecism, as talk of carcinogens might be to a man riddled with cancer? For the neatly mown grass terminated a few paces from where we stood in a ragged tear that zigged towards one static home, then zagged away from its neighbour.

'Me, wurried? No, lad,' he laughed. 'There's a good forty-six feet there. It's him oop there should wurry, he's only got twelve and he isn't even chained!'

I looked where he pointed and saw the unchained fool and the beckoning crevice.

'See,' the English bulldog resumed, 'it goes pretty regular; true, I did lose nine feet last year, but that were exceptional.'

I shook my head, bedevilled by such sangfroid: 'But look, with that crack coming in there, and this one over here, won't it—'

'Oh aye, it'll even up – these hard standings'll be gone before the year's out.'

He nodded to the concrete platforms teetering over the abyss; they had the evil air of concentration camp ruins.

'So,' I said, 'what happened to the static homes that were on them?'

'Well, they joost move us back when we get too near – winch us oop, move us back. It's all in the contract, like – part of the deal.'

Move us back, part of the deal. Death came wading through the sea fret; at first it was featureless, a blur of black robe and steel scythe, then it was right before me, elbows planted on the cliff edge the way any normally sized person might lean upon a bar. Death's skull loomed, ivory in its house-sized hood, and it stretched out a bony grabber to wrench Aspen from its hard standing, then place it on a vacant square three rows back.

Glimpsed over my retreating shoulder, this looked to be a tender act, the merciful forestalling of these retirees' inevitable decline, then fall. But it came at a cost, for Death completed this outsized chequers move by snatching up the two static homes it had taken and casting them into the sea. The cacophony – the pitiful screams, the smash and the clatter – stayed with me for a while, then they became the seagulls' ordinary savagery, the mist drew back from the horizon, and there were no personifications to be seen except the turbines with their blades feathered, standing sentinel and still.

Stalks swarmed on the wide deck of a wheat field, then marched to the brink, where fluting away from their roots were buttresses and cornices of quick-setting mud. Away in their dense ranks the parentheses inscribed by last winter's tractors referenced the remaining rags of mist, and so seemed like earthy vapour trails scored in a green-gold sky.

Ten yards of beach hauled themselves clear from the long fetch of the waves – I longed to descend, yet feared being trapped between cliff and sea. But then a dead porpoise swam into view, and as there was a way to scrabble down nearby I took it, then knelt on the shingle to contemplate its gouged flanks and parched spiracle. It was too silly to impute all evils to the turbines – no sea creature could have leapt into their blades – but the wounds seemed to have been made by a boatman's gaff and there were few fishermen abroad on the water – although plenty of contractors.

I scrabbled back up and the cliff went on. The dead porpoise had shaken me and to steady myself I consulted my notebook, which suggested I try this mental exercise: On my holiday I took with me a neurofibrillary tangle that was awkward to manoeuvre – like a large bunch of twisted wire – and when I reached a gate or a stile I would have to wrangle it over, often tearing my clothing as the loose ends caught in the loops of my wicking T-shirt. Then there were the UPVC windows, three of them framed in white plastic, 140cm x 260cm, far too unwieldy for a walking tour. Not forgetting the parish records of Hornsea Burton, Hornsea Beck and Southorpe – the soggy ledgers from which leaves kept dropping, each veined with the calligraphy of birth, death and marriage; they were God-fearing parishes, these, yet all were sucked upon by the sea's salty mouth, rod after rod, until they were dissolute. Finally, there was the rubber figurine, which, if meant as a child's toy, was scarcely fit for purpose, being – despite its three-inch stature – a bulky, imposing thing, garbed in a skin-tight Churchillian siren suit, and, most disturbing of all, with a pig's head, not a man's.

The North Cliff Boat Club stood fifty feet above the waves, its yard a jumble of fibreglass hulls trapped behind corrugated iron and barbed wire. To escape into the sea the craft would have to be manhandled over the fence, then dragged down a steep concrete slipway – and what pleasure could there be in that?

The path drew me capriciously along a choked alley between two caravan parks, bindweed caught then snapped between my ankles, my clothes snagged at brambles and snatched up burrs, my bare arms lunged at nettles – then I found myself on the long dusty road into Hornsea, sweating in the noonday sun, as some obese people gathered round a cake stall beside the fire station waddled towards me and then past.

A street of redbrick two-up, two-downs, the deeply conservative impasto of road markings in yellow and white, the Floral Hall with '1911' worked into its pediment – I had hoped, devoutly, for the respite of the town, the smell of car exhaust in the tarshadow of Nonconformist chapels, string shopping bags dangling along the high street. Instead, Hornsea Mere appeared between Belle-Époque yews, and, while I saw that model boats were abroad on its sweet waters, I knew that below them lay the Cainozoic mush of drowned woodlands and impacted reed beds, all the ebb and flow of millennia.

Along the high street there were no string shopping bags, only people yanking money from the cash points and running the next relay leg to the shops. I paused by the window of a second-hand one: 35mm cameras, some Spode. Inside tweed jackets clubbed together on hangars. As soon as the door tinged shut I hid behind a freestanding bookcase stuffed with paperbacks – but the tall, potbellied man who supervised the place hadn't noticed me; he was involved with a peer in a corduroy cap. The pair were unwrapping a series of objects swathed in green recycling bags. The shopkeeper's sleeves were rolled up almost to his armpits and his arms disturbed me.

I took a book from the case at random; it was *Why Didn't They Ask Evans?* by Agatha Christie. The cover depicted a seagull nesting at the edge of a cliff; between its legs were a speckled egg and a golf ball. Down below, a man in a two-piece suit was plunging, tie flapping, and with more gulls bothering his blank face. The illustrator, working in pen and wash, had placed a nasty black outcrop in the waters, waters he had also embellished with the black swirls of an impact that was *yet to occur*.

The sixth impression of a Fontana paperback published in 1972, I had read it in this very edition, concurrently with my father, when we were rained in during a Cornish walking tour. Can there ever have been anywhere more subdued than that parlour, with its carriage clock's gold-balled gimbals slow-revolving on the mantelpiece, and the superfluity of Windsor and wing chairs? We had lingered over breakfast as long as we could, my father, as was his way, elaborately buttering a single, mouthful-sized section of toast, then anointing it with marmalade, before finally and reverently consuming it. The rain lulled outside gathering its strength, then gushed. My father went out to negotiate with the lady of the house – we were permitted to stay but confined to the parlour, where we sat all that long day, either side of an electric fire, its bars furry with summer dust, and read alternate chapters of the Christie, the contest being – with my father there always had to be competition – to see who could guess the murderer first.

Night fell with the rain. A flyer in the bus shelter promised a choral performance at the village hall. We sallied out along oilskin roads from Trebetherick to Rock. I was so bored by then that even the red-faced farmer's wives belting out Handel pleased me, while as for my dad—

'These might interest you.'

'I'm sorry?'

'These may interest you – these here.'

The Elastoplast he had wrapped around the bridge of his spectacles fitted precisely in the groove of his frown. His eyes – of an awesome mildness – held me as he leant forward over the counter. At the base of the triangle formed by his forearms, between the heels of his liver-spotted hands, were five wood carvings of etiolated human figures. They were perhaps a foot to eighteen inches long and lay in a pile like outsized spillikins. There was also a larger piece of wood: one end curved into a stern, while the prow had been whittled into a serpent's streamlined head. There were also three discs that, if shields, were to scale with the figures. To one side lay a little heap of what looked like spare limbs – or possibly clubs.

The man wearing the corduroy cap had gone. Outside the lunchtime shoppers had evaporated, while in front of the newsagent opposite a handwritten shout for the *Hornsea Echo* lamented: THREE SISTERS DISAPPEAR IN BEWHOLME. 'Pick one up,' the shopkeeper ordered me. 'D'you recognize it?'

Fragments of quartzite had been rammed into the figure's roughly carved pinhead, a head reduced by bronze blade to its essential planes: a sharp chin, a triangular nose, the oval slot of a mouth. It lay on its back in my palm. The wood was warm to the touch, fine-fissured pine. I hefted the figurine – it was perfectly balanced, more like a tool than anything decorative.

I guessed it must be very old, although the neoteny of the head, the armless shoulder sockets, the notched crotch and legs that tapered to a point also called to mind wavering aliens silhouetted in the molten light spilling from the cracked shell of a flying saucer.

I gingerly set the figure down on the counter and said, 'I think I'd remember *that*.'

Then I was sitting on the seawall watching the tide lap back from muddy shingle. The wall was in three smooth tiers, with orange-painted steel gates set on mammoth hinges in the uppermost one. The sunlight was bright enough to strike sparks on the wavelets, yet overall visibility was only a couple of hundred yards, the sea mist enclosing what might be – for all I knew – an isolated section of coral reef. I peered closely at the smooth whiteness between my thighs – was it concrete, or the massively compacted exoskeletons of myriad antediluvian crustaceans?

I was getting out my oat cakes and the sweating cheese I'd bought in Skipsea, when a family came trundling out of the mist and sat right beside me. There was a chocolate-smeared three-year-old in a pushchair, its feet trailing along the path. Too bloody big for it, I thought, it'll end up fat as its mother – who was mountainous in a bright red blouse and black slacks. A sixtyish mother-in-law was in attendance, her senior hair set hard. Her hovering around the pushchair was a mute agony: she mustn't *interfere*, although everything her daughter-in-law did was *wrong as wrong could be*.

A short way off, on the steel stairway down to the strand, a skinny husband in a bowling shirt fiddled with a tacky kite. The six-year-old boy pestering him was equally skinny – all bone struts, stringy tendons and plastic skin. I watched them get tangled up in each other, while I removed from my rucksack my tea-making kit, a paperback thriller and a small oilcloth bundle, which when I unrolled it contained what appeared to be the detachable wooden penises of some Bronze Age figurines.

'D'you want yer bap now?' The mountainous mummy thrust the white roll at the child in the pushchair.

'I thought, maybe—' the mother-in-law ventured, then was silenced by a furious glare.

'Go on, 'ave yer bap now!' the mother insisted, kneading love and hatred together.

'Ah, well,' the mother-in-law sighed.

'Whaddya mean by that?' the mother snapped, and as the mother-in-law quailed I thought it will always be thus, until one or the other of them dies.

I couldn't remember acquiring the Agatha Christie or the bundle of wooden penises. I knew that on my holiday I had taken with me a formerly lascivious madman, a neurofibrillary tangle, a pig-headed rubber figurine and a dead porpoise rescued from the long fetch of the German Ocean – but these?

While I was playing the memory game the skinny husband came up to get his own bap, abandoning the older kid to crunch along the shingle, the kite nipping at his heels.

'Oh, it's you,' the man said when he saw me. 'What're you doing up this way again?'

I was grateful to him for two things: first, his bowling shirt, which was lilac with a blue revere collar, cuffs and pocket-facing; it was also monogrammed 'Derek' across the breast pocket. Secondly, there was Derek's low-key reaction to what I assumed must be a quite a coincidence. I imagined he was responding intuitively to my blank expression, and fed me this easy question so I could skirt whatever mutual history we had, leaving it for him to unearth later.

I began explaining that I was taking a few days out to walk the Holderness coast, but no sooner had I begun talking than Derek interrupted me, turning to the uncongenial woman-mountain and blurting, 'Look, it's 'im who came round that evening we 'ad the bees.'

'Oh, ho!' she laughed. 'It's you – I didn't even notice you sitting there all quiet, like. 'Ow yer doin'? Still writing your cra-azy books?'

Her sudden warmth was overpowering – I thought, how sad she has so little of this for her own, and also for an instant – could I spill it all out? My deteriorating memory – the quixotic quest for the man in the scrap of photograph I'd found in the gutter of St Rule Street? Might I throw myself on the soft mercy of her bosom?

'It weren't 'til well after midnight that the police got hold of some feller who knew how to deal wi' it,' Derek was saying.

In the course of a few more exchanges I gathered this: that he had gone to see me give a book reading at the Pave Café in Hull the previous summer. She – Karen, that is – would've gone too, were it not for a swarm of bees that had blanketed the front of the house: 'The babysitter were absolutely bloody terrified.' I, however, had risen to the challenge, and when I heard the tale accompanied Derek home and gave an impromptu recital in the kitchen, 'While me an' my mate drank oor gin.'

As this was transpiring the mother-in-law, released from her daughter-in-law's cage of contempt, escaped with the pushchair. Wheeling it twenty yards off, she snatched back the child's bap and began vigorously to wipe the chocolate from its mouth with an index finger cowled in saliva-dampened cloth.

My lips felt sore and I was walking along the cliff top. The tide was still too high to risk the beach. Another caravan park rolled towards me, but this time there was no fencing between the static homes – which were arranged side-on – and the precipice. Hard standings overhung the abyss – and one had recently collapsed together with the ruptured diaphragm of a paddling pool, the shards of fake-marble planters, a toilet seat and a yucca, which still alive had replanted itself in the mudface, near to a swollen and putrefying hand – or rubber glove.

The dregs of an army camp marched through the badlands towards me. There were overgrown trenches and ramparts studded with sentinel towers, redbrick revetments crumbled into the ruderals, and the heat shimmered over the hedgerows – crystal stairs for flies to shimmy on. The black outline of a man punched a hole in a tower's doorway. A gun nut. Spent all morning at home, up in his bedroom. 'Gary!' his old man called up. ''Ave you 'ad yer breakfast, oor what?' Or *what*. He came along the flatland from Rolston on a mountain bike, a shotgun slung around one shoulder, a .22 rifle round the other, the pockets of his unseasonable parka bulging with ammunition. He stands in the doorway watching me come on in my Union Army-blue uniform T-shirt, my head full of deep-laid plans for world Zionist domination. He stands stock still, not wanting to aim then track me, but postponing the ecstasy of fluid movement, and so on I come, at every pace expecting his big chin to bristle from the shadows, the nostrils of his shotgun to sneeze snotty lead, his parenthetic shoulders to shrug with the recoil – and so bracket my expiration.

It wasn't until I was within ten paces of the tower that the gun nut resolved into nothing but the outline of a man bashed in the old steel door. I went on, quaking, and debouched into the road by Mappleton village hall, a Wesleyan chapel dated 1830. Along the road a car slowed beside me and the driver asked if I knew of a petrol station nearby; I said I didn't, walked on and discovered a jolly little Prius dealership around the next bend, its eco-bunting limp on this hot afternoon, the cars hunched and shiny, the prices exorbitant.

Down a lane, past raggle-taggle cottages, I came upon a declivity leading to the beach. The tide had turned; looking south I could pick out a route worming around the mud slid down, so, despite the prominent signs warning of unexploded ordinance, I set off into the daymare of my own relentless velleity.

At first there were a few dog walkers, some swimmers waist-high in the churned cream waves and a pod of sunbathers cast ashore on cushions of sea-worn concrete – but soon enough I was utterly alone, picking my way between pinnacles of dried mud studded with pebbles of all colours, from bone-white through eggshell to carmine, mahogany and black. To my right the cliff swooped up, to my left the sea rippled away, while before my eyes the sea fret coiled and shredded – a miasma at once nothingy and permanent; as each buttress of hardened mud formed the flats of this set, so the mist appeared always on the point of being whisked away to reveal the audience of giants seated in the deep.

During the Second War there had been extensive defences along this stretch of the coast; now sections of wall – concrete *Z*'s, *L*'s and double *U*'s, bearded with reinforcing – and even entire blockhouses were embedded in the beach. For a while the mudface was scattered with a selection of the things I had brought with me on my holiday – girders, spars, plastic sheeting, the neuritic plaques, the senile plaques, the braindruse – which, while soiled, nonetheless anchored this liminal desert to the world up above, to the kitchens still fitted, the carports yet intact, beside the bungalows that crouched well away from the edge. Soon enough, though, these relics of the distant present had tumbled by, while the fret still draped offshore, hiding the turbines, and the only player was me, walking on the spot as one shingle spit then the next revolved towards me, each a miniature Spurn Head.

If before I had been held by the loess, now it sucked me in; I had only to let my glimpse penetrate its moist gashes for the entire body to shiver, then contort, as if it were a monstrous and living thing. The heat mounted, the beery waves frothed on the rim of the land, my vain boots ate my feet, while, incontinently, the Andante of Mahler's Sixth began to syringe my ears – at first a slow seep of syrupy violins and sucrose melody, but then, with recursive eddies of flute and woodwind, larger flows of sound began sloshing around my brainpan, rocking then floating my hollow soul.

Spooked, I gripped the plastic water bottle that had served me for the entire walk as *something to hold on to*, the all-too-real limb of that phantom body, the Other, who walked beside me yet said nought. The bottle crackled – the Andante flooded on, its cascades of sweet sadness spurting through my eyes, mouth and nose. I put the bottle down on a mud plinth, hoping its mundane shape would trump all this amorphous weirdness. This didn't work: the Mahler became more turbulent; I slid across glassy sound-boils, whipping into whirlpools of timpani

– massed triangles, cow bells and old hubcaps smitten with fenders: 'Zing! Boom! Tan-ta-ra!' A cartoon Cleopatra was hauled towards me reclining on a pyramidal juggernaut drawn by naked and burnished Nubians. 'Zing! Boom! Tan-ta-ra!' And although she vanished into the haze, once she was gone the patterns of the pebbles, the gulls twisting into the sky at my approach, the very winding of the sea fret – all these phenomena assumed a demented congruence with the Andante, responding to its every glissade.

It got worse, the mud Romantically writhing, the sandbars flip-flopping, the very rods and cones of my optic nerves made visible, frenziedly dancing to the brassy blare of the movement's crescendo – until all was blissfully and terribly silenced by the bomb: which lay, small and rusted, a few sustained glockenspiel notes and oboe tones curling into silence around it. I'd nearly trodden on the *fucking thing* and sat down abruptly, my rucksack marrying my back to the sand, so that I lay panting, parenthesized by my calves.

When I got upright again, I saw there was a shoal of these death fish beached along the tide line – perhaps a hundred in all. Fear renders the body down so that each movement becomes clarified, so, keeping close to the cliff face, I tiptoed past the bombs to the accompaniment of the arrhythmic rasping of my breath in my ears, and atonal cries desiring my life to be not just longer – but *forever*.

Then the beach was a hard flat pan. Up above on the bluffs stood the stark forms of ruined military installations about to surrender. My bowels slackened and I squatted, back to the cliff, to add my lava to the glacial till. Standing to wipe myself, I saw two small figures coming on along the beach, maybe a quarter of a mile distant. It had been so long since I'd seen another human that, for the aeons until we met, I speculated on what life forms these might be – were they the luminous beings, descended now, their gossamer wings folded into yellow nylon jackets?

It was a Yorkshireman – rotund but hard, like a well-inflated beach ball, his smooth-shaven face cut into by the shadow of his baseball cap. Both he and his son – aged perhaps thirteen – were wearing Hull City football shirts; the black-and-yellow stripes widened over their tummies, then narrowed at the broad leather belts they wore, dangling with chisels and hammers. They rolled towards me across the bled, so at ease that I could not bear to let them pass – had to seize them, tap into their reservoir of honeyed love. As I drew level I cried out, 'I saw a bomb back there!'

'Oh, aye,' the man said. 'What were it like?'

He had three gold front teeth, two incisors and a canine; also a heavy gold chain in the fold of his thick neck – these I registered, rather than his relaxed manner, so ran on nervously: 'You see all those signs warning of unexploded ordinance all the time, but I never think anything of them – then I nearly trod on this *bomb*.'

'Aye,' he reiterated, 'what were it like?'

'Um . . . well,' I flustered, 'I dunno, about this long,' I held out my hands to bracket an implausible catch, 'and sorta bomb-shaped – with tailfins.'

'Four of 'em, squared off?'

'Y-yes, four fins, square ones.'

'That'll be a tank-buster, an A10. I've come out here after a high tide and seen thousands of 'em.'

'There were at least a hundred of them back there!' We were both taken aback by my vehemence. 'Are they, y'know, *live*?'

'Soom are, uthers 're joost dummies – practice bombs.'

The boy stayed a way off, took a rubber-handled hammer from his belt and swung it idly at a mud outcrop – in the seconds it took to connect I saw this as an orbit within an orbit, the boy as a sun, the father as a satellite, myself at the aphelion, the whole as an orrery designed to explain the emotional pull that children exert—

The hammer struck, cleanly splitting the mud to reveal its pebbly lode and we all staggered two steps sideways as the beach jerked beneath our feet. Over the fossicker's left shoulder a section of the cliff face dematerialized into dirty fret that boiled towards the sea. I couldn't understand what had happened, but the man – turning to look so that the gold chain was spat from his neck folds – said casually, 'That were a big one.'

'Was it a bomb?' I gasped.

He laughed, 'That? No, it were only an ordinary fall, haven't you seen wun yet? 'Ow long you bin walking?'

The shock of the cliff fall seemed to have jolted my memory and without needing to consult my notebook I was able to explain I'd come from Skipsea that day, and Bempton via Flamborough Head the one before. Thrilled by my own lucidity, I rambled on about the Holderness coast, its strangeness, and how there must be some odd connection between its progressive engulfment and the ignorance of the wider world.

The fossicker was also thrown into loquacity by the cliff fall and spoke of his fossil hunting, how the Yorkshire coast was perfect for this, exhibiting three successive strata – the Jurassic, the Cretaceous, the Cainozoic – exposed successively from Whitby in the north to the Humber estuary, and how he himself had found, 'All sorts. I dug up a whole bloody bison in Tunstall mere last year and a fossilized tree the year before.'

He told me that he and his family lived in Goole, and I pictured them there at once: sitting in a conservatory tacked on to the back of a small terraced house beside the docks. The fossicker sat watching the racing on television, the fossilized bison serving him as an awkward sofa. The boy stood by a full-length UPVC window lazily swinging his steel hammer until it hit the TV set, which neatly split, spilling its ancient micro-circuitry of ammonites and trilobites. The father-god and the son-god looked on, one substance, at peace.

Before they walked on the fossicker urged me to visit the sound mirror at Kilnsea. 'It's right queer,' he said. 'Dirty great big concrete thing – but wunderfully smooth, y'know what it were for?'

I didn't.

'Zeppelins, they say if you put your ear to it you could hear a zeppelin four minutes before it reached the coast. Four minutes! What good were that?'

What good indeed. I was alone – the boy and his father were a fast-fading memory, then nothing but the sinusoids of their footprints in the sand, crossing and recrossing into the beige distance. All they had left me was this awful data: that the cliff could fall – and it could fall *on me*. How dense I must have been to have come this far, contemplating all the erosion that had gone before, yet never taking it personally.

The beach narrowed once more until it became a defile between the solidified brown tsunami to my right and the green waves to the left. Narrowed until I was picking my way among fossilized chunks of the earth's own shit – that was it! I was to die like this, butt-fucked by frigid Ceres. All along I'd had it wrong – there was a grandeur to the static homes and the caravans toppling over the cliff, whereas to be crushed beneath this anthropomorphic *muck*, where was the romance in that?

I stopped for my hoosh of oat cake and tea beside a sinking pillbox, gingerly removing boots then socks as a polar explorer might – fearful lest a digit come away. THAT'S LIFE read the graffito above me. I hated the mud now – if it was shape-shifting its transitions were only from one prosaic thing to the next. I looked upon it and saw the hooked noses and chins of storybook witches poking round the archivolt of a chintzy grotto.

I rebandaged my feet, sheathed them in their leather man-traps, packed the rucksack, shouldered it and went on. At a point where the cliff had slumped into two plateaux I saw a way to scramble up – and so did, desperate for reassurance that I was not the sole civilized man left alive on a planet ruled by apes. All I discovered were the wavering legions of wheat, the superstructures of copses cruising along the horizon, enigmatic barns – in short, a world now altogether alien to me, so I slid down once more and set off south along the beach, keeping close to the water's edge, where one silky wave overlapped the next and the birds' footprints could be read as hieroglyphs: 'Bird foot, bird foot, bird foot, bird foot,' they said.

The afternoon grew duller yet clearer as all the golden sea fret was sucked up into a pewter sky. A line of turbines appeared offshore – very high, at least 400 feet. I supposed they must be part of a renewable energy programme, fostered by a civilization acutely conscious of the fragility of the global ecology, and sensitive to its legacy – the habitat of all those generations to come. The mud was just mud. I thought of nothing – and came upon a seal pup stranded above the tidal wrack, with its strips and stalks and frills of seaweed, the rubber goods of Nature.

The pup's dirty-white fur was crawling with sea lice, and flies were at its mouth and nostrils. As soon as it registered my presence the poor mite writhed with fear and entreaty, its breath coming in harsh little rasps. *Help me*, the pup implored, speaking through the brown eyes agonizingly bored in its doggy brow. *Help me, please do something – anything!*

All the anger and the nihilism, all the alienation and disgust, all the friendships neglected and the lovers abandoned, all the children abused and neglected, all the trans-generational misery of a row that had continued for decade upon decade, sustained by senseless bickering, all of the oily repulsion that kept me from *them* was crammed into the gap between my palms and the pup's flanks. All I had to do was squat down and take this baby in my arms – for it was a baby now, a baby with chubby pink legs, tightly encircled by invisible threads. It had a rotting stub of umbilical cord pinched in a yellow plastic clip around which the flies swirled, while those snubby-putty features were almost . . . my own.

I knelt down and slowly – so as to not alarm the mite – examined it from its hind flippers to its earless head, but could discover no sign of injury or trauma. The seal pup continued to rasp and writhe, I felt the protein-rich milk of sentiment rising up my throat – what to do? If I tried to lift it would it bite me? Should I put it back in the sea, or carry it along the beach to a dispensary for sick animals where an intersex volunteer in a round-collared tunic would feed it formula from a bottle? Or, given it was a member of protected species, would disturbing it in any way be an offence? Would I find myself in the dock – not, I suspected, for the first time – of a magistrates' court panelled with medium-density fibreboard, my head tilted back on my shoulders, searching for the squiggle of judgement in the flaking paint?

Was there no one besides me to take on the responsibility of the seal pup? I looked out to sea where the turbines stood, complacent and at ease. I took four paces towards them, stopped and brought a handful of cold water to my hot salt brow. I straightened up and silently railed: all those technicians, engineers and workers – yet there was no help available for the seal pup. As I watched a tender cast off from one of the turbines and made course for the Humber mouth – they would be drinking Shits-on-the-Grass in the old town tonight.

I turned back. The seal pup had a kitchen knife rammed to the hilt into what would have been the small of its back were it a human child. How could I have missed this when I examined the creature? And where was the murderer? Still, at least I'd found out what ailed it – the only mystery was why this parenthesis of blubber still encapsulated life at all. I cast around for a rock with which to smash in its brains and put it out of my misery – but there were only pebbles and clods; besides, I'd probably just *fuck it up* and leave the seal pup to writhe still more horribly. In another seven hours the tide would be in – that would decide the matter; Nature would forge her course, a mudslide, pushing before it the churned-up slurry of lived lives.

# 4
# The Sound Mirror

'Good evening.'

'Evening.'

'D'you mind my asking, what's the name of the nearest village?'

'Village?'

He was incredulous – although there were credulous twins in the mirrored lenses of his goggle sunglasses. His hair was bleached at the ends, his wife's was dark at the roots – she hung back a few yards, troubled by a couple of small sons in tracksuits who butted at her belly and thighs. It struck me that he might think I meant Ringborough, Monkwike or Sand-le-Mere, hamlets long since ground down to silt, and that if he pointed the way towards the shoals to which these place names once applied, I'd strip off and start wading out.

'Well . . . place, then.'

'Tunstall d'you mean?'

Over his shoulder I could see a battle group of earth movers standing on the brow of a low hill that they appeared to have carved from the cliff. What was this, a projecting horn of the Withernsea sea defences? The tracks of the earth movers zippered across the beach's cloth of gold – in the evening sunlight all shadows were needlessly prolonged.

'Um, yeah – but how far is Withernsea?'

'In a car five minutes, but ahv no ahdëah on foot.'

This was my re-entry to the cities of the plain – I felt it went well, my simplicity provocative of his candour. A mile or so on I took to the low bluffs, then, soon enough, Withernsea lighthouse rose up judiciously from a huddle of houses inland. Next came the sea defences, a steel-and-concrete rampart stretching for hundreds of yards, grossly out of scale with the low-rise blocks of flats and poky houses it had been thrown up to protect.

My feet were incandescent, and with each forward pace I abandoned another husk of myself – the burnt-out shell of a man I had once been, which upon falling to the pathway fluttered into ash. A pair of boys – perhaps eleven-years-old and starveling thin – rose from a bench and flapped after me. The castellated gateway of the long vanished pier ushered in the tired waves. 'Oi, mister!' one of the boys cried. 'Your laces're undone.' I ignored the scallywag, then: 'Oi, mister, there's sum wooden cocks fallen ahtuv yer rucksack – could be Iron Age, more likely late Bronze Age.'

I stopped, and together with the obliging lads gathered up the curls of petrified wood, which had a smoky patina. I'd no idea where they had come from, or why they had been lodged in the webbing pocket of my rucksack – looking down into the palm of my hand, where one lay, old and enigmatic, it occurred to me that this was a prompt for a tragic history, that inscribed by the cracks in the pine were the strophe and antistrophe of my own past. I explained this to the boys, then together we chanted: 'On my holiday I took with me a dying seal pup, a rusted flight of metal stairs leading to a beach, a rubber figurine – such as child might play with – wearing a blue siren suit and with a pig's head –', but that was all I could remember and when I looked up from the parenthetic penis the boys had gone.

I crept into the town, passing 7's Smiles – an amusement parlour, Trixter's Joke Shop & Fancy Dress and a bowling alley. Shop fronts were hiding under the skirts of the older Victorian buildings – it all looked permanent enough, yet I knew Withernsea had waltzed backwards from the waves, that the esplanade had once been the high street, that the current high street had once been a back alley. An enormous plaice was bracketed by seaweed on the gable end of a building, beside the chip shop there was a Chinese, and beside the Chinese the Bengal Lancer was picketed. A square-headed Bengali put me in the window and I looked around appreciatively at the red cloths strewn with white and yellow rice. He brought me a menu and I began to ask him, 'Why relocate from one flood zone—' Then was interrupted by the table of teenagers on the far side of the restaurant: 'If you wanna real laff watch *Jackass*.'

'Ooh, no, Ah don't think that's foony.'

I found a paperback in my rucksack and began to read: *What rotten luck there was in the world! A swirl of mist on a fine evening, a false step – and life came to an end.* Two middle-aged men were seated beside me in the window and they pawed at their menus with callused hands. *The pallor of approaching death couldn't disguise the deep tan of the skin.* Outside in the gloaming three large combine harvesters charged past scattering clods and chaff.

'Ahl av that wun lahk the boxer,' said the younger of the men.

'Boxer?' his companion replied – he was seated so close to me I could have put an arm around the nylon shoulders of his windcheater, and in a way it seemed rude not to.

*Bobby shuddered and brought his eyes up again to the face. An attractive face, humorous, determined, resourceful—*

'Jalfrezi.'

'Boxer?'

'Aye, y'know – Joe Frazier.'

*The eyes, he thought, were probably blue –*

*And just as he reached that point in his thoughts, the eyes suddenly opened.*

'Chicken jalfrezi.'

*They were watchful and at the same time seemed to be asking a question.*

*Bobby got up quickly and came towards the man.*

They were riggers working on a civil engineering contract of some kind. From what they said I gathered the work was dangerous, requiring them to ascend hundreds of feet in cradles. I couldn't understand why, but the site they were working on was fundamentally unstable. I pictured an alien planet, its colloidal surface shifting and buckling in a near-infinite series of peaks and troughs that seemed always on the verge of an apprehensible pattern – yet never quite there.

'. . . an Audi TT' – they were discussing their gaffer, a German – 'that don't even leave the garage.'

''E's got three fookin' cars.'

*Before he got there the other spoke. His voice was not weak – it came out clear and resonant.*

'Least we're not at the beck and bluddy call uv wassisface.'

'Oo?'

'That scoolptur chap oo's got the turbine in at Bridlington – they say 'e's a complete fookin' nooter.'

*'Why didn't they ask Evans?' he said.*

*And then a queer little shudder passed over him, the eyelids dropped, the jaw fell . . .*

*The man was dead.*

A woman was charging across the road towards the Bengal Lancer. She had a fake tan the colour of the Holderness mud and her enormous breasts and belly – veiled by the diaphanous sea fret of a three-tiered white blouse – rotationally slumped. Her scary makeup recalled eyes painted on the prows of Athenian ships. I drew the waiter into me conspiratorially by his small arm. 'For Chrissakes,' I said as she tinkle-banged through the door. 'Whatever you do, don't feed her.'

Punctured, the waiter hissed embarrassment.

Then I was walking out of Withernsea, tending inland, the concrete stanchions of chain-link fences the only things I had ever known in the warm sodium-orange silence of suburban nightfall, the chocolate bar bought from the convenience store where I stopped to ask directions the only solid thing I had ever hungered for, the agony of my blistered feet and the nettle stings pricking my calves the only sensations I had ever felt, as the headlights of oncoming cars planted magenta blooms on the retinas of my dilated eyes.

Beyond the final caravan park the village of Hollym appeared as a black smudge of woodland on the night. Then I was on a long lane footing past a flint church. I sat down on the bench outside the Plough Inn and rolled a cigarette, and was joined by a second smoke-sucker who didn't speak but paced up and down, thumbs in his waistcoat pockets, while behind us the bar billiards rumbled and clacked.

'Steve was a geography teacher in Stanford-le-Hope for thirty years, but once the kids were off to uni we began looking around. To begin with we ignored the ad – because of the new house, we didn't fancy that.'

Another rumble of bar billiards – this time from below. The two of us stood looking at the two narrow single beds, the three white towels, the Country Crunch biscuits, the individual UHT milk cartons, the tea bags and sugar in sachets. She wasn't exactly friendly, yet competent in the domestic science of pimping.

'Well,' she said in answer to a question I couldn't recall asking, 'I think the farmers are philosophical about the loss of their land.'

What does she know, I thought. Here in Hollym she's a good mile from the sea; even given the faster rate of erosion down drift from the Withernsea defences it'll still be 400 years before the German Ocean marches into the Plough Inn, bellowing, 'I don't need a drink – I am the fucking drink!'

Her brown perm floated away along the corridor . . . *mouse droppings, rotting lino, an old knitting pattern used to plug a broken pane in the shed where Uncle Charlie did it.* She had left me with careful instructions on how to unlock the two doors when I left in the morning, then relock them and post the keys back in. She had left me with an individual box of cornflakes and a small jug of milk.

The plastic sheet in the shower stall clung to me as the shower head became lachrymose over my raw feet. Shriven, I put myself into the right-hand bed and shoved a radio I'd found in my rucksack under the clean, thin pillow. There was a cup of tea I couldn't for the life of me remember making cooling on the bedside table – next to it the unopened Country Crunch. In the night the Archbishop's wife whispered through striped cotton, 'I don't know how he's feeling, he's not here.'

Having walked for four centuries I came to the cliff edge only to discover that it wasn't there; instead a cartographer's black ink line was ruled across the field strips. Distance was time, while beyond a screen of crack willows a small mere rippled in the morning sunlight. I struck out to the north-east, heading for the villages of Newsham and Sisterkirke. The going was soft between the tilled strips and soon enough my boots were balled in mud. Away to the north-west, above the unseen Wolds, a cloud host flew, wings outspread. There must have been hail as well as rain in the night because here and there the wheat was mashed to the ground in swirls of stalks; stalks that, when I stooped to examine an ear, I saw were rotten. White grubs wriggled obscenely from the spikelets.

The wind got up, and within sight of Newsham church spire I came upon a gaggle of peasants herding their livestock before them – a few white geese, but mostly motos, their thin withers bloody from the willow switches the peasant women wielded. The motos' baby faces were contorted with the effort of trotting through the waterlogged fields.

''S'all gone,' the lead moto lisped as it rushed past me, and when the peasants drew level they affirmed this simply by their own flight and the tawdry vessels of Christ's feast they lugged with them: a tarnished brass ewer and bowl, two hefty leather-bound volumes – the Holy Bible and the parish records. Of their priest there was no sign.

I detained an old man by the sleeve of his smock. ''E stayed in the church last night,' he told me while the others hurried by. 'Praying, asking God to deliver the village from the sea.' As an afterthought he added: 'Silly cunt. Come sunup the nave were down on the beach. All our owsez 'n' all – but God's got nowt t'do wi' it.'

'Really.' I was keen to interrogate this advanced thinker further. 'Then what do you imagine he *feels* about the loss of your village?'

'I don't know how he's feeling,' Jane Williams whispered, the motion of the news having rolled her back beneath me. 'He's not here.'

It was grey dawn and the stiff spear threw me to the partitioned bathroom, where I waited on cold lino until I was able to piss. Back in the winding sheet I lay listening to an owl impersonate a man impersonating the hooting of an owl. Then I rose again, and twitching back the curtains saw a misty back garden lined with trestle tables, each one stabbed by a collapsed sunshade.

I rose once more and returned to the bathroom. There was a small window in the wall above the sink and a man I'd never seen before was looking through it straight at me. He was gaunt and somehow shifty, with lines of incompetence around his eyes – not laughter. We stared at one another in silence for a few minutes, while I took in the saliva, dried white, at the corners of his saturnine mouth. The fellow seemed so confused and drowsy that I felt no fear or exposure. Nonetheless, I quit the bathroom and went into the corridor to have a word with him – but he must have fled at my approach.

Then crept back again, because when I regained the sink he was at the window once more. Tiring of his little game, I undid the catch at the side of the frame and closed the shutter, in the process exposing a curious recess in which three small shelves held individual bars of soap, a tooth mug and a box of pink tissues, its thin cardboard printed with a photograph of a pink rose. So, looking at these items, I shaved myself by touch alone.

After I'd eaten the cornflakes someone had thoughtfully provided, drunk a cup of Nescafé, then taken a miserable shit, I opened the little shutter in the bathroom to see if the man was still there. He was, but appeared fresher-faced, and with a fast-scabbing nick in his Adam's apple that suggested he'd recently shaved. It was the same as before: the two of us enmeshed in a doleful stare; then, unhesitatingly, he reached out his hand towards me, and I, not hesitating either, extended mine to him. On to my open palm rolled a curious little figurine – a child's toy, presumably, although there was nothing playful about it. The blue Churchillian siren suit with a pig's head rising from its high collar was redolent of unnatural experiments conducted in secret government laboratories. I had never seen the figurine before, yet sensed that it had talismanic properties, and was a gift the giving of which had to be respected.

The stranger and I nodded curtly to one another, then simultaneously stepped away from the window.

\*     \*     \*

I found myself on the outskirts of a village that was shrouded in dense morning mist with no awareness of how I might have got there. I was dressed appropriately for a walking tour in green Gore-Tex trousers, thick socks, viciously uncomfortable leather boots, a blue wicking T-shirt and a black cagoule. It was chilly and although the trees and hedges had a midsummer density for a while I equivocated: was the cobweb stretched between the bars of a gate jewelled with frost or dew?

I couldn't remember my name, where I had come from or where I was going. I didn't know whether I was old or young. I unfastened my trousers and pulled them and my underpants down enough to expose a penis between blanched thighs – so discovered I was a man, and a white one. One memory I also retained: that *both* doors had to have been locked before I left wherever it was I'd been and the keys then posted back into the building. Had I done this?

A neoprene pouch sagged in the half-masted folds of my nether garments. I unzipped it, discovered a digital camera and prodded it on. Adjusting it so I could access the images already saved on its memory card, I flicked through them. My hunch had been correct: there were pictures of a lock with a hand inserting a key in it, then the same hand poked inside a letterbox. I compared the hand in the photo with the one on the end of my arm – they matched.

Replacing the camera and rearranging my clothing, I discovered a paper napkin on which was scrawled a crude map with arrows, approximate distances and a wavy line for the seaside. No other plan presented itself – I was an enigma to myself, swathed in the silence of this strange place; nevertheless, in choosing to follow the map forward, along the lane between the knapped-flint walls, I knew that I conformed to the paradigm for people like me – white men like me. At a crossroads a simple roundel annulled limits on speed but my pace remained constant as I moved into open country. Whoever had bequeathed me these feet had done me no favours, as with every step they cut into me like knives.

Peacocks roosted on the pantiled roof of a cottage – how did I know these terms? Away in the unvarying stubble a hare searched for a shadow to box, and the sodden umbels of the cow parsley were as still as any living thing could be. I reached a T-junction and obeying the napkin turned to the right. Now, in back of wide verges, bungalows lay behind privet hedges; beside a carport I glimpsed a trampoline festooned in old police crime scene tape. A blackbird fidgeted in a hawthorn, a blackboard was scratch-marked 'Clematis', 'Alpines', 'Laxton Fortunes' – all items priced at 50p.

A stile hopped towards me, crept under me, and I was on a drainage ditch the banks of which were massed with marsh marigolds, yarrow, thistles and nettles – all their flowers monochrome in the mist, all their scent as fresh as air freshener. I went on and in due course a pillbox canted in a cleft came upon me; here the path terminated in a muddy chute that slid me the twenty feet down to the beach.

No sooner had my smouldering feet been stubbed out in the grubby sand than I felt at ease: extinguished. I set off towards the south, moving swiftly along the tide line, and soon became utterly absorbed by the way the wrack of seaweed and driftwood resolved into a jumble of letters, which then became legible as words: *amygoid nucleus, sucli of cortex, senile and neuritic plaques, senile and braindruse.*

The disc of the sun appeared high up in the eastern quadrant of the sky, a duct sucking in the sea fret – but, suck as it might, visibility remained only a few score yards, with the world remaining all that was at my hurting feet. Amnesia was a belief system – an ideology all its own. I believed, fervently, in my inability to recall anything of significance, and this functioned as a heuristic, allowing me to operate effectively in a world that to anyone armed with prior knowledge would be frighteningly incomprehensible.

No one could be more desolate than I, the not-not other faced by an increasing threat level: the beach widening and the cliffs rising, the misshapen mud lumps sucking in the shallows – then, far off, a small group of figures pinned in the mist. Long minutes passed but it was still not possible to judge their size – were they toys or Titans? They stood at the water's edge, legs parted, arms held away from the body, swirling all around the nothing made visible. Five of them – so still, with what could be a boat or a canoe pulled up on the shingle at their feet. They inched up on me, so slow they had surrounded me before I ceased expecting lonely sea fishermen and acknowledged that these were wooden figures, none higher than my knee.

Some had arms missing – two round shields lay beside the rough-adzed boat. The figures were obviously of either ancient or aboriginal manufacture – and they possessed a humming resonance. Propped up there, so that the quartzite pebbles embedded in their pinheads were fixed upon where the horizon ought to be, the socket holes in their low pelvises yawned horribly.

It felt as if a small child had leapt upon my back. I turned and turned again, futile as a cat, to see what was there, then realized it was a parasitizing rucksack; then realized I was wreathed in lavatory chain. The madman sat a short way off, me yet not, his clothes in tatters, drool in his beard, his sack of manhood dusted with sand. He tugged the chain gently, and so I unwound myself and took off the rucksack. Together we went through it, taking out nylon bags packed with stuff: a mobile phone, a notebook, a radio the madman clicked, listened to for a few moments, then, after the flute and crackle of static, chucked to one side. He scattered the clothing and, crushing the oat cakes in his dirty hands, rubbed the crumbs into his bare chest. There was nothing in this portable world that he wanted, nothing until he discovered the small pine spars and curls in the oilskin bundle; these he urged me – none too gently – to insert: some into the figures' pelvic sockets, others into their vacant arm holes. The last one I let fall to the beach – what was the point, now?

The madman dragged me to my feet, prodded me until I strapped the empty rucksack to my back. Its unzipped compartments gaped – smelly canvas mouths. He pushed me – so that I might lead him.

If I had had any notion of why it was that I was travelling this lowering and excremental shore, I would've had to say that the trip had gone badly – but I didn't, so only went on until an industrial installation floated slowly by behind a ballast of dragons' teeth. The haloed safety lights, the alien elbows of steel piping, the cyber-pregnancy of a gas tank – the resources needed to fabricate all these were nowhere to be found on this planetoid, which was a mere 200 yards in diameter. They must have been mined from asteroids, assembled in space – crazy ideas of de-evolving gripped me, so painful were my feet. Why should I not remove my useless wooden arms from their sockets, slip into a blubbery body stocking and flip off into the comforting swell?

The beach narrowed once more, the cliffs soared, the sharp triangles of undercut hard standing appeared, silhouetted against the non-Euclidean sky. I came upon two mates, fishing and sharing a can of morning cider. They stood on a tarmac slab, their rods stuck in the muck. By reason of their summery drinking I knew it was getting hotter – we were companions in the sauna, and so I stopped to ask, the coffee sea sipping the soles of my boots, 'Is there much more beach along this way?'

'No,' the bald one in the white T-shirt answered. 'Yer awl ahtuv it now, lad. But if ewe go oop the cliff, like, u can walk along there.'

I thanked him and went on – but he was wrong: the cliff top had run for only fifty yards beneath my feet when it revealed itself to be nought but a headland, so I was exiled back down to what was no longer a beach at all, only a broad ledge of mud, with teeth cut out of it by longshore drift. Infective fluid surged into these inlets, swirling around the carcasses of rusted engines and jaundiced white goods.

Sand dunes sighed in from the west, their flanks creeping with marram grass, their hummocks and vales networked with paths of wooden slats wired apart. A sign directed me away from a PROTECTED SITE where terns were nesting. Their small white bodies blasted their black heads into grey space; then they fell to earth and resumed their positions, fluffuzzling up beside thistles and Flora margarine tubs. Could this go on indefinitely? Ignorant as I was, I doubted it – besides, who was the second who walked alongside me, skipping through the misty drapes, taunting the periphery of my vision? When I did the head-count there was only the one – still, there he was, sometimes dragging behind, other times scampering ahead along the muddy ledge. I didn't trust him.

I came upon an entire forty-foot-long blockhouse that had been abandoned on the beach by the retreating land. Beyond this a phantasmagorical confusion of military concrete – beige discs, rectangles, triangles and trapezoids – was aping a promontory. What was all this – the shattered remains an accident-prone temple?

Clambering about on the heap were a couple of kids, a yapping terrier and a bored dad. I joined them on a ramp that tended at a 20-degree angle to the German Ocean.

'D'you know where the sound mirror is?' I asked without preamble or forethought.

'You don't want to go bothering with that,' the dad said, his tone so sharp that at first I thought he was warning off the terrier, which was gnawing at a stalk of seaweed. But no: he meant me.

'Oh, why's that, then?'

'It's nowt but a stupid lump of concrete – and there's enough of 'em here.'

'I thought it was an early-warning device – for zeppelin raids during the First War. They say if you put your ear up against it you can hear . . .' I trailed off, because all of this had come to me unbidden, and I had no idea what could be heard in a sound mirror.

'Aye, that's right,' the dad said snidely. 'What *would* you hear – fook awl, there's fook awl to hear, here, nowt except those fookin turbines out there.' He jerked a thumb at the crescent of sea.

'Turbines?' I queried, but one of the kids had come up to show him something she'd found and he dismissed me with some cursory directions.

To make my way through the caravan park, then along the lane that skirted the bird reserve. There I found a noticeboard

that had trapped a heterogeneous flock of seafowl behind its glass, and next to it a handmade way marker that pointed towards THE SOUND MIRROR, and added hopefully, CREAM TEAS.

Out in the wheat field the sound mirror bloomed. Softened by the sea fret it was movingly lovely. The circular depression in its seaward side suggested that somewhere nearby hovered the enormous and comforting breast that had moulded it. I laid my cheek where it once had been and suckled on the sounds: the gull squeak and peewit, the distant groan of heavy machinery, the cries of children, the groans of the dispossessed, and the entreaties of those about to die. Were these the warnings of the deadly paravane, at that very moment being towed through the choppy skies towards me, passing over the silt that was once Northorpe and Hoton? I didn't know, and besides, even – even! – if I were able to recognize these harbingers I still would not have heeded them, for in the four minutes it took for the zeppelin to arrive, I would've forgotten all about it.

# 5

# The Struldbrug

'D'you mind my asking, but what're you fishing for?'

'Dunno, it's my first time here.'

Here being the tidal flats of the Isle of the Dead, exposed now that filmic civilization is ebbing away, and washed up upon them this marriage on the half shell – a blue nylon one, six feet across, ribbed with fibreglass poles. When I strolled past its lip, there they were – the meaty beings secondarily reliant on the suck of the current, siphoning it in through a taut nylon line and a long bent rod. They were in their fifties, she seated on a folding chair with truncated legs; he on the sand, his ankles boyishly crossed, a cigarette cupped in the half shell of his hand.

'I thought your gear looked new—'

'No, not my first time *ever* – I fish up and down the coast the whole time.'

Sturdy pride to buoy him up, the shell upended, a coracle now in which they paddle up and down the Holderness.

'And what do you catch?'

'This time of t'year, bass.'

Big-mouthed Billy-man, nailed to a plaque. Spasming at the waist, I walked away, my head hammering at the point of my shoulder, then, luminously ascended to a knoll from where I saw the reddest Nissan saloon parked in a sandy car park, beyond it a footprinted shore disappearing into the mist, and over to the right a line of telegraph poles and gorse bushes, the dorsal crest of a peninsula:

Spurn Head.

This much I did know: I had arrived at this wavering landmass, flipped this way and that by the sea for millennia, the tail of the East Riding lashing at Old Kilnsea, Ravenser and Ravenser Odd, so scattering their people on the face of the deep. Ravenser, or Ravensburg, or Ravenseret – it was once one of the wealthiest ports in the kingdom. It returned two members to parliament, held two markets a week and mounted an annual fair that lasted for over a month. 'Away with me in post to Ravenspurgh!' cries Northumberland in the opening scene of Act Two of *Richard the Second*; however, it's Ravenspurgh that's been had away, dissolved so completely that by the 1580s there was nothing left, and Shakespeare was name-checking an Atlantis. The last reference to the town was in Leland's sixteenth-century *Itinerary*, and presumably by then, Richard Reedbarowe, the hermit of the chapel of Ravenserporne, was long gone.

As early as the 1350s, the chronicler of Meaux wrote, 'When the inundations of the sea and of the Humber had destroyed the foundations of the chapel of Ravenserre Odd, built in honour of the Blessed Virgin Mary, so that the corpses and bones of the dead there buried horribly appeared, and the same inundations daily threatened the destruction of the said town, sacrilegious persons carried off and alienated certain ornaments of the said chapel, without our due consent, and disposed of them for their own pleasure—'

The rubber figurine, with the head of a pig, dressed in a blue Churchillian siren suit; the detachable penises and arms, carved from pinewood, of late Bronze Age votary objects; the neurofibrillary tangle and the amyloid visible as apple-green yellow birefringence; the UPVC windows and the water colours salvaged from the slidden studio at Skipsea; the madman holding a handful of individual UHT milk pots to his face – all mine, he mutters, all mine.

*What brings you up here, to an area of land almost equal to that upon which London stands, but which has now been swept away?*

*Oh, pleasure, pleasure! What else should bring one anywhere? Eating as usual, I see, Algy?*

Eaten up by introspection, I frogmarched myself on along the spit; the last few incisive nibbles would soon have done with the amyloid, the core of the present would be consumed, and the simple past would be all that there is, or ever can be. A line of wooden piles stood – stand – in the surf, spiny with iron spikes upon which seaweed and shreds of fishing nets have caught. What was – is – this, some futile attempt to fix the shifting mass to the bedrock? Or were – are – they, the staves of musical notation, a very late Romanticism of surging chords, gut-wrenching melodies and lofty crescendos, the entire gleaming metropolis of sounds long since sunk, church bells withal, beneath the shallow German Ocean?

A Struldbrug came towards me, his tattered clothing – hose, doublet, shirt and jerkin – as wispy as the sea fret. He paused fifty paces away, panting, one arm against a pile for support – his bent back and the curving upright parenthesizing the waves – then came on again, the black spot above his left eyebrow a gun barrel levelled at me. My impulse was to run, however . . . too late, he was upon me, his palsied claw rattling my shoulder, as he thrust his face into mine. Its features fell like wormy clods from the winding sheet of ancient skin.

From his clothing I judged him to be above 600 years old, but whether the mushy sounds that fell from his mouth were the authentic accents of the late medieval tongue, or only the consequence of toothlessness, I couldn't say. There were a few words I could make out – playce, cum, stä – by which, combined with his erratic gestures, I understood that he wished me to accompany him to his abode. I was sorely tempted – my feet were killing me – but then, through the curtains of mist being swept up by unseen cables, there came hurrying a pair of attendants wearing blue siren suits.

They spotted me and the Struldbrug, adjusted their course and made straight for us, coming up puffing.

''E's a sly wun, 'e is,' the first attendant said, although whether to me or as a general observation was ambiguous. He had a piggy head, this fellow, and his wide nostrils quivered, sucking in everything.

'C'mon ewe daft booger,' his equally piggy colleague said. 'Yul miss ewer soup, woncha.'

Taking the Struldbrug by either arm, they began to lead him away. Across their shoulders both attendants had the words DEMENTIA ADVISORY picked out in white letters. But the old man kept on babbling. 'Playce! Cum! Stä!' and trying to break away, so they stopped and the pig-headed figure in the Churchillian siren suit called back, ''E wants yet t'cum oop t'clinic. Willya, lad? It'll mekk 'im ever so 'appy.'

On my walking tour – a journey I made without maps – I forgot who I was and where I was going. Nevertheless, I carried with me for the entire time a damp and writhing burden of guilt, together with the mental picture of a baby lying in the wrack at the high tide mark, with a kitchen knife planted between its shoulder blades. I acquired a handful of carved wooden penises and arms – late Bronze Age, I thought – that I made a gift of to some fishermen I met. And I bought an Agatha Christie thriller in a junk shop in Hornsea that I read a few pages of before discarding in a bin, beside the shower block in a caravan park.

The lead attendant explained everything as we padded along the beach, trying to maintain headway despite the Struldbrug, who kept veering off, his anachronistic clothes flapped mournfully in the breeze. On we went towards the lighthouse, which was climbing out of its humid raiment so that it stood, if not exactly proud, at least prominent against the fast-bluing sky.

'There's bin a memory clinic out on Spurn for a while now,' the attendant said. 'There was always a lot of older folk in Holderness anyway – retirees an' that – but when the noombers wi' Altzheimer's began to get . . . well, out of 'and, like, the clinic were the logical place to put 'em, so the facility were expanded.'

Despite the Struldbrug's wayward progress, we had gained the dunes and picked our way through the muffled defiles, our ankles scratched by the lyme grass and sea holly. There was homely flybuzz and butterflies swirling in the warming air, then, from top of an acclivity, we could see the whole hummocky panhandle.

'It's glacial, yer see,' the second attendant was moved to explain. 'The point, that is – it's a glacial moraine, so it's stable. It's only the beach that moves around. Any road' – he threw his arm wide to bracket the mismatched buildings, some prefabs, some concrete, some stone, that were huddled at the foot of the lighthouse – 'there were all these here lying empty, so it were a logical idea to put the clinic here. Besides, it's less institutional.'

'Less instëtewshunal – that were it.' His colleague snorted. 'Patients can get aht, tek the air. It's dead restful here – calm, like – and if they aren't too distressed they can have the run of the place. Sort of folk who cwm aht to Spurn, well, they're nature lovers, twitchers – oonderstandin' when it cums dahn t'it.'

'They've gotta be!' the other fellow laughed bitterly. 'Chances are there's wunnov their own here, or they're headed this way themselves. How many is it now with t'dementia, over two million – and rising all the time.'

'Rising all the time,' said the first, kicking out at a lump of oily driftwood with his boot. The Struldbrug groaned upon impact, and I wondered if over the centuries he had come to identify somatically with things older than humans, wind and wave weathered trees – perhaps Spurn Head itself.

'What,' I asked, 'happens if the patients do get too distressed?'

The first looked at me curiously and a little contemptuously; at times the fletch of a man's cartilaginous ear is too much to take, along with the toothbrush bristles in the corner of his jaw, and the slow-roasting shoulders bundled in blue cloth. 'Do-too, do-too, do-too-too,' he prated, incorporating my syllables into a parody of just such distress; then, seeing I wasn't going to rise to it, or laugh, he went on: 'Bull Sands Fort, out there in the Umber. Filthy big place bang on a sandbank, it were built in the First War – eyronickle, really, weren't ready 'til nineteen-nineteen when the show was over.

'Any road, if any of oor lot get too tricky, like, it's off to Bull Sands wi' 'em. I've not been out meself, but they say' – he shuddered – 'it ain't pretty – ain't pretty at all.'

'And the Struldbrug?' I felt no compunction talking of the aged one as if he weren't right by us, because in a way he wasn't, riding his tempest of time with his ragged wings of linen and leather; what could he grasp of mayflies such as us and our dandelion clock concerns?

''Im?' The lipless mouth widened revealing peg teeth. ''E's no trubble – YER NO TRUBBLE, ARE YER?' he bellowed at the hapless Struldbrug, who hung so slack now I was reminded of a cadaver strung upon wires. 'No,' the piggy warder said, resuming at a more reasonable level, 'over my dead body duzz 'e go aht t'Bull Sands—' Then he stopped short, shivering at the absurdity of what he'd just said. 'Whatever. Anyway, he's a mascot 'e is – bin 'ere before the clinic, before the new lighthouse – before the old wun inall. 'E was probably 'ere when the light were joost an iron basket fulla burning faggots lifted by a lever.'

'How old d'you think he is?' I ventured. 'His clothes look medieval.'

'Medieval!' the warder guffawed. 'Don't be soft, lad – 'ow could they last? No, these togs are theatrical clobber; soom joker put them on 'im back in the day – the fifties weren't it?'

'Aye,' his companion concurred, 'the fifties.'

The bigger piggier warder gathered the cloth above either hip of his siren suit in his trotters and adopted an oratorical stance, turning so as show his DEMENTIA ADVISORY to me. It was clear, on this most obscurely ephemeral of days, that I was about to be privileged with an insight into deep and pellucid time.

'Soom folk,' the warder said, 'claim 'e's the old hermit that lived here in the fifteenth century, the wun mentioned in the chronicle of Mo. Personally, I don't believe it. My granddad, well, before 'e lost 'is own bluddy marbles, 'e told me what the Struldbrug were like when 'e were a nipper. Back then this chap 'ere still 'ad a tooth in 'is head. Now, that wouldn't put 'im much over the two-hundred mark.'

The sea fret had finally and entirely dispersed. The Struldbrug's horny toes scrabbled in the sand, the yellow flowering birefringence hung on the neurofibrillary tangle of the gorse, the berries of the sea buckthorn were as shiny-yellow as benzodiazepine capsules. The wallpaper of the sky wrapped around our little colloquy, and for a moment it fooled me with its cloudy furbelows into thinking the three-bladed buckthorns were painted along the skirting board of the nursery, then I regained my sense of scale and grasped that these were massive wind turbines, a long parenthetic curve of them, tending towards the point of Spurn Head. How could I have not noticed these things during my tramp along the coast? Or even heard about them before I left . . . before I left . . . wherever it was that I had left.

'You're coming on down to the memory clinic with uz and the Struldbrug now – that's what yer doing,' the dementia advisor said in answer to a question I couldn't recall having posed.

'Aye,' his number two pitched in, "course you canav a cuppa and sum cayk.'

'Cayk! Cayk!' the Struldbrug crowed.

'What other facilities are there at the . . . memory clinic?' My voice swooped up into the interrogative, borne on thermals of hot, moist distress.

'There're digital enhancement programmes and neural-activated webcam systems—'

I whimpered, and the senior advisor silenced his subordinate with a glare, then reassured me, 'Aye, and there's uz, uz dementia advisors to help you learn it all, after all, it can be a lot to take on board.'

We were within a few hundred paces of the clinic now, and it seemed to me that I must be a merman, for there were daggers thrust into the soles of my newborn feet, the attendants held me under either arm and I'd all but surrendered the power of speech when, seeing that the Struldbrug had lurched on ahead, I broke away and ran after him.

The ancient clattered along a walkway between thick gorse, and although I soon lost him I also lost my pursuers. I could hear them wandering around in the crannies between the bushes – one of them must have picked up a stick, because there was swishing, smiting and cracking as he cried, 'Cummon ahtuv it you daft booger!' and 'No cake fer you if you don't cum soon!' But they soon tired of looking for us, and one of the dementia advisors called to the other, 'I'm fed oop. He'll cum back when 'e's 'ungree.'

I was left alone in the desiccated undergrowth and crawled out from the sandy cave beneath a root system, then limped through this fine dust of ages towards a crest from where I could see the whole semicircular sweep of the beach. The Struldbrug was down there already, paddling in the shallows, his shaggy head dangling low. I wondered what he could be looking for so intently, and felt frustrated by the pointlessness of asking him.

I took off the empty rucksack, unlaced the stabbing boots and cast them aside, to be followed by T-shirt, trousers, smalls unlaundered for the entire trip, all of which I left behind me on top of the gorse bushes, like the pathetic unpacking of a plane-crash victim, compelled by Death. All I hung on to was a notebook. I needn't have felt frustrated, because as I walked towards the Struldbrug I grasped what it was that he sought, first peering into the ripples, then rearing back: the end of the peninsula. The shoreline curved so symmetrically that the exact point where the sea met the waters of the estuary was impossible to gauge.

I shared his obsession, and so the two of us moved back and forth in the shallows, crossing and recrossing, intent on the elusive terminus. After some time we had achieved a consensus and stood confronting one another – I naked, he in his rags. I dared to look upon his medieval features. *The next stop is Victoria, change here for District, Circle and Piccadilly lines and mainline rail services* . . . I opened the notebook and a scrap of black-and-white photograph fell on to the water between us and floated there. I stooped to peer at a scraggy beard, an attempt at a quiff, a row of optics. I looked up at the Struldbrug and thought I could see a resemblance, but when I glanced back at the scrap it had been spun away by the wavelets, leaving me behind, paddling in the Now.

# Afterword

On 17 July 2008 I was making my children supper in the basement kitchen of our terraced house in Stockwell, South London, when I heard a commotion in the street outside and the demented shriek of emergency services sirens. When I opened the front door I found some of my neighbours already standing on the front steps of their houses, the street was full of police cars, and an ambulance was parked further up. Very quickly it became clear that a young man had been attacked and stabbed immediately outside the house by a group of youths; he had staggered up the road and collapsed about a hundred yards further on. Paramedics and a doctor who lived locally fought to save his life, but he died three hours later. He was eighteen years old, his name was Frederick Moody Boateng, and he was the twenty-first teenage fatality from a stabbing in London that year.

Freddy's family lived six doors up from us, and although I'd nodded to him in the street we'd never exchanged a word. In the immediate aftermath of the murder, shocked local people said the usual things about the senselessness of the attack. It was thought the assailants might also have been at a spontaneous water fight in Hyde Park that Freddy had attended that day, and that something had happened there that caused them to lay in wait for him. The suppressed premise, of course, was whether Freddy was a 'good' or a 'bad' boy.

Soon enough another narrative emerged: Freddy had been in trouble before, the doorman in the nearby flats alleged that he had been there immediately before the knifing, and someone else said that rocks of crack cocaine had been found on him. The man in the local park who does youth football coaching told me that Freddy had asked to participate in his sessions, but that 'He was mixed up in drugs, so I told him no. I won't take anyone who can't stay out of trouble.'

Three young men stood trial for the killing in January 2009, all on charges of affray. It was understood that the police had been unable to get sufficient evidence for a murder charge, and besides the actual knifeman was said to have fled to Jamaica. In the event, none of the three accused received more than a three-year sentence. This barely made the news anyway – by then the focus of attention had long since moved on, and there were tens if not scores of stories with more obviously moralistic dramatic arcs to satisfy English connoisseurs of murder.

But Freddy's killing stayed with me by reason of proximity alone: this was not murder considered as one of the fine arts, but homicide as interior decoration. The crime scene tape decked the street for a week or more. For the first couple of days we had to be escorted to and from our house by police officers. Then there was the shrine created by Freddy's friends at the end of the block, with its blooms dying in cellophane, his name outlined in tea lights, and a sad little assemblage of cards, water pistols and handwritten poems. The kids stood vigil for him, at first every night, then weekly, then monthly. There was the funeral, a memorial service – the family were active in a local church – and a march protesting against the epidemic of knife crime. All of these gatherings forced an awareness of community on the inhabitants of this very typical – and typically polyglot – inner London residential street.

I felt an obscure shame about the murder – or, rather, about my detachment from the immediate environment, let alone the wider world. I wasn't remotely interested in the morality tale used to impose 'sense' on this young man's death; I thought instead of the city, its anonymity, its criss-cross currents of physical mortality and psychic violence. Over the preceding few years I had a growing sense of the room where I typed being encircled by homicides: the woman whose smouldering corpse was found in the local park – the victim of an 'honour' killing; the young woman strangled in her workplace shower down the road in Vauxhall; the kid shot in his flat at Clapham North by gang members; the doorman of a club on the Wandsworth Road shot in a drive-by; and, of course, the young Brazilian electrician shot by police seven times at point-blank range in the nearby tube station.

All works of fiction represent terrains across which characters travel, and while the writer maps these he is down there on the ground, orienting by compass – whether moral or otherwise – and the familial resemblances of faces, landmarks and geographical features. Only towards the end of the journey, when he climbs the last hill, does he look back to survey the entire territory; only then does he understand the nature of the particular route undertaken.

When I reached the end of this book – so contorted, wayward and melancholic – I looked back and saw my father-in-law's death from cancer in November 2007, Freddy Moody's murder in July 2008, and the death of J. G. Ballard in April of 2009. The mental pathologies that underlie the three memoirs – obsessive-compulsive disorder for 'Very

Little', psychosis for 'Walking to Hollywood' and Alzheimer's for 'Spurn Head' – are themselves displacements of a single phenomenon.

*W. W. S., London, 2009*

## A NOTE ON THE TYPE

The text of this book is set Adobe Garamond. It is one of several versions of Garamond based on the designs of Claude Garamond. It is thought that Garamond based his font on Bembo, cut in 1495 by Francesco Griffo in collaboration with the Italian printer Aldus Manutius. Garamond types were first used in books printed in Paris around 1532. Many of the present-day versions of this type are based on the *Typi Academiae* of Jean Jannon cut in Sedan in 1615.

Claude Garamond was born in Paris in 1480. He learned how to cut type from his father and by the age of fifteen he was able to fashion steel punches the size of a pica with great precision. At the age of sixty he was commissioned by King Francis I to design a Greek alphabet, and for this he was given the honourable title of royal type founder. He died in 1561.

# ALSO AVAILABLE BY WILL SELF

# THE QUANTITY THEORY OF INSANITY

'He writes like a devil'
**MAIL ON SUNDAY**

This is the sparkling debut with which Will Self burst onto the literary scene. In it, we discover a superhumanly dull tribe of Amazonians, the terrible, seductive secret of Ward 9 and why you are right to think that London is full of dead people. Full of his trademark jagged-edge satire and dark wit, this short-story collection is acerbic, hilarious and, most of all, utterly unique in its imaginative vision.

'Very funny and very good, with that unmistakable sign of the genuine comic writer's absurdity that unfurls logically from absurdity, but always as a mirror of what we are living in – and wish we didn't'
**DORIS LESSING**

# THE BUTT

'Self writes here with an adroit impersonation of coarse exuberance that makes *The Butt* as readable as a blokeish airport novel … Ingenious'
**SUNDAY TELEGRAPH**

When Tom Brodzinski finally decides to give up smoking during a family holiday in a weird, unnamed land, a moment's inattention becomes his undoing. Flipping the butt of his last cigarette off the balcony of the holiday apartment, it lands on the head of the elderly Reggie Lincoln, and burns him. Despite Brodzinski's liberal attitudes and good intentions, the local authorities treat his action as an assault. Soon the full weight of the courts and tribal custom is brought to bear. What follows is a journey through a fantastically distorted world, a country that is part Australia, part Iraq and entirely the heart of distinctively modern darkness.

'*The Butt* is Self's most gripping and disturbing novel in years'
**HARPER'S BAZAAR**

B L O O M S B U R Y

# MY IDEA OF FUN

'This is a brilliant first novel, obscene, funny, opulently written, and, of course,
agonisingly moral'
**OBSERVER**

Ian Wharton is having devilish and murderous thoughts, courtesy of the
influence of Mr Broadhurst – companion, confidant and the manifestation of
Ian's mental illness – who is now apparently being carried around in his wife's
womb. How he got there isn't important (though Dr Gyggle, Ian's psychiatrist,
might disagree), but what he wants from Ian certainly is…

'No one else I can think of writes about contemporary Britain with such elan,
energy and witty intelligence. Rejoice'
**NICHOLAS LEZARD, GUARDIAN**

# GREY AREA

'Brilliantly original, Will Self is one of those rare writers whose imaginations
change for ever the way we see the world'
**J.G. BALLARD**

The stories in this bizarre and disturbing collection include the revelation of
the eight people who control the whole of London life; a nightmare vision of
Soho where every waiter is an unpublished novelist; a poetic tour of the British
motorway; and a heady night in the home of a bickering couple. This is a truly
inimitable showcase of short stories.

'A demon lover, a model village and office paraphernalia are springboards for
Self's bizarre flights of fancy … this collection explores strange worlds which
have mutated out of our own'
**TIBOR FISCHER, FINANCIAL TIMES**

BLOOMSBURY

# GREAT APES

'A brick dropped into the stagnant pond of contemporary English prose'
**NEW STATESMAN**

When Simon Dykes wakes one morning, he discovers that his girlfriend has turned into a chimpanzee. And, to his horror, so has the rest of humanity. His bizarre delusion that he is 'human' brings Simon to the attention of eminent psychologist (and chimp), Dr Zack Busner. For, with this fascinating case, Busner thinks he may finally make his reputation as a truly great ape.

'Exultantly hallucinogenic ... achieves the rare feat of temporarily altering the reader's perspective'
**GUARDIAN**

# COCK & BULL

'Imagine a film of Kafka's *Metamorphosis* scripted by William Burroughs and shot by David Cronenberg ... pure delight to verbal perverts everywhere'
**SUNDAY TIMES**

In *Cock: A Novelette*, Carol is dissatisfied with her sex life, and her effete husband's drinking problem is not helping. Then, one evening while he is out, Carol discovers something unexpected about herself. Then there is *Bull: A Farce*. John Bull is a man's man: A sports writer, a rugby player, a drinker. But he's about to wake up to something of an anatomical surprise...

'Mordant, acute ... exquisitely cunning ... the funniest book about late onset hermaphroditism you'll read all year'
**INDEPENDENT**

BLOOMSBURY

# THE SWEET SMELL OF PSYCHOSIS

'A tour de force'
**TIME OUT**

Thrust into the seedy underworld of hack reporters and Soho drinking dens, young Richard Hermes is skidding down a cocaine slope of self-destruction in pursuit of the impossibly beautiful socialite-cum-columnist Ursula Bentley. But between Richard and his object of desire stands his omnipresent nemesis, the lubricious Bell, doyen of late night radio shows, provider of drugs and gossip, and ringmaster of the Sealink Club. Erudite and witty as ever, this hilarious novella is vintage Self at his acerbic, incisive best, brilliantly illustrated by Martin Rowson's sharp, dark, satirical pen.

'Self is the master of the art of a telling sentence'
**OBSERVER**

# JUNK MAIL

'An explosive collection'
**J.G. BALLARD, GUARDIAN**

Martin Amis, William Burroughs and Damien Hirst; East End crack dens, cocaine and hallucinogens; English culture, satanic abuse and severed heads in liquid nitrogen. Punctuated by his other-worldly cartoons, *Junk Mail* is a Self-selection of his most brilliant essays; an innovative and irreverent trawl through a landscape of drugs, literature, politics, art and motorways.

'Locking antlers with his personal gods of British fiction, we finally get the undivided Self in all his maddening brilliance'
**SPECTATOR**

**ORDER YOUR COPY:** BY PHONE +44 (0)1256 302 699; BY EMAIL: DIRECT@MACMILLAN.CO.UK
DELIVERY IS USUALLY 3–5 WORKING DAYS. FREE POSTAGE AND PACKAGING FOR ORDERS OVER £20.

**ONLINE:** WWW.BLOOMSBURY.COM/BOOKSHOP
PRICES AND AVAILABILITY SUBJECT TO CHANGE WITHOUT NOTICE.

WWW.BLOOMSBURY.COM/WILLSELF